CASEBOOK SERIES

JANE AUSTEN: *Emma* (Revised) David Lodge
JANE AUSTEN: *'Northanger Abbey' & 'Persuasion'* B. C. Southam
JANE AUSTEN: *'Sense and Sensibility', 'Pride and Prejudice' & 'Mansfield Park'* B. C. Southam
BECKETT: *Waiting for Godot* Ruby Cohn
WILLIAM BLAKE: *Songs of Innocence and Experience* Margaret Bottrall
CHARLOTTE BRONTE: *'Jane Eyre' & 'Villette'* Miriam Allott
EMILY BRONTE: *Wuthering Heights* (Revised) Miriam Allott
BROWNING: *'Men and Women' & Other Poems* J. R. Watson
CHAUCER: *The Canterbury Tales* J. J. Anderson
COLERIDGE: *'The Ancient Mariner' & Other Poems* Alun R. Jones & W. Tydeman
CONRAD: *'Heart of Darkness', 'Nostromo' & 'Under Western Eyes'* C. B. Cox
CONRAD: *The Secret Agent* Ian Watt
DICKENS: *Bleak House* A. E. Dyson
DICKENS: *'Hard Times', 'Great Expectations' & 'Our Mutual Friend'* Norman Page
DICKENS: *'Dombey and Son' & 'Little Dorrit'* Alan Shelston
DONNE: *Songs and Sonets* Julian Lovelock
GEORGE ELIOT: *Middlemarch* Patrick Swinden
GEORGE ELIOT: *'The Mill on the Floss' & 'Silas Marner'* R. P. Draper
T. S. ELIOT: *Four Quartets* Bernard Bergonzi
T. S. ELIOT: *'Prufrock', 'Gerontion' & 'Ash Wednesday'* B. C. Southam
T. S. ELIOT: *The Waste Land* C. B. Cox & Arnold P. Hinchliffe
T. S. ELIOT: *Plays* Arnold P. Hinchliffe
HENRY FIELDING: *Tom Jones* Neil Compton
E.M. FORSTER: *A Passage to India* Malcolm Bradbury
WILLIAM GOLDING: *Novels 1954–64* Norman Page
HARDY: *The Tragic Novels* (Revised) R. P. Draper
HARDY: *Poems* James Gibson & Trevor Johnson
HARDY: *Three Pastoral Novels* R. P. Draper
GERARD MANLEY HOPKINS: *Poems* Margaret Bottrall
HENRY JAMES: *'Washington Square' & 'The Portrait of a Lady'* Alan Shelton
JONSON: *Volpone* Jonas A. Barish
JONSON: *'Every Man in his Humour' & 'The Alchemist'* R. V. Holdsworth
JAMES JOYCE: *'Dubliners' & 'A Portrait of the Artist as a Young Man'* Morris Beja
KEATS: *Odes* G.S. Fraser
KEATS: *Narrative Poems* John Spencer Hill
D.H. LAWRENCE: *Sons and Lovers* Gamini Salgado
D.H. LAWRENCE: *'The Rainbow' & 'Women in Love'* Colin Clarke
LOWRY: *Under the Volcano* Gordon Bowker
MARLOWE: *Doctor Faustus* John Jump
MARLOWE: *'Tamburlaine the Great', 'Edward II' & 'The Jew of Malta'* J. R. Brown
MARLOWE: *Poems* Arthur Pollard
MAUPASSANT: *In the Hall of Mirrors* T. Harris
MILTON: *Paradise Lost* A. E. Dyson & Julian Lovelock
O'CASEY: *'Juno and the Paycock', 'The Plough and the Stars' & 'The Shadow of a Gunman'* Ronald Ayling
EUGENE O'NEILL: *Three Plays* Normand Berlin
JOHN OSBORNE: *Look Back in Anger* John Russell Taylor
PINTER: *'The Birthday Party' & Other Plays* Michael Scott
POPE: *The Rape of the Lock* John Dixon Hunt
SHAKESPEARE: *A Midsummer Night's Dream* Antony Price
SHAKESPEARE: *Antony and Cleopatra* (Revised) John Russell Brown
SHAKESPEARE: *Coriolanus* B. A. Brockman

SHAKESPEARE: *Early Tragedies* Neil Taylor & Bryan Loughrey
SHAKESPEARE: *Hamlet* John Jump
SHAKESPEARE: *Henry IV Parts I and II* G.K. Hunter
SHAKESPEARE: *Henry V* Michael Quinn
SHAKESPEARE: *Julius Caesar* Peter Ure
SHAKESPEARE: *King Lear* (Revised) Frank Kermode
SHAKESPEARE: *Macbeth* (Revised) John Wain
SHAKESPEARE: *Measure for Measure* C. K. Stead
SHAKESPEARE: *The Merchant of Venice* John Wilders
SHAKESPEARE: *'Much Ado About Nothing' & 'As You Like It'* John Russell Brown
SHAKESPEARE: *Othello* (Revised) John Wain
SHAKESPEARE: *Richard II* Nicholas Brooke
SHAKESPEARE: *The Sonnets* Peter Jones
SHAKESPEARE: *The Tempest* (Revised) D. J. Palmer
SHAKESPEARE: *Troilus and Cressida* Priscilla Martin
SHAKESPEARE: *Twelfth Night* D. J. Palmer
SHAKESPEARE: *The Winter's Tale* Kenneth Muir
SPENSER: *The Faerie Queene* Peter Bayley
SHERIDAN: *Comedies* Peter Davison
STOPPARD: *'Rosencrantz and Guildenstern are Dead', 'Jumpers' & 'Travesties'* T. Bareham
SWIFT: *Gulliver's Travels* Richard Gravil
SYNGE: *Four Plays* Ronald Ayling
TENNYSON: *In Memoriam* John Dixon Hunt
THACKERAY: *Vanity Fair* Arthur Pollard
TROLLOPE: *The Barsetshire Novels* T. Bareham
WEBSTER: *'The White Devil' & 'The Duchess of Malfi'* R. V. Holdsworth
WILDE: *Comedies* William Tydeman
VIRGINIA WOOLF: *To the Lighthouse* Morris Beja
WORDSWORTH: *Lyrical Ballads* Alun R. Jones & William Tydeman
WORDSWORTH: *The 1807 Poems* Alun R. Jones
WORDSWORTH: *The Prelude* W. J. Harvey & Richard Gravil
YEATS: *Poems 1919–35* Elizabeth Cullingford
YEATS: *Last Poems* Jon Stallworthy

Issues in Contemporary Critical Theory Peter Barry
Thirties Poets: 'The Auden Group' Ronald Carter
Tragedy: Developments in Criticism R.P. Draper
The Epic Ronald Draper
Poetry Criticism and Practice: Developments since the Symbolists A.E. Dyson
Three Contemporary Poets: Gunn, Hughes, Thomas A.E. Dyson
Elizabethan Poetry: Lyrical & Narrative Gerald Hammond
The Metaphysical Poets Gerald Hammond
Medieval English Drama Peter Happé
The English Novel: Developments in Criticism since Henry James Stephen Hazell
Poetry of the First World War Dominic Hibberd
The Romantic Imagination John Spencer Hill
Drama Criticism: Developments since Ibsen Arnold P. Hinchliffe
Three Jacobean Revenge Tragedies R.V. Holdsworth
The Pastoral Mode Bryan Loughrey
The Language of Literature Norman Page
Comedy: Developments in Criticism D.J. Palmer
Studying Shakespeare John Russell Brown
The Gothic Novel Victor Sage
Pre-Romantic Poetry J.R. Watson

Shakespeare
The Tempest

A CASEBOOK
EDITED BY

D. J. PALMER

First published 1968 by
THE MACMILLAN PRESS LTD
Houndmills, Basingstoke, Hampshire RG21 2XS
and London
Companies and representatives
throughout the world

ISBN 0–333–53361–5 hardcover
ISBN 0–333–53362–3 paperback

A catalogue record for this book is available from the British Library.

Thirteenth reprint 1990
Revised edition 1991
Reprinted 1993, 1994

Printed in Hong Kong

CONTENTS

SOURCES AND ACKNOWLEDGEMENTS

The editor and publishers wish to thank the following for permission to use copyright material:

PART I

The John Dryden and Sir William Davenant version of *The Tempest* (1670); John Dryden's Preface to *Troilus and Cressida* (1679); Nicholas Rowe, *Some Account of the Life &c. of Mr. William Shakespeare* (1709); Joseph Warton, from *The Adventurer*, no. 93 and no. 97 (1753); Dr Johnson's Note on *The Tempest*, Act I, scene iv, from *The Works of William Shakespeare* (1765); S. T. Coleridge's Ninth Lecture from *Lectures on Shakespeare and Milton* (1811) and an extract from *Literary Remains* (pub. 1836); William Hazlitt, *Characters of Shakespeare's Plays* (1817); Edward Dowden, *Shakespere – His Mind and Art* (1875); Henry James's Introduction to *The Tempest*, first published in *The Complete Works of William Shakespeare*, vol. XVI of the Renaissance Edition (1907); extract from 'Caliban to the Audience', from *The Sea and the Mirror* in *For the Time Being* (Faber & Faber Ltd, Random House Inc., 1945).

PART 2

John Middleton Murry, *Shakespeare* (Jonathan Cape Ltd and The Society of Authors); E. M. W. Tillyard, *Shakespeare's Last Plays* (Miss Angela Tillyard and Chatto & Windus Ltd); G. Wilson Knight, *The Crown of Life* (Methuen & Co. Ltd, Barnes & Noble Inc.); Reuben A. Brower, *The Fields of Light* (Oxford University Press Inc., New York; © Oxford University Press Inc. 1951); Frank Kermode (ed.), *The Tempest* (1954) in *The Arden Edition of the Works of William Shakespeare* (Methuen & Co. Ltd, Harvard University

Press; Frances Barker and Peter Hulme, 'Nymphs and Reapers heavily vanish: the discursive contexts of *The Tempest*' in *Alternative Shakespeares*, edited by John Drakakis, Methuen & Co. (1985), by permission of Routledge; Leslie A. Fiedler, extract from *The Stranger in Shakespeare*, Croom Helm (1973), by permission of Routledge; Trevor R. Griffiths, 'Caliban and Colonialism', *The Yearbook of English Studies*, vol. 13 (1983), .by permission of The Modern Humanities Research Association; Frances Yates, extract from *Shakespeare's Last Plays: A New Approach*, Routledge and Kegan Paul (1975), by permission of Peters Fraser and Dunlop Group Ltd on behalf of the author.

Every effort has been made to trace all the copyright holders but if any have been inadvertently overlooked the publishers will be pleased to make the necessary arrangement at the first opportunity.

GENERAL EDITOR'S PREFACE

Each of this series of Casebooks concerns either one well-known and influential work of literature or two or three closely linked works. The main section consists of critical readings, mostly modern, brought together from journals and books. A selection of reviews and comments by the author's contemporaries is also included, and sometimes comments from the author himself. The Editor's Introduction charts the reputation of the work from its first appearance until the present time.

What is the purpose of such a collection? Chiefly, to assist reading. Our first response to literature may be, or seem to be, 'personal'. Certain qualities of vigour, profundity, beauty or 'truth to experience' strike us, and the work gains a foothold in our mind. Later, an isolated phrase or passage may return to haunt or illuminate. Where did we hear that? we wonder – it could scarcely be better put.

In these and similar ways appreciation begins, but major literature prompts to very much more. There are certain facts we need to know if we are to understand properly. Who were the author's original readers, and what assumptions did he share with them? What was his theory of literature? Was he committed to a particular historical situation, or to a set of beliefs? We need historians as well as critics to help us with this. But there are also more purely literary factors to take account of: the work's structure and rhetoric; its symbols and archetypes; its tone, genre and texture; its use of language; the words on the page. In all these matters critics can inform and enrich our individual responses by offering imaginative recreations of their own.

For the life of a book is not, after all, merely 'personal'; it is more like a tripartite dialogue, between a writer living 'then', a reader living 'now', and whatever forces of survival and honour link the two. Criticism is the public manifestation of this dialogue, a witness to the continuing power of literature to arouse and excite. It illuminates the possibilities and regards of the dialogue, pushing 'interpretation' as far forward as it can go.

And here, indeed, is the rub: how far can it go? Where does 'interpretation' end and nonsense begin? Why is one interpretation superior to another, and why does each age need to interpret for itself? The critic knows that his insights have value only in so far as they serve the text, and that he must take account of views differing sharply from his own. He knows that his own writing will be judged as well as the work he writes about, so that he cannot simply assert inner illumination or a differing taste.

The critical forum is a place of vigorous conflict and disagreement, but there is nothing in this to cause dismay. What is attested is the complexity of human experience and the richness of literature, not any chaos or relativity of taste. A critic is better seen, no doubt, as an explorer than as an 'authority', but explorers ought to be, and usually are, well equipped. The effect of good criticism is to convince us of what C. S. Lewis called 'the enormous extension of our being which we owe to authors'. A Casebook will be justified only if it helps to promote the same end.

A single volume can represent no more than a small selection of critical opinions. Some critics have been excluded for reasons of space, and it is hoped that readers will follow up the further suggestions in the Select Bibliography. Other contributions have been severed from their original context, to which some readers may wish to return. Indeed, if they take a hint from the critics represented here, they certainly will.

A. E. DYSON

INTRODUCTION

I

The Tempest was Shakespeare's last play, excluding his contributions to *Henry VIII* and *The Two Noble Kinsmen.* The first recorded performance took place at Court on 1 November 1611: 'Hallomas nyght was presented att Whithall before y[e] kinges Maiestie, a play Called the Tempest.' From Shakespeare's use in the play of certain documents relating to the Virginia Company, published in the previous autumn, it seems likely that *The Tempest* was written during 1611. It was not printed during Shakespeare's lifetime and first appeared in the Folio of 1623, where the text shows signs of careful editorial preparation. Although we have no direct evidence about its contemporary popularity, the fact that Shakespeare's fellows, in collecting his dramatic work for publication, thought *The Tempest* worthy to stand as the first play in the Folio, suggests that as qualified judges they held a high opinion of its merits and of its appeal to current taste.

Theories that *The Tempest* was an earlier play revived and refurbished for some Court occasion are no longer widely believed. Such hypotheses usually involved the suspicion that the masque in Act IV was not an integral part of the play, but an interlude inserted into the main structure in order to celebrate a Court wedding or betrothal. E. K. Chambers convincingly disposed of these arguments in his essay 'The Integrity of *The Tempest*'; and other critics have since shown how the betrothal masque relates directly to the main dramatic interests of the play. *The Tempest* was performed again at Court in the winter of 1612–13 as part of the entertainments celebrating the marriage of Princess Elizabeth to the Elector Palatine, which took place on 14 February 1613; but it was one of several plays presented for these festivities, and there are no grounds for supposing the masque of Act IV to have been more than a happy coincidence in its appropriateness to that occasion.

The Tempest as a whole shows the influence on Shakespeare's dramatic techniques of the Court Masque, a form of private entertainment which reached new heights of splendour and lavishness under James I, who was more extravagant, and whose queen was more enthusiastic, than his predecessor in promoting such shows at royal expense. The emphasis of the masques upon music and spectacle, and their use of improbable settings and supernatural figures, are reflected in Shakespeare's play. The acting company of which he was a leading member had strengthened its links with the Court since Elizabeth's day, first by receiving the patronage of the new monarch (signified by the title of the King's Men, which had been their's since 1603), and later by their acquisition in 1608 of the 'private' indoor theatre at Blackfriars, frequented by a more exclusive, courtly audience.

Thus by 1611, although the King's Men still occupied the larger public playhouse at the Globe for most of the year, they were also catering to a narrower social élite in Blackfriars and with performances at Court. It has been argued that the romantic plays written by Shakespeare at the close of his career reflect these changing circumstances and illustrate Shakespeare's readiness, as ever, to exploit new trends in dramatic taste and fashion. Similarities of a general kind have been observed between these plays and the Italianate tragi-comedies of Beaumont and Fletcher, who also wrote for the King's Men, and whose work in these same years was enjoying great success among those who considered themselves sophisticated and refined. Nevertheless it is possible to exaggerate the importance of the courtly audience in searching for an explanation of Shakespeare's last plays; the fact remains that the first references we have to performances of *Cymbeline* and *The Winter's Tale* relate them to the Globe, and therefore we should not assume that Shakespeare was incapable of pleasing both popular and courtly tastes with the same play, or that *The Tempest* was 'caviare to the general'.

II

While the dramatic form of *The Tempest* can be shown to reflect theatrical innovations of its day, no source has been found for the plot of the play. Analogies to the story abound in folktale and romance, and the central situations have been compared with certain *scenari* written for the contemporary *commedia dell' arte* in Italy. No direct relationship between *The Tempest* and any of such analogues has been established, however, and, reluctant as critics are to credit Shakespeare's inventive powers in this respect, it seems as though we must suppose that on this occasion Shakespeare composed his own version of a story whose elements are conventional and familiar enough to be regarded as the common property of romance. The only 'sources' of the play (if we mean something more specific than influences of a general kind) are three documents in the Virginia Company's papers relating to a shipwreck on the Bermudas in 1609; Montaigne's essay 'Of the Caniballes'; and, for Prospero's speech renouncing his magic arts, the *Metamorphoses* of Ovid. Of these, the papers concerning the Bermudas shipwreck are perhaps the most important, because they may well have been the true 'occasion' of Shakespeare's play. The three documents are Sylvester Jourdain's *A Discovery of the Bermudas* (1610), the London Council of Virginia's *A True Declaration of the Estate of the Colonie in Virginia* (1610), and a letter from William Strachey to the Council, dated 1609, later published in 1625 as *A True Reportory of the Wracke and Redemption of Sir Thomas Gates, Knight.* Each of these papers tells of the expedition which left England in May 1609 under the command of Sir Thomas Gates and Sir George Summers, carrying five hundred colonists bound for Virginia. The ship bearing both Gates and Summers was separated from the others in a storm and was wrecked on the coast of the Bermudas. All on board reached shore safely and stayed on the island until May 1610, when they left to continue their voyage to Virginia. News of their survival, and of the beauty and fertility of the island, was reported to the Company by Jourdain and Strachey, each of whom had shared the fate of the shipwrecked colonists. The adventure was seen as a miraculous deliverance from disaster, and the island discovered seemed a new Paradise. The Virginia Company published Jourdain's account, together with its own *True Declaration*, which also related a recent uprising in Virginia and its successful quelling by the governor. Shakespeare seems to have made more use of Strachey's then unpublished account, however, and he might well have had access to this private communication through his acquaintance with leading members of the Company, such as the Earl of Southampton and Sir Dudley Digges (whose brother Leonard was to write commemorative verses for the 1623 Folio).

The narratives of the Bermudas shipwreck and of mutiny in the colony probably lie behind several details and 'authentic' touches in

Shakespeare's play, but the most interesting link between them and *The Tempest* is the way in which the colonists interpreted their adventures in pious terms illustrating the goodness of divine providence. It may at first seem a far cry from the realism of the Virginia Company's publicity to the fantasy world of romance, but Professor Kermode, in his Introduction to the New Arden edition of the play, has shown how attitudes to the New World were conditioned by the ideas of the Old World. Marvell's poem 'The Bermudas', written in the 1650s, expresses the same tendency to assimilate the modern experiences of colonisation to the ancient biblical or classical beliefs concerning providential voyages, primitive mankind, and unspoiled nature. Consequently Montaigne's essay 'Of the Caniballes' is not very remote from the preoccupations of Jourdain and Strachey in their reports. For Montaigne is reflecting upon such travellers' tales about the savages of the New World, and the theme of his essay is the moral superiority of uncivilised man. Shakespeare's use of Montaigne in *The Tempest* is not confined to the close verbal parallels between the essay and Gonzalo's speech on the ideal commonwealth, for the ideas of Montaigne's primitivism permeate many aspects of the play. Caliban may derive his name from a simple anagram of 'cannibal', and the contrasts with the drunken sailors and with the corrupt Antonio, which reflect so favourably upon him, are in line with Montaigne's attitude. Some of the nobility and generosity attributed by Montaigne to primitive chieftains in war also seems to have rubbed off on Prospero. But in other respects Shakespeare's point of view is more complex than that of the essay: Gonzalo's raptures are treated ironically, and Caliban, in his brutality and cunning, is scarcely an idealised representation of the savage. To Montaigne's comparisons between the virtues of primitivism and the vices of civilisation Shakespeare adds a series of contrasts between the baser instincts of untutored nature and the higher values of a life ordered by reason and honour.

In Renaissance literature these ideas were particularly associated with the pastoral convention, and Professor Kermode has argued convincingly that *The Tempest* is primarily a pastoral play, composed on the theme of Nature and Art. In this context 'Art' embraces all aspects of man's endeavour to improve on Nature, not competing with her, but co-operating in order to sustain a life worthy of his rational and moral nature. Civilisation, government, and the values of society, breeding, education, and virtue, are achieved by Art. Thus Prospero's magic powers, which Miranda calls his 'art', are seen as the human improvement of nature, raised to its highest level; his control over the spirits of earth, air, and water is derived from his learning and virtue, unlike that of the witch Sycorax, whose powers were diabolical. Thus, too, Miranda and Ferdinand are contrasted with Caliban, since their royal blood gives them an innate nobility lacking in the monstrous offspring of a witch and a demon; while, on the other hand, Antonio and Sebastian show how noble birth may be betrayed by unnatural vices. Caliban is ineducable, as Prospero realises, but Antonio's breeding makes him the more dangerous enemy; Caliban will sue for mercy, but Antonio remains unreconciled. By means of parallels and contrasts of this kind the carefully balanced structure of *The Tempest* expresses the traditional concern of pastoral with the antithesis of primitive and sophisticated planes of existence. The pastoral convention itself is a product of this duality, being essentially a highly artificial image of an ideal simplicity.

The Tempest is consequently a very subtle composition of realism and fantasy. From one point of view it is a topical play closely related to the discovery of the New World and to the literature of colonisation. At the same time it derives from the world of folk-tale and make-believe, being a romantic story of a magician and his daughter the princess, with the inevitable happy ending. It is both a charming entertainment, full of music and stage-spectacle, and a serious philosophical drama employing the concepts of its day in distinguishing virtue's true simplicity from baseness and deception. Yet again, it is a play of severely restricted compass and symmetrical form, although so comprehensive that it ranges through the scale of creation from a sub-human brute to the spirits of the air, between which extremes the mechanicals, the courtiers, the members of royalty, children and their fathers, each occupies an appropriate station. Such seeming contradictions pay tribute to the artistry with which Shakespeare has blended the elements of his work. The complexity of Shakespeare's pattern is illustrated by Caliban. In that he cannot respond to Prospero's attempts to teach him, he is a foil to Miranda; in that he resents the tasks imposed upon him by Prospero, he is a foil to Ferdinand; in that he plots with Trinculo and Stephano, he is a foil to Antonio; in that he urges his fellow conspirators to ignore the flashy clothes left by Prospero to distract them, he is a foil to Stephano and Trinculo. He is both villain and clown – in one respect an unnatural hybrid monster, in another sense the savage man of pastoral tradition; and he might even be claimed as the only American in Shakespeare. The whole is greater than the sum of its parts.

III

It is this sensitive poise of *The Tempest* – between sheer enchantment and the issues of the real world – which makes the play a great work of art, and yet which is most difficult to analyse or represent. The particular balance and tone of the work have almost always eluded critics, and the history of *Tempest* criticism chiefly reveals the changes of emphasis upon this or that aspect of the play.

Even within the half-century that separated Shakespeare's play from the version composed by Dryden and Davenant in 1667, the cultural climate had changed so sharply that while Dryden was able to feel the Shakespearean harmony, he was unable to reproduce it. This quality in the original *Tempest* receives its tribute from Dryden in his Prologue to the new version:

> But *Shakespear's* Magick could not copy'd be;
> Within that Circle none durst walk but he.

Perhaps Dryden's witty metaphorical identification of Shakespeare with Prospero in this famous couplet anticipates the later romantic interpretations of *The Tempest* as an autobiographical work. The fact remains that the Dryden and Davenant adaptation is a poor thing compared with Shakespeare's play, as Dryden half-confesses. Milton's *Comus* (1634) is much closer to the spirit of *The Tempest* than this crude piece of work, though the comparison between the Dryden and Davenant version and the original is instructive. To please the tastes of the Restoration the spectacular elements were elaborated and the comic potentialities of Miranda's ignorance of the opposite sex exploited to the full. Indeed, as the excerpts included in this volume show, Dryden and Davenant completely recast the play by multiplying the sexual partnerships, giving Miranda a sister, Dorinda, who has similarly never seen a man other than her father, and balancing this situation by introducing Hippolito as Prospero's young ward, who has never set eyes on a woman. In addition Ariel and Caliban each have female counterparts. Shakespeare's main action involving the confrontation of Prospero with his enemies is thus rendered subordinate to a farce, in which dramatic conflict is generated by sexual jealousy, and amusement, if that is the right word, is chiefly dependent on *doubles entendres* at the expense of sexual naivety. The only element which strikes a less frivolous note is the political satire provided by the quarrels between Trinculo, Stephano, Mustacho and Ventoso, in their attempts to set up a rival régime to that of Prospero. Dryden and Davenant's version is not only a much simpler and more superficial play than Shakespeare's, it represents a marked coarsening and vulgarising of the original. The solemnity with which Shakespeare treats conceptions of chastity and honour has been replaced by some rather cheap sniggers about virginity. The differences between the two plays reveal that profounder changes than literary fashions separated Shakespeare from the Restoration.

Neo-classical critics of the later seventeenth and the eighteenth centuries showed little awareness of the philosophical themes in *The Tempest*, but recognised its appeal as a charming fantasy. Since so many of the conceptions and attitudes underlying Shakespeare's work belong to a view of the world which had become outmoded and forgotten, Ben Jonson's strictures on Shakespeare's want of learning gained currency, and the author of *The Tempest* was regarded as an untutored genius of prodigious imaginative power, whose natural abilities compensated for an assumed deficiency in book-learning. Dryden's admiration for *The Tempest*, acknowledged in the Preface to *Troilus and Cressida*, was based on a view of the play as a triumph of sheer poetic invention. According to this view, Shakespeare had succeeded precisely because he needed no learning, but only his imagination, to create such an original and fanciful romance. In particular, Dryden singled out for praise the character of Caliban, as a creature of an entirely new species, not to be found in nature, and one whom Shakespeare had appropriately endowed with a new language. Dryden's encomium was echoed throughout the Augustan period in virtually the same terms; we find it reiterated by Addison, that reliable index to contemporary taste, in *The Spectator* for 19 January 1712:

> It shews a greater Genius in *Shakespear* to have drawn his *Calyban*, than his *Hotspur* or *Julius Caesar*: The one was to be supplied out of his own Imagination, whereas the other might have been formed upon Tradition, History and Observation.

Dr Johnson did his best to crush what must have been quite a cliché by his time (1765), asserting rather testily that there was nothing peculiar to Caliban's language which anyone of similar sentiments and in similar circumstances would not utter. The fact that *The Tempest* obeys the unities of action, place and time gratified neo-classical tastes, but it was thought to spring more from accident than design on Shakespeare's part.

Joseph Warton's essays on the play in 1753 mainly elaborate the familiar eighteenth-century response, although there is a distinctively new emphasis, and a relatively new word, in his observation that 'He has there given the reins to his boundless imagination, and has carried the romantic, the wonderful, and the wild, to the most pleasing extravagance'. We seem with Warton to be on the verge of Romanticism; nevertheless the critics of the Romantic generation show less interest in the fanciful extravagance of the play than in its harmony of design and in the ideal truths apprehended by poetic vision.

Coleridge's affirmation that *The Tempest* 'addresses itself entirely to the imagination' bears only a superficial resemblance to the emphasis of eighteenth-century commentaries, for the word 'imagination' itself has developed new implications, and his lectures on the play explore deeper significances than the older critics were aware of. The Romantic conception of *The Tempest* as a dramatic poem reflected a more philosophical interest in its meaning. Like Coleridge, Hazlitt paid tribute to the unifying and idealising power of imagination revealed in the play. And like Coleridge, Lamb thought the play too profound, too exalted, for its effects to be properly conveyed by the crudities of theatrical performance:

> Much has been said, and deservedly, in reprobation of the vile mixture which Dryden has thrown into the Tempest: doubtless without some such vicious alloy, the impure ears of that age would never have sate out to hear so much innocence of love as is contained in the sweet courtship of Ferdinand and Miranda. But is the Tempest of Shakespeare at all a subject for stage representation? It is one thing to read of an enchanter, and to believe the wondrous tale while we are reading it; but to have a conjuror brought before us in his conjuring-gown, with his spirits about him, which none but himself and some hundred of favoured spectators before the curtain are supposed to see, involves such a quantity of the *hateful incredible*, that all our reverence for the author cannot hinder us from perceiving such gross attempts upon the senses to be in the highest degree childish and

inefficient. Spirits and fairies cannot be represented, they cannot even be painted, – they can only be believed. But the elaborate and anxious provision of scenery, which the luxury of the age demands, in these cases works a quite contrary effect to what is intended. That which in comedy, or plays of familiar life, adds so much to the life of the imitation, in plays which appeal to the higher faculties, positively destroys the illusion which it is introduced to aid.[1]

We shall be less astonished at this failure to appreciate the eminent stageworthiness of *The Tempest* when we recall that in Lamb's day – and throughout the nineteenth century – methods of production were dominated by a concern for gross literalism and decorative detail on the grandest scale. The encumbrances of the naturalistic stage, in terms of which Lamb was thinking, were quite inappropriate to Shakespeare. Charles Kean's production of *The Tempest* in 1857 was just such a travesty, to judge from his self-congratulatory programme-note:

> The scenic appliances of the play are of a more extensive and complicated nature than ever has been attempted in any theatre in Europe, requiring the aid of one hundred and forty operatives nightly, who, unseen by the audience, are engaged in working the machinery and carrying out the various effects.

The fabric of this vision must have been an unwieldy parody of that presented to Ferdinand and Miranda. It was not until the end of the nineteenth century, when William Poel made his audiences begin to realise the advantages of the kind of open stage for which Shakespeare had originally written, and so rid Shakespearean productions of extravagant scenic distractions, that the poetic quality of the plays could be shown as theatrically effective.

After the high Romantic interest in the play as a product of the poetic imagination, *The Tempest* became for many Victorians above all an allegory of Shakespeare's own artistic genius. For them, there was no boundary between art and life, and Prospero, the supreme master of visions, was identified with his creator, nowhere more so than in his great speech, 'Our revels now are ended', which was interpreted as Shakespeare's own farewell to the stage. Thus Edward Dowden finds in Prospero's benign reconciliation and

[1] Charles Lamb, *On the Tragedies of Shakespeare, considered with reference to their fitness for Stage Representation* (1811).

resignation of magic power an expression of Shakespeare's thoughts on 'passing from his service as artist to his service as English country gentleman'.

Exasperation with such pseudo-autobiographical liberties provoked Lytton Strachey roundly to assert, in his notorious essay of 1906 on 'Shakespeare's Final Period', that the poet was 'bored with people, bored with real life, bored with drama, bored, in fact, with everything except poetry and poetical dreams'. Henry James' meditation on the play appeared in the following year, using the Prospero-Shakespeare analogue to question the differences between literature and life, and W. H. Auden, through the comic-grotesque ventriloquism of Caliban, distinguishes between the 'felicitous pattern' we expect Art to provide and the haphazard 'embarrassing copresence of the absolutely natural'. The fact that James and Auden were themselves creative writers is a reminder of the capacity of *The Tempest* to inspire original artists, poets, painters and composers, to go off from the play at tangents of their own.

Twentieth-century interpretations of the play are generally more aware of its discordant and disturbing elements. Middleton Murry accepts that 'Prospero is, to some extent, an imaginative paradigm of Shakespeare himself in his function of poet', but he recognises the disillusion that circumscribes the poet's vision of mankind. E. M. W. Tillyard presents a fallible Prospero, still embittered by his recollection of past failure and betrayal, and looking to Ferdinand and Miranda to sustain 'a new order of things'. For G. Wilson Knight, the play recalls many images and metaphorical patterns in Shakespeare's previous work, including the tragedies as well as the comedies, and Prospero, like Shakespeare in his poetry, 'labours to master and assimilate that unassuaged bitterness and sense of rejection so normal a lot to humanity'. If a metaphysical and allegorical mistiness still clings to these interpretations from the first half of the century, Reuben Brower's detailed study of the play's metaphorical design clarifies even its dream-like qualities and makes them yield to a less subjective analysis.

The most authoritative and comprehensive modern view of *The Tempest*, and one which finally dispenses with the Prospero–Shakespeare analogue, is Frank Kermode's Introduction to his Arden edition of the play. By identifying it as belonging to the genre of pastoral romance, Kermode gives central importance to the antithesis of Art and Nature as the play's ordering principle. The primitivism of Montaigne's essay. 'Of the Caniballes', which we know to have been one of Shakespeare's sources, is traced to the same roots in literary tradition, as interest in the old question of nature *versus* nurture was rekindled by the Renaissance discovery of the savages of the New World. Kermode, anticipated in this by Middlcton Murry, tends to side with the civilised Art of Prospero against the ugly brutality of Caliban and to suppose that 'the black and mutilated cannibal must be the natural slave of the European gentleman', particularly when that gentleman is as virtuous and as learned as Prospero. A very different interpretation of the encounter is taken by Leslie Fiedler, for whom Caliban represents all the victims of colonial suppression and exploitation by a master-race, preserving for some future release those anarchic energies of 'a dark divinity which the master of arts had failed to take into account'. Fiedler writes with the hindsight of the twentieth century, and therefore his case is anachronistic, but, as we shall see, it is one that currently prevails.

The nature of Prospero's magic is further distinguished from the powers of his creator in Frances Yates' derivation of his learning from the curious currents of Renaissance scientific thought, with their mixture of ancient esoteric lore and early modern mathematical technology. 'It is inevitable and unavoidable,' she claims, 'in thinking of Prospero to bring in the name of John Dee, the great mathematical magus of whom Shakespeare must have known'. This bold speculation introduces us to a chain of hypothetical topical allusions which are no less fascinating for bringing the play out of the shadows of allegory and fairy tale.

Two final extracts reflect the recent shift of critical interest towards Caliban as the key to interpretation. Trevor R. Griffiths' revealing account of Caliban on the stage and his critical reception there from the Edwardian period to our own day relates performances of the role to the change from Imperialist to Postimperialist attitudes towards race and class. F. R. Benson, for instance, is described as preparing for the part by studying monkeys in the zoo, to give his Caliban a suggestion of the Darwinian 'missing link', a grotesquely bestial character who is subjugated by right and necessity. Beerbohm Tree's Caliban was also 'the ignorant native to whom the colonist Prospero had brought an enlightenment'. But in Jonathan Miller's production in 1970, which emphasised the colonial possibilities of the play, Caliban was taken seriously, together with Ariel, as embodying opposing responses of native black populations to European settlers. In 1978 a reviewer castigated a Stratford production for its failure 'in mining the play's political-colonial sub-text', although the same production was praised by another critic for a Caliban who was 'no deformed monster but a Man Friday conscious of his usurped rights'.

Francis Barker and Peter Hulme point out that the play's concerns with usurpation and liberation extend beyond the Prospero–Caliban relationship and that Prospero's disturbance at remembering Caliban's plot and his interruption of the masque are of particular significance. His reaction 'represents his disquiet at the irruption into consciousness of an unconscious anxiety concerning the grounding of his legitimacy, both as producer of his plays and, *a fortiore*, as governor of the island'. Prospero's perception and his version of events, in other words, are not to be taken at face value. Indeed, the text of the play may be used as 'the quelling of a fundamental disquiet concerning its own functions within the projects of colonialist discourse', its supposed autotelic unity 'marked and fissured' by an interplay of multiple discourses. Barker and Hulme are in no doubt that we are dealing with a play of political realism and not, as Coleridge thought, one that 'addresses itself entirely to the imaginative faculty'.

PART ONE

Adaptations, and Extracts from Earlier Critics, 1670–1945

John Dryden and Sir William Davenant
The Tempest (1670)

Act II Scene ii

Cypress trees and a Cave

Enter PROSPERO *alone*

Prosp. 'Tis not yet fit to let my daughters know,
I keep the infant duke of Mantua
So near them in this isle;
Whose father, dying, bequeathed him to my care;
Till my false brother (when he designed to usurp
My dukedom from me) exposed him to that fate,
He meant for me.
By calculation of his birth, I saw
Death threat'ning him, if, till some time were past,
He should behold the face of any woman:
And now the danger's nigh. – Hippolito!

Enter HIPPOLITO

Hip. Sir, I attend your pleasure.
Prosp. How I have loved thee, from thy infancy,
Heaven knows, and thou thyself canst bear me witness;
Therefore accuse not me of thy restraint.
Hip. Since I knew life, you've kept me in a rock;
And you, this day, have hurried me from thence,
Only to change my prison, not to free me.
I murmur not, but I may wonder at it.
Prosp. O, gentle youth! fate waits for thee abroad;
A black star threatens thee; and death, unseen,
Stands ready to devour thee.
Hip. You taught me
Not to fear him in any of his shapes: –
Let me meet death rather than be a prisoner.
Prosp. 'Tis pity he should seize thy tender youth.
Hip. Sir, I have often heard you say, no creature
Lived in this isle, but those which man was lord of.
Why, then, should I fear?
Prosp. But here are creatures which I named not to thee,
Who share man's sovereignty by nature's laws,
And oft depose him from it.

Hip. What are those creatures, sir?
Prosp. Those dangerous enemies of men, called women.
Hip. Women! I never heard of them before. –
What are women like?
Prosp. Imagine something between young men and angels;
Fatally beauteous, and have killing eyes;
Their voices charm beyond the nightingale's;
They are all enchantment: Those, who once behold them,
Are made their slaves for ever.
Hip. Then I will wink, and fight with them.
Prosp. 'Tis but in vain;
They'll haunt you in your very sleep.
Hip. Then I'll revenge it on them when I wake.
Prosp. You are without all possibility of revenge;
They are so beautiful, that you can ne'er attempt,
Nor wish, to hurt them.
Hip. Are they so beautiful?
Prosp. Calm sleep is not so soft, not winter suns,
Nor summer shades, so pleasant.
Hip. Can they be fairer than the plumes of swans?
Or more delightful than the peacock's feathers?
Or than the gloss upon the necks of doves?
Or have more various beauty than the rainbow? –
These I have seen, and, without danger, wondered at.
Prosp. All these are far below them: Nature made
Nothing but woman dangerous and fair.
Therefore if you should chance to see them,
Avoid them straight, I charge you.
Hip. Well, since you say they are so dangerous,
I'll so far shun them, as I may with safety
Of the unblemished honour, which you taught me.
But let them not provoke me, for I'm sure
I shall not then forbear them.
Prosp. Go in, and read the book I gave you last.
To-morrow I may bring you better news.
Hip. I shall obey you, sir. [*Exit* HIP.
Prosp. So, so; I hope this lesson has secured him,
For I have been constrained to change his lodging
From yonder rock, where first I bred him up,
And here have brought him home to my own cell,
Because the shipwreck happened near his mansion.
I hope he will not stir beyond his limits,
For hitherto he hath been all obedience:
The planets seem to smile on my designs,
And yet there is one sullen cloud behind:
I would it were dispersed!

Enter MIRANDA *and* DORINDA

How, my daughters!
I thought I had instructed them enough:
Children! retire; why do you walk this way?

Mir. It is within our bounds, sir.

Prosp. But both take heed, that path is very dangerous;
remember what I told you.

Dor. Is the man that way, sir?

Prosp. All that you can imagine ill is there,
The curled lion, and the rugged bear,
Are not so dreadful as that man.

Mir. Oh me, why stay we here then?

Dor. I'll keep far enough from his den, I warrant him.

Mir. But you have told me, sir, you are a man;
And yet you are not dreadful.

Prosp. Ay, child; but I
Am a tame man; old men are tame by nature,
But all the danger lies in a wild young man.

Dor. Do they run wild about the woods?

Prosp. No, they are wild within doors, in chambers, and in closets.

Dor. But, father, I would stroak them, and make them gentle;
then sure they would not hurt me.

Prosp. You must not trust them, child: No woman can come near them, but she feels a pain, full nine months. Well, I must in; for new affairs require my presence: Be you, Miranda, your sister's guardian.

[*Exit* PROS.

Dor. Come, sister, shall we walk the other way?
The man will catch us else: We have but two legs,
And he, perhaps, has four.

Mir. Well, sister, though he have; yet look about you.

Dor. Come back! that way is towards his den.

Mir. Let me alone; I'll venture first, for sure he can
Devour but one of us at once.

Dor. How dare you venture?

Mir. We'll find him sitting like a hare in's form,
And he shall not see us.

Dor. Ay, but you know my father charged us both.

Mir. But who shall tell him on't? we'll keep each other's counsel.

Dor. I dare not, for the world.

Mir. But how shall we hereafter shun him, if we do not know him first?

Dor. Nay, I confess I would fain see him too. I find it in my nature, because my father has forbidden me.

Mir. Ay, there's it; sister; if he had said nothing, I had been quiet. Go softly, and if you see him first, be quick, and beckon me away.

Dor. Well, if he does catch me, I'll humble myself to him, and ask him pardon, as I do my father, when I have done a fault.

Mir. And if I can but escape with life, I had rather be in pain nine months, as my father threatened, than lose my longing.

[*Exeunt*.

Scene iii

Enter HIPPOLITO

Hip. Prospero has often said, that nature makes
Nothing in vain: Why then are women made?
Are they to suck the poison of the earth,
As gaudy coloured serpents are? I'll ask
That question, when next I see him here.

Enter MIRANDA *and* DORINDA *peeping*

Dor. O sister, there it is! it walks about
Like one of us.
Mir. Ay, just so, and has legs as we have too.
Hip. It strangely puzzles me: Yet 'tis most likely,
Women are somewhat between men and spirits.
Dor. Hark! it talks: – sure this is not it my father meant,
For this is just like one of us: Methinks,
I am not half so much afraid on't as
I was; see, now it turns this way.
Mir. Heaven! what a goodly thing it is!
Dor. I'll go nearer it.
Mir. O no, 'tis dangerous, sister! I'll go to it.
I would not for the world that you should venture.
My father charged me to secure you from it.
Dor. I warrant you this is a tame man; dear sister,
He'll not hurt me, I see it by his looks.
Mir. Indeed he will! but go back, and he shall eat me first: Fie, are you not ashamed to be so inquisitive?
Dor. You chide me for it, and would give him yourself.
Mir. Come back, or I will tell my father.
Observe how he begins to stare already!
I'll meet the danger first, and then call you.
Dor. Nay, sister, you shall never vanquish me in kindness. I'll venture you no more than you will me.
Prosp. [*within*] Miranda, child, where are you?
Mir. Do you not hear my father call? Go in.
Dor. 'Twas you he named, not me; I will but say my prayers, and follow you immediately.
Mir. Well, sister, you'll repent it. [*Exit* MIR.
Dor. Though I die for it, I must have the other peep.
Hip. What thing is that? [*Seeing her*.] Sure 'tis some infant of

The sun, dressed in his father's gayest beams,
And comes to play with birds: My sight is dazzled,
And yet I find I'm loth to shut my eyes:
I must go nearer it; – but stay a while;
May it not be that beauteous murderer, woman,
Which I was charged to shun? Speak, what art thou,
Thou shining vision!

Dor. Alas, I know not; but I'm told I am
A woman; do not hurt me, pray, fair thing.

Hip. I'd sooner tear my eyes out, than consent
To do you any harm; though I was told,
A woman was my enemy.

Dor. I never knew
What 'twas to be an enemy, nor can I e'er
Prove so to that, which looks like you: For though
I've been charged by him (whom yet I ne'er disobeyed,)
To shun your presence, yet I'd rather die
Than lose it; therefore, I hope you will not have the heart
To hurt me: Though I fear you are a man,
The dangerous thing of which I have been warned.
Pray, tell me what you are?

Hip. I must confess, I was informed I am a man;
But if I fright you, I shall wish I were some other creature.
I was bid to fear you too.

Dor. Ah me! Heaven grant we be not poison to
Each other! Alas, can we not meet, but we must die?

Hip. I hope not so! for, when two poisonous creatures,
Both of the same kind, meet, yet neither dies.
I've seen two serpents harmless to each other,
Though they have twined into a mutual knot:
If we have any venom in us, sure, we cannot be
More poisonous, when we meet, than serpents are.
You have a hand like mine – may I not gently touch it?
[*Takes her hand.*

Dor. I've touched my father's and sister's hands,
And felt no pain; but now, alas! there's something,
When I touch yours, which makes me sigh: Just so
I've seen two turtles mourning when they met:
Yet mine's a pleasing grief; and so, methought,
Was theirs: For still they mourned, and still they seemed
To murmur too, and yet they often met.

Hip. Oh heavens! I have the same sense too: your hand,
Methinks, goes through me; I feel it at my heart,
And find it pleases, though it pains me.

Prosp. [*within*] Dorinda!

Dor. My father calls again; ah, I must leave you.

Hip. Alas, I'm subject to the same command.

Dor. This is my first offence against my father,
Which he, by severing us, too cruelly does punish.
Hip. And this is my first trespass too: But he
Hath more offended truth, than we have him:
He said our meeting would destructive be,
But I no death, but in our parting, see. [*Exeunt severally.*

John Dryden The Character of Caliban (1679)

To return once more to Shakespeare; no man ever drew so many characters, or generally distinguished them better from one another, excepting only Jonson. I will instance but in one, to show the copiousness of his invention; it is that of Caliban, or the monster, in *The Tempest*. He seems there to have created a person which was not in nature, a boldness which, at first sight, would appear intolerable; for he makes him a species of himself, begotten by an incubus on a witch; but this, as I have elsewhere proved, is not wholly beyond the bounds of credibility, at least the vulgar still believe it. We have the separated notions of a spirit, and of a witch; (and spirits, according to Plato, are vested with a subtle body; according to some of his followers, have different sexes;) therefore, as from the distinct apprehensions of a horse, and of a man, imagination has formed a centaur; so, from those of an incubus and a sorceress, Shakespeare has produced his monster. Whether or no his generation can be defended, I leave to philosophy; but of this I am certain, that the poet has most judiciously furnished him with a person, a language, and a character, which will suit him, both by father's and mother's side: he has all the discontents, and malice of a witch, and of a devil, besides a convenient proportion of the deadly sins; gluttony, sloth, and lust, are manifest; the dejectedness of a slave is likewise given him, and the ignorance of one bred up in a desert island. His person is monstrous, and he is the product of unnatural lust; and his language is as hobgoblin as his person; in all things he is distinguished from other mortals.

Nicholas Rowe Solemn and Poetical Magic (1709)

But certainly the greatness of this Author's Genius do's no where so much appear, as where he gives his Imagination an entire Loose, and raises his Fancy to a flight above Mankind and the Limits of the visible World. Such as his Attempts in *The Tempest, Midsummer-Night's Dream, Macbeth* and *Hamlet*. Of these, *The Tempest*, however it comes to be plac'd the first by the former Publishers of his Works, can never have been the first written by him: It seems to me as perfect in its Kind, as almost any thing we have of his. One may observe, that the Unities are kept here with an Exactness uncommon to the Liberties of his Writing: Tho' that was what, I suppose, he valu'd himself least upon, since his Excellencies were all of another Kind. I am very sensible that he do's, in this Play, depart too much from that likeness to Truth which ought to be observ'd in these sort of Writings; yet he do's it so very finely, that one is easily drawn in to have more Faith for his sake, than Reason does well allow of. His Magick has something in it very Solemn and very Poetical: And that extravagant Character of *Caliban* is mighty well sustain'd, shews a wonderful Invention in the Author, who could strike out such a particular wild Image, and is certainly one of the finest and most uncommon Grotesques that was ever seen. The Observation, which I have been inform'd* three very great Men concurr'd in making upon this Part, was extremely just. *That* Shakespear *had not only found out a new Character in his* Caliban, *but had also devis'd and adapted a new manner of Language for that Character*. Among the particular Beauties of this Piece, I think one may be allow'd to point out the Tale of *Prospero* in the First Act; his Speech to *Ferdinand* in the Fourth, upon the breaking up the Masque of *Juno* and *Ceres*; and that in the Fifth, where he dissolves his Charms, and resolves to break his Magick Rod. This Play has been alter'd by *Sir William D'Avenant* and Mr. *Dryden*; and tho' I won't Arraign the Judgment of those two great Men, yet I think I may be allow'd to say, that there are some things left out by them,

* *Ld.* Falkland, *Ld. C. J.* Vaughan, *and Mr.* Selden.

that might, and even ought to have been kept in. Mr. *Dryden* was an Admirer of our Author, and, indeed, he owed him a great deal, as those who have read them both may very easily observe.

Joseph Warton 'Amazing wildness of fancy' (1753)

As Shakespeare is sometimes blameable for the conduct of his fables, which have no unity; and sometimes for his diction, which is obscure and turgid; so his characteristical excellencies may possibly be reduced to these three general heads: 'his lively creative imagination; his strokes of nature and passion; and his preservation of the consistency of his characters'. These excellencies, particularly the last, are of so much importance in the drama, that they amply compensate for his transgressions against the rules of Time and Place, which being of a more mechanical nature, are often strictly observed by a genius of the lowest order; but to portray characters naturally, and to preserve them uniformly, requires such an intimate knowledge of the heart of man, and is so rare a portion of felicity, as to have been enjoyed, perhaps, only by two writers, Homer and Shakespeare.

Of all the plays of Shakespeare, *The Tempest* is the most striking instance of his creative power. He has there given the reins to his boundless imagination, and has carried the romantic, the wonderful, and the wild, to the most pleasing extravagance. The scene is a desolate island; and the characters the most new and singular that can well be conceived: a prince who practises magic, an attendant spirit, a monster the son of a witch, and a young lady who had been brought to this solitude in her infancy, and had never beheld a man except her father.

As I have affirmed that Shakespeare's chief excellence is the consistency of his characters, I will exemplify the truth of this remark, by pointing out some master-strokes of this nature in the drama before us.

The poet artfully acquaints us that Prospero is a magician, by the first words which his daughter Miranda speaks to him:

> If by your art, my dearest father, you have
> Put the wild waters in this roar, allay them:

which intimate that the tempest described in the preceding scene, was the effect of Prospero's power. The manner in which he was driven from his dukedom of Milan, and landed afterwards on this solitary island, accompanied only by his daughter, is immediately introduced in a short and natural narration.

The offices of his attendant Spirit, Ariel, are enumerated with amazing wildness of fancy, and yet with equal propriety: his employment is said to be,

> ——To tread the ooze
> Of the salt deep;
> To run upon the sharp wind of the north;
> To do me business in the veins o' th' earth,
> When it is bak'd with frost;
> ——to dive into the fire; to ride
> On the curl'd clouds.

In describing the place in which he has concealed the Neapolitan ship, Ariel expresses the secrecy of its situation by the following circumstance, which artfully glances at another of his services;

> ——In the deep nook, where once
> Thou call'dst me up at midnight, to fetch dew
> From the still-vext Bermudas.

Ariel, being one of those elves or spirits, 'whose pastime is to make midnight mushrooms, and who rejoice to listen to the solemn curfew'; by whose assistance Prospero has bedimm'd the sun at noon-tide,

> And 'twixt the green sea and the azur'd vault,
> Set roaring war;

has a set of ideas and images peculiar to his station and office; a beauty of the same kind with that which is so justly admired in the Adam of Milton, whose manners and sentiments are all Paradisaical. How delightfully and how suitably to his character, are the habitations and pastimes of this invisible being pointed out in the following exquisite song!

Where the bee sucks, there suck I:
In a cowslip's bell I lie;
There I couch when owls do cry.
On the bat's back I do fly,
After sun-set, merrily,
Merrily merrily shall I live now,
Under the blossom that hangs on the bough.

Mr. Pope, whose imagination has been thought by some the least of his excellencies, has, doubtless, conceived and carried on the machinery in his 'Rape of the Lock', with vast exuberance of fancy. The images, customs, and employments of his Sylphs, are exactly adapted to their natures, are peculiar and appropriated, are all, if I may be allowed the expression, Sylphish. The enumeration of the punishments they were to undergo, if they neglected their charge, would, on account of its poetry and propriety, and especially the mixture of oblique satire, be superior to any circumstances in Shakespeare's Ariel, if we could suppose Pope to have been unacquainted with *The Tempest*, when he wrote this part of his accomplished poem.

——She did confine thee
Into a cloven pine; within which rift
Imprison'd, thou didst painfully remain
A dozen years: within which space she dy'd,
And left thee there; where thou didst vent thy groans,
As fast as mill-wheels strike.

If thou more murmur'st, I will rend an oak,
And peg thee in his knotty entrails, 'till
Thou'st howl'd away twelve winters.

For this, be sure, to-night thou shalt have cramps,
Side-stitches that shall pen thy breath up: urchins
Shall, for that vast of night that they may work,
All exercise on thee; thou shalt be pinch'd
As thick as honey-combs, each pinch more stinging
Than bees that made 'em.

If thou neglect'st or dost unwillingly
What I command, I'll rack thee with old cramps;
Fill all thy bones with aches: make thee roar,
That beasts shall tremble at thy din.

Shakespeare

Whatever spirit, careless of his charge,
Forsakes his post or leaves the Fair at large,
Shall feel sharp vengeance soon o'ertake his sins,
Be stopp'd in vials, or transfix'd with pins;
Or plung'd in lakes of bitter washes lie,
Or wedg'd whole ages in a bodkin's eye:
Gums and pomatums shall his flight restrain,
While clog'd he beats his silken wings in vain;
Or allum styptics with contracting pow'r,
Shrink his thin essence like a shrivell'd flow'r:
Or as Ixion fix'd, the wretch shall feel
The giddy motion of the whirling wheel;
In fumes of burning chocolate shall glow,
And tremble at the sea that froths below!

Pope

The method which is taken to induce Ferdinand to believe that his father was drown'd in the late tempest, is exceedingly solemn and striking. He is sitting upon a solitary rock, and weeping over-against the place where he imagined his father was wrecked, when he suddenly hears with astonishment aërial music creep by him upon the waters, and the Spirit gives him the following information in words not proper for any but a Spirit to utter:

Full fathom five thy father lies:
Of his bones are coral made:
Those are pearls that were his eyes:
Nothing of him that doth fade,
But doth suffer a sea-change,
Into something rich and strange.

And then follows a most lively circumstance;

Sea-nymphs hourly ring his knell.
Hark! now I hear them – Ding-dong-bell!

This is so truly poetical, that one can scarce forbear exclaiming with Ferdinand,

This is no mortal business, nor no sound
That the earth owns! –

The happy versatility of Shakespeare's genius enables him to excel in lyric as well as in dramatic poesy.

But the poet rises still higher in his management of this character of Ariel, by making a moral use of it, that is, I think, incomparable, and the greatest effort of his art. Ariel informs Prospero, that he has fulfilled his orders, and punished his brother and companions so severely, that if he himself was now to behold their sufferings, he would greatly compassionate them. To which Prospero answers,

– Dost thou think so, Spirit?
Ariel. Mine would, Sir, were I human.
Prospero. And mine shall.

He then takes occasion, with wonderful dexterity and humanity, to draw an argument from the incorporeality of Ariel, for the justice and necessity of pity and forgiveness:

Hast thou, which art but air, a touch, a feeling
Of their afflictions; and shall not myself,
One of their kind, that relish all as sharply,
Passion'd as they, be kindlier mov'd than thou art?

The poet is a more powerful magician than his own Prospero: we are transported into fairy land; we are rapt in a delicious dream, from which it is misery to be disturbed; all around is enchantment!

Joseph Warton Remarks on the Creation of Character (1753)

Χρὴ δὲ χαὶ ἐν τοῖς ἤθεσιν ὥσπερ χαὶ ἐν τῆ τῶν ὦραγμάτων συστάσει, ἀεὶ ζητεῖν, ἤ τὲ ἀναγχαὶον, ἤ τὸ εἰχος.

ARISTOTLE, *Poetics*

As well in the conduct of the manners as in the constitution of the fable, we must always endeavour to produce either what is necessary or what is probable.

'Whoever ventures', says Horace, 'to form a character totally original, let him endeavour to preserve it with uniformity and consistency; but the formation of an original character is a work of great difficulty and hazard.' In this arduous and uncommon task, however, Shakespeare has wonderfully succeeded in his *Tempest*: the monster Calyban is the creature of his own imagination, in the formation of which he could derive no assistance from observation or experience.

Calyban is the son of a witch, begotten by a demon: the sorceries of his mother were so terrible, that her countrymen banished her into this desart island as unfit for human society: in conformity, therefore, to this diabolical propagation, he is represented as a prodigy of cruelty, malice, pride, ignorance, idleness, gluttony, and lust. He is introduced with great propriety, cursing Prospero and Miranda whom he had endeavoured to defile; and his execrations are artfully contrived to have reference to the occupation of his mother:

> As wicked dew, as e'er my mother brush'd
> With raven's feather from unwholesome fen,
> Drop on you both!——
> ——All the charms
> Of Sycorax, toads, beetles, bats, light on you!

His kindness is, afterwards, expressed as much in character, as his hatred, by an enumeration of offices, that could be of value only in a desolate island, and in the estimation of a savage:

> I pr'ythee, let me bring thee where crabs grow;
> And I with my long nails will dig the pig-nuts;
> Shew thee a jay's nest; and instruct thee how
> To snare the nimble marmazet. I'll bring thee
> To clust'ring filberds; and sometimes I'll get thee
> Young sea-malls from the rock——
> I'll shew thee the best springs; I'll pluck thee berries;
> I'll fish for thee, and get thee wood enough.

Which last is, indeed, a circumstance of great use in a place, where to be defended from the cold was neither easy nor usual; and it has a farther peculiar beauty, because the gathering wood was the occupation to which Calyban was subjected by Prospero, who, therefore, deemed it a service of high importance.

The gross ignorance of this monster is represented with delicate judgment; he knew not the names of the sun and moon, which he calls the bigger light and the less; and he believes that Stephano was the man in the moon, whom his mistress had often shewn him: and when Prospero reminds him that he first taught him to pronounce articulately, his answer is full of malevolence and rage:

> You taught me language; and my profit on't
> Is, I know how to curse:——

the properest return for such a fiend to make for such a favour. The spirits whom he supposes to be employed by Prospero perpetually to torment him, and the many forms and different methods they take for this purpose, are described with the utmost liveliness and force of fancy:

> Sometimes like apes, that moe and chatter at me,
> And after bite me; then like hedge hogs, which
> Lie tumbling in my bare-foot way, and mount
> Their pricks at my foot-fall: sometimes am I
> All wound with adders, who with cloven tongues
> Do hiss me into madness.

It is scarcely possible for any speech to be more expressive of the manners and sentiments, than that in which our poet has painted the brutal barbarity and unfeeling savageness of this son of Sycorax, by making him enumerate, with a kind of horrible delight, the various ways in which it was possible for the drunken sailors to surprize and kill his master:

> ——There thou may'st brain him,
> Having first seiz'd his books; or with a log
> Batter his skull; or paunch him with a stake;
> Or cut his wezand with thy knife——

He adds, in allusion to his own abominable attempt, 'above all be sure to secure the daughter; whose beauty, he tells them, is incomparable'. The charms of Miranda could not be more exalted, than by extorting this testimony from so insensible a monster.

Shakespeare seems to be the only poet who possesses the power of uniting poetry with propriety of character; of which I know not an instance more striking, than the image Calyban makes use of to express silence, which is at once highly poetical, and exactly suited to the wildness of the speaker:

> Pray you tread softly, that the blind mole may not
> Hear a foot-fall.——

I always lament that our author has not preserved this fierce and implacable spirit in Calyban, to the end of the play; instead of which, he has, I think, injudiciously put into his mouth, words that imply repentance and understanding:

> —— I'll be wise hereafter
> And seek for grace. What a thrice double ass
> Was I, to take this drunkard for a God,
> And worship this dull fool?

It must not be forgotten, that Shakespeare has artfully taken occasion from this extraordinary character, which is finely contrasted to the mildness and obedience of Ariel, obliquely to satirize the prevailing passion for new and wonderful sights, which has rendered the English so ridiculous. 'Were I in England now,' says Trinculo, on first discovering Calyban, 'and had but this fish painted, not an holiday fool there but would give a piece of silver. – When they will not give a doit to relieve a lame beggar, they will lay out ten to see a dead Indian.'

Such is the inexhaustible plenty of our poet's invention, that he has exhibited another character in this play, entirely his own; that of the lovely and innocent Miranda.

When Prospero first gives her a sight of prince Ferdinand, she eagerly exclaims,

> ——What is't? a spirit?
> Lord, how it looks about! Believe me, Sir,
> It carries a brave form. But 'tis a spirit.

Her imagining that as he was so beautiful he must necessarily be one of her father's aërial agents, is a stroke of nature worthy admiration: as are likewise her intreaties to her father not to use him harshly, by the power of his art;

> Why speaks my father so ungently? This
> Is the third man that e'er I saw; the first
> That e'er I sigh'd for!——

Here we perceive the beginning of that passion, which Prospero was desirous she should feel for the prince; and which she afterwards more fully expresses upon an occasion which displays at once the tenderness, the innocence, and the simplicity of her character. She discovers her lover employed in the laborious task of carrying wood, which Prospero had enjoined him to perform. 'Would', says she, 'the lightning had burnt up those logs, that you are enjoined to pile!'

——If you'll sit down,
I'll bear your logs the while. Pray give me that,
I'll carry't to the pile.——
——You look wearily.

It is by selecting such little and almost imperceptible circumstances that Shakespeare has more truly painted the passions than any other writer: affection is more powerfully expressed by this simple wish and offer of assistance, than by the unnatural eloquence and witticisms of Dryden, or the amorous declamations of Rowe.

The resentment of Prospero for the matchless cruelty and wicked usurpation of his brother; his parental affection and solicitude for the welfare of his daughter, the heiress of his dukedom; and the awful solemnity of his character, as a skilful magician; are all along preserved with equal consistency, dignity, and decorum. One part of his behaviour deserves to be particularly pointed out: during the exhibition of a mask with which he had ordered Ariel to entertain Ferdinand and Miranda, he starts suddenly from the recollection of the conspiracy of Calyban and his confederates against his life, and dismisses his attendant spirits, who instantly vanish to a hollow and confused noise. He appears to be greatly moved; and suitably to this agitation of mind, which his danger has excited, he takes occasion, from the sudden disappearance of the visionary scene, to moralize on the dissolution of all things:

——These our actors
As I foretold you, were all spirits: and
Are melted into air, into thin air.
And, like the baseless fabric of this vision,
The cloud-capt towers, the gorgeous palaces,
The solemn temples, the great globe itself,
Yea, all which it inherit, shall dissolve;
And, like this unsubstantial pageant faded,
Leave not a rack behind——

To these noble images he adds a short but comprehensive observation on human life, not excelled by any passage of the moral and sententious Euripides:

——We are such stuff
As dreams are made on; and our little life
Is rounded with a sleep!——

Thus admirably is an uniformity of character, that leading beauty in dramatic poesy, preserved throughout *The Tempest*. And it may be farther remarked, that the unities of action, of place, and of time, are in this play, though almost constantly violated by Shakespeare, exactly observed. The action is one, great, and entire, the restoration of Prospero to his dukedom; this business is transacted in the compass of a small island, and in or near the cave of Prospero; though, indeed, it had been more artful and regular to have confined it to this single spot; and the time which the action takes up, is only equal to that of the representation; an excellence which ought always to be aimed at in every well-conducted fable, and for the want of which a variety of the most entertaining incidents can scarcely atone.

Samuel Johnson Caliban's Language (1765)

It was a tradition, it seems, that Lord *Falkland*, Lord *C.J. Vaughan*, and Mr. *Seldon* concurred in observing, that *Shakespear* had not only found out a new character in his *Caliban*, but had also devised and adapted a *new manner of language* for that character. – WARBURTON

Whence these criticks derived the notion of a new language appropriated to *Caliban* I cannot find: They certainly mistook brutality of sentiment for uncouthness of words. *Caliban* had learned to speak of *Prospero* and his daughter, he had no names for the sun and moon before their arrival, and could not have invented a language of his own without more understanding than *Shakespear* has thought it proper to bestow upon him. His diction is indeed somewhat clouded by the gloominess of his temper and the malignity of his purposes; but let any other being entertain the same thoughts and he will find them easily issue in the same expressions.

S. T. Coleridge An Analysis of Act I (1811)

Although I have affirmed that all Shakespeare's characters are ideal, and the result of his own meditation, yet a just separation may be made of those in which the ideal is most prominent – where it is put forward more intensely – where we are made more conscious of the ideal, though in truth they possess no more nor less ideality; and of those which, though equally idealized, the delusion upon the mind is of their being real. The characters in the various plays may be separated into those where the real is disguised in the ideal, and those where the ideal is concealed from us by the real. The difference is made by the different powers of mind employed by the poet in the representation.

At present I shall only speak of dramas where the ideal is predominant; and chiefly for this reason – that those plays have been attacked with the greatest violence. The objections to them are not the growth of our own country, but of France – the judgment of monkeys, by some wonderful phenomenon, put into the mouths of people shaped like men. These creatures have informed us that Shakespeare is a miraculous monster, in whom many heterogeneous components were thrown together, producing a discordant mass of genius – an irregular and ill-assorted structure of gigantic proportions.

Among the ideal plays, I will take *The Tempest*, by way of example. Various others might be mentioned, but it is impossible to go through every drama, and what I remark on *The Tempest* will apply to all Shakespeare's productions of the same class.

In this play Shakespeare has especially appealed to the imagination, and he has constructed a plot well adapted to the purpose. According to his scheme, he did not appeal to any sensuous impression (the word 'sensuous' is authorized by Milton) of time and place, but to the imagination, and it is to be borne in mind, that of old, and as regards mere scenery, his works may be said to have been recited rather than acted – that is to say, description and narration supplied the place of visual exhibition: the audience was told to fancy that they saw what they only heard described; the painting was not in colours, but in words.

This is particularly to be noted in the first scene – a storm and its confusion on board the king's ship. The highest and the lowest characters are brought together, and with what excellence! Much of the genius of Shakespeare is displayed in these happy combinations – the highest and the lowest, the gayest and the saddest; he is not droll in one scene and melancholy in another, but often both the one and the other in the same scene. Laughter is made to swell the tear of sorrow, and to throw, as it were, a poetic light upon it, while the tear mingles tenderness with the laughter. Shakespeare has evinced the power, which above all other men he possessed, that of introducing the profoundest sentiments of wisdom, where they would be least expected, yet where they are most truly natural. One admirable secret of his art is, that separate speeches frequently do not appear to have been occasioned by those which preceded, and which are consequent upon each other, but to have arisen out of the peculiar character of the speaker.

Before I go further, I may take the opportunity of explaining what is meant by mechanic and organic regularity. In the former the copy must appear as if it had come out of the same mould with the original; in the latter there is a law which all the parts obey, conforming themselves to the outward symbols and manifestations of the essential principle. If we look to the growth of trees, for instance, we shall observe that trees of the same kind vary considerably, according to the circumstances of soil, air, or position; yet we are able to decide at once whether they are oaks, elms, or poplars.

So with Shakespeare's characters: he shows us the life and principle of each being with organic regularity. The Boatswain, in the first scene of *The Tempest*, when the bonds of reverence are thrown off as a sense of danger impresses all, gives a loose to his feelings, and thus pours forth his vulgar mind to the old Counsellor: –

'Hence! What care these roarers for the name of King? To cabin: silence! trouble us not.'

Gonzalo replies –'Good; yet remember whom thou hast aboard.' To which the Boatswain answers – 'None that I more love than myself. You are a counsellor: if you can command these elements to silence, and work the peace of the present, we will not hand a rope more; use your authority: if you cannot, give thanks that you have lived so long, and make yourself ready in your cabin for the mischance of the hour, if it so hap. – Cheerly, good hearts! – Out of our way, I say.'

An ordinary dramatist would, after this speech, have represented Gonzalo as moralizing, or saying something connected with the Boatswain's language; for ordinary dramatists are not men of genius: they combine their ideas by association, or by logical affinity; but the vital writer, who makes men on the stage what they are in nature, in a moment transports himself into the very being of each personage, and, instead of cutting out artificial puppets, he brings before us the men themselves. Therefore, Gonzalo soliloquizes, – 'I have great comfort from this fellow: methinks, he hath no drowning mark upon him; his complexion is perfect gallows. Stand fast, good fate, to his hanging! make the rope of his destiny our cable, for our own doth little advantage. If he be not born to be hanged, our case is miserable.'

In this part of the scene we see the true sailor with his contempt of danger, and the old counsellor with his high feeling, who, instead of condescending to notice the words just addressed to him, turns off, meditating with himself, and drawing some comfort to his own mind, by trifling with the ill expression of the boatswain's face, founding upon it a hope of safety.

Shakespeare had pre-determined to make the plot of this play such as to involve a certain number of low characters, and at the beginning he pitched the note of the whole. The first scene was meant as a lively commencement of the story; the reader is prepared for something that is to be developed, and in the next scene he brings forward Prospero and Miranda. How is this done? By giving to his favourite character, Miranda, a sentence which at once expresses the violence and fury of the storm, such as it might appear to a witness on the land, and at the same time displays the tenderness of her feelings – the exquisite feelings of a female brought up in a desert, but with all the advantages of education, all that could be communicated by a wise and affectionate father. She possesses all the delicacy of innocence, yet with all the powers of her mind unweakened by the combats of life. Miranda exclaims: –

> O! I have suffered
> With those that I saw suffer: a brave vessel,
> Who had, no doubt, some noble creatures in her,
> Dash'd all to pieces.

The doubt here intimated could have occurred to no mind but to that of Miranda, who had been bred up in the island with her father and a monster only: she did not know, as others do, what sort of creatures were in a ship; others never would have introduced it as a conjecture. This shows, that while Shakespeare is displaying his vast excellence, he never fails to insert some touch or other, which is not merely characteristic of the particular person, but combines two things – the person, and the circumstances acting upon the person. She proceeds: –

> O! the cry did knock
> Against my very heart. Poor souls! they perish'd.
> Had I been any god of power, I would
> Have sunk the sea within the earth, or e'er
> It should the good ship so have swallow'd, and
> The fraughting souls within her.

She still dwells upon that which was most wanting to the completeness of her nature – these fellow creatures from whom she appeared banished, with only one relict to keep them alive, not in her memory, but in her imagination.

Another proof of excellent judgment in the poet, for I am now principally adverting to that point, is to be found in the preparation of the reader for what is to follow. Prospero is introduced, first in his magic robe, which, with the assistance of his daughter, he lays aside, and we then know him to be a being possessed of supernatural powers. He then instructs Miranda in the story of their arrival in the island, and this is conducted in such a manner, that the reader never conjectures the technical use the poet has made of the relation, by informing the auditor of what it is necessary for him to know.

The next step is the warning by Prospero, that he means, for particular purposes, to lull his daughter to sleep; and here he exhibits the earliest and mildest proof of magical power. In ordinary and vulgar plays we should have had some person brought upon the stage, whom nobody knows or cares anything about, to let the audience into the secret. Prospero having cast a sleep upon his daughter, by that sleep stops the narrative at the very moment when it was necessary to break it off, in order to excite curiosity, and yet to give the memory and understanding sufficient to carry on the progress of the history uninterruptedly.

Here I cannot help noticing a fine touch of Shakespeare's

knowledge of human nature, and generally of the great laws of the human mind: I mean Miranda's infant remembrance. Prospero asks her –

> Canst thou remember
> A time before we came unto this cell?
> I do not think thou canst, for then thou wast not
> Out three years old.

Miranda answers,

> Certainly, sir, I can.

Prospero inquires,

> By what? by any other house or person?
> Of any thing the image tell me, that
> Hath kept with thy remembrance.

To which Miranda returns,

> 'Tis far off;
> And rather like a dream than an assurance
> That my remembrance warrants. Had I not
> Four or five women once, that tended me? (I ii)

This is exquisite! In general, our remembrances of early life arise from vivid colours, especially if we have seen them in motion: for instance, persons when grown up will remember a bright green door, seen when they were quite young; but Miranda, who was somewhat older, recollected four or five women who tended her. She might know men from her father, and her remembrance of the past might be worn out by the present object, but women she only knew by herself, by the contemplation of her own figure in the fountain, and she recalled to her mind what had been. It was not, that she had seen such and such grandees, or such and such peeresses, but she remembered to have seen something like the reflection of herself: it was not herself, and it brought back to her mind what she had seen most like herself.

In my opinion the picturesque power displayed by Shakespeare, of all the poets that ever lived, is only equalled, if equalled, by Milton and Dante. The presence of genius is not shown in elaborating a picture: we have had many specimens of this sort of work in modern poems, where all is so dutchified, if I may use the word, by the most minute touches, that the reader naturally asks why words, and not painting, are used? I know a young lady of much taste, who observed, that in reading recent versified accounts of voyages and travels, she, by a sort of instinct, cast her eyes on the opposite page, for coloured prints of what was so patiently and punctually described.

The power of poetry is, by a single word perhaps, to instil that energy into the mind, which compels the imagination to produce the picture. Prospero tells Miranda,

> One midnight,
> Fated to the purpose, did Antonio open
> The gates of Milan; and i' the dead of darkness,
> The ministers for the purpose hurried thence
> Me, and thy crying self.

Here, by introducing a single happy epithet, 'crying', in the last line, a complete picture is presented to the mind, and in the production of such pictures the power of genius consists.

In reference to preparation, it will be observed that the storm, and all that precedes the tale, as well as the tale itself, serve to develop completely the main character of the drama, as well as the design of Prospero. The manner in which the heroine is charmed asleep fits us for what follows, goes beyond our ordinary belief, and gradually leads us to the appearance and disclosure of a being of the most fanciful and delicate texture, like Prospero, preternaturally gifted.

In this way the entrance of Ariel, if not absolutely forethought by the reader, was foreshewn by the writer: in addition, we may remark, that the moral feeling called forth by the sweet words of Miranda,

> Alack, what trouble
> Was I then to you!

in which she considered only the sufferings and sorrows of her father, puts the reader in a frame of mind to exert his imagination in favour of an object so innocent and interesting. The poet makes him wish that, if supernatural agency were to be employed, it should be used for a being so young and lovely. 'The wish is father to the thought', and Ariel is introduced. Here, what is called poetic faith is required and created, and our common notions of philosophy give way before it: this feeling may be said to be much stronger than historic faith, since for the exercise of poetic faith the mind is previously prepared. I make this remark, though somewhat digressive, in order to lead to a future subject of these lectures – the poems of Milton. When adverting to those, I shall have to explain farther the distinction between the two.

Many Scriptural poems have been written with so much of Scripture in them, that what is not Scripture appears to be not true, and like mingling lies with the most sacred revelations. Now Milton, on the other hand, has taken for his subject that one point of Scripture of which we have the mere fact recorded, and upon this he has most judiciously constructed his whole fable. So of Shakespeare's *King Lear*: we have little historic evidence to guide or confine us, and the few facts handed down to us, and admirably employed by the poet, are sufficient, while we read, to put an end to all doubt as to the credibility of the story. It is idle to say that this or that incident is improbable, because history, as far as it goes, tells us that the fact was so and so. Four or five lines in the Bible include the whole that is said of Milton's story, and the Poet has called up that poetic faith, that conviction of the mind, which is necessary to make that seem true, which otherwise might have been deemed almost fabulous.

But to return to *The Tempest*, and to the wondrous creation of Ariel. If a doubt could ever be entertained whether Shakespeare was a great poet, acting upon laws arising out of his own nature, and not without law, as has sometimes been idly asserted, that doubt must be removed by the character of Ariel. The very first words uttered by this being introduce the spirit, not as an angel, above man; not a gnome, or a fiend, below man; but while the poet gives him the faculties and the advantages of reason, he divests him of all mortal character, not positively, it is true, but negatively. In air he lives, from air he derives his being, in air he acts; and all his colours and properties seem to have been obtained from the rainbow and the skies. There is nothing about Ariel that cannot be conceived to exist either at sun-rise or at sun-set: hence all that belongs to Ariel belongs to the delight the mind is capable of receiving from the most lovely external appearances. His answers to Prospero are directly to the question, and nothing beyond; or where he expatiates, which is not unfrequently, it is to himself and upon his own delights, or upon the unnatural situation in which he is placed, though under a kindly power and to good ends.

Shakespeare has properly made Ariel's very first speech characteristic of him. After he has described the manner in which he had raised the storm and produced its harmless consequences, we find that Ariel is discontented – that he has been freed, it is true, from a cruel confinement, but still that he is bound to obey Prospero, and to execute any commands imposed upon him. We feel that such a state of bondage is almost unnatural to him, yet we see that it is delightful for him to be so employed. – It is as if we were to command one of the winds in a different direction to that which nature dictates, or one of the waves, now rising and now sinking, to recede before it bursts upon the shore: such is the feeling we experience, when we learn that a being like Ariel is commanded to fulfil any mortal behest.

When, however, Shakespeare contrasts the treatment of Ariel by Prospero with that of Sycorax, we are sensible that the liberated spirit ought to be grateful, and Ariel does feel and acknowledge the obligation; he immediately assumes the airy being, with a mind so elastically correspondent, that when once a feeling has passed from it, not a trace is left behind.

Is there anything in nature from which Shakespeare caught the idea of this delicate and delightful being, with such child-like simplicity, yet with such preternatural powers? He is neither born of heaven, nor of earth; but, as it were, between both, like a May-blossom kept suspended in air by the fanning breeze, which prevents it from falling to the ground, and only finally, and by compulsion, touching earth. This reluctance of the Sylph to be under the command even of Prospero is kept up through the whole play, and in the exercise of his admirable judgment Shakespeare has availed himself of it, in order to give Ariel an interest in the event, looking forward to that moment when he was to gain his last and only reward – simple and eternal liberty.

Another instance of admirable judgment and excellent preparation is to be found in the creature contrasted with Ariel – Caliban; who is described in such a manner by Prospero, as to lead us to expect the appearance of a foul, unnatural monster. He is not seen at once: his voice is heard; this is the preparation; he was too offensive to be seen first in all his deformity, and in nature we do not receive so much disgust from sound as from sight. After we have heard

Caliban's voice he does not enter, until Ariel has entered like a water-nymph. All the strength of contrast is thus acquired without any of the shock of abruptness, or of that unpleasant sensation, which we experience when the object presented is in any way hateful to our vision.

The character of Caliban is wonderfully conceived: he is a sort of creature of the earth, as Ariel is a sort of creature of the air. He partakes of the qualities of the brute, but is distinguished from brutes in two ways: – by having mere understanding without moral reason; and by not possessing the instincts which pertain to absolute animals. Still, Caliban is in some respects a noble being: the poet has raised him far above contempt: he is a man in the sense of the imagination: all the images he uses are drawn from nature, and are highly poetical; they fit in with the images of Ariel. Caliban gives us images from the earth, Ariel images from the air. Caliban talks of the difficulty of finding fresh water, of the situation of morasses, and of other circumstances which even brute instinct, without reason, could comprehend. No mean figure is employed, no mean passion displayed, beyond animal passion, and repugnance to command.

The manner in which the lovers are introduced is equally wonderful, and it is the last point I shall now mention in reference to this, almost miraculous, drama. The same judgment is observable in every scene, still preparing, still inviting, and still gratifying, like a finished piece of music. I have omitted to notice one thing, and you must give me leave to advert to it before I proceed: I mean the conspiracy against the life of Alonzo. I want to shew you how well the poet prepares the feelings of the reader for this plot, which was to execute the most detestable of all crimes, and which, in another play, Shakespeare has called 'the murder of sleep'.

Antonio and Sebastian at first had no such intention: it was suggested by the magical sleep cast on Alonzo and Gonzalo; but they are previously introduced scoffing and scorning at what was said by others, without regard to age or situation – without any sense of admiration for the excellent truths they heard delivered, but giving themselves up entirely to the malignant and unsocial feelings, which induced them to listen to everything that was said, not for the sake of profiting by the learning and experience of others, but of hearing something that might gratify vanity and self-love, by making them believe that the person speaking was inferior to themselves.

This, let me remark, is one of the grand characteristics of a villain; and it would not be so much a presentiment, as an anticipation of hell, for men to suppose that all mankind were as wicked as themselves, or might be so, if they were not too great fools. Pope, you are perhaps aware, objected to this conspiracy; but in my mind, if it could be omitted, the play would lose a charm which nothing could supply.

Many, indeed innumerable, beautiful passages might be quoted from this play, independently of the astonishing scheme of its construction. Every body will call to mind the grandeur of the language of Prospero in that divine speech, where he takes leave of his magic art; and were I to indulge myself by repetitions of the kind, I should descend from the character of a lecturer to that of a mere reciter. Before I terminate, I may particularly recall one short passage, which has fallen under the very severe, but inconsiderate, censure of Pope and Arbuthnot,* who pronounce it a piece of the grossest bombast. Prospero thus addresses his daughter, directing her attention to Ferdinand:

> The fringed curtains of thine eye advance,
> And say what thou seest yond. (I ii)

Taking these words as a periphrase of – 'Look what is coming yonder,' it certainly may to some appear to border on the ridiculous, and to fall under the rule I formerly laid down, – that whatever, without injury, can be translated into a foreign language in simple terms, ought to be in simple terms in the original language; but it is to be borne in mind, that different modes of expression frequently arise from difference of situation and education: a blackguard would use very different words, to express the same thing, to those a gentleman would employ, yet both would be natural and proper; difference of feeling gives rise to difference of language: a gentleman speaks in polished terms, with due regard to his own rank and position, while a blackguard, a person little better than half a brute, speaks like half a brute, showing no respect for himself, nor for others.

But I am content to try the lines I have just quoted by the introduction to them; and then, I think, you will admit, that nothing could be more fit and appropriate than such language. How does

* *Memoirs of Martinus Scriblerus*, Book II ('The Art of Sinking in Poetry') ch. xii.

Prospero introduce them? He has just told Miranda a wonderful story, which deeply affected her, and filled her with surprise and astonishment, and for his own purposes he afterwards lulls her to sleep. When she awakes, Shakespeare has made her wholly inattentive to the present, but wrapped up in the past. An actress, who understands the character of Miranda, would have her eyes cast down, and her eyelids almost covering them, while she was, as it were, living in her dream. At this moment Prospero sees Ferdinand, and wishes to point him out to his daughter, not only with great, but with scenic solemnity, he standing before her, and before the spectator, in the dignified character of a great magician. Something was to appear to Miranda on the sudden, and as unexpectedly as if the hero of a drama were to be on the stage at the instant when the curtain is elevated. It is under such circumstances that Prospero says, in a tone calculated at once to arouse his daughter's attention,

> The fringed curtains of thine eye advance,
> And say what thou seest yond.

Turning from the sight of Ferdinand to his thoughtful daughter, his attention was first struck by the downcast appearance of her eyes and eyelids; and, in my humble opinion, the solemnity of the phraseology assigned to Prospero is completely in character, recollecting his preternatural capacity, in which the most familiar objects in nature present themselves in a mysterious point of view. It is much easier to find fault with a writer by reference to former notions and experience, than to sit down and read him, recollecting his purpose, connecting one feeling with another, and judging of his words and phrases, in proportion as they convey the sentiments of the persons represented.

Of Miranda we may say, that she possesses in herself all the ideal beauties that could be imagined by the greatest poet of any age or country; but it is not my purpose now, so much to point out the high poetic powers of Shakespeare, as to illustrate his exquisite judgment, and it is solely with this design that I have noticed a passage with which, it seems to me, some critics, and those among the best, have been unreasonably dissatisfied. If Shakespeare be the wonder of the ignorant, he is, and ought to be, much more the wonder of the learned: not only from profundity of thought, but from his astonishing and intuitive knowledge of what man must be at all times, and under all circumstances, he is rather to be looked upon as a prophet than as a poet. Yet, with all these unbounded powers, with all this might and majesty of genius, he makes us feel as if he were unconscious of himself, and of his high destiny, disguising the half god in the simplicity of a child.

S. T. Coleridge 'The moved and sympathetic imagination' (pub. 1836)

[*The Tempest*] addresses itself entirely to the imaginative faculty; and although the illusion may be assisted by the effect on the senses of the complicated scenery and decorations of modern times yet this sort of assistance is dangerous. For the principal and only genuine excitement ought to come from within, – from the moved and sympathetic imagination; whereas, where so much is addressed to the mere external senses of seeing and hearing, the spiritual vision is apt to languish, and the attraction from without will withdraw the mind from the proper and only legitimate interest which is intended to spring from within.

The romance opens with a busy scene admirably appropriate to the kind of drama, and giving, as it were, the keynote to the whole harmony. It prepares and initiates the excitement required for the entire piece, and yet does not demand anything from the spectators, which their previous habits had not fitted them to understand. It is the bustle of a tempest, from which the real horrors are abstracted; – therefore it is poetical, though not in strictness natural – (the distinction to which I have so often alluded) – and is purposely restrained from concentering the interest on itself, but used merely as an induction or tuning for what is to follow.

In the second scene, Prospero's speeches, till the entrance of Ariel, contain the finest example I remember of retrospective narration for the purpose of exciting immediate interest, and putting the audience in possession of all the information necessary for the understanding of the plot. Observe, too, the perfect probability of the moment chosen by Prospero (the very Shakespeare himself, as it were, of the tempest) to open out the truth to his daughter, his own romantic bearing, and how completely any thing that might have been disagreeable to us in the magician, is reconciled and shaded in the humanity and natural feelings of the father. In the very first speech of Miranda the simplicity and tenderness of her character are at once laid open; – it would have been lost in direct contact with the agitation of the first scene. The opinion once prevailed, but, happily, is now abandoned, that Fletcher alone wrote for women; – the truth is, that with very few, and those partial, exceptions, the female characters in the plays of Beaumont and Fletcher are, when of the light kind, not decent; when heroic, complete viragos. But in Shakespeare all the elements of womanhood are holy, and there is the sweet, yet dignified feeling of all that *continuates* society, as sense of ancestry and of sex, with a purity unassailable by sophistry, because it rests not in the analytic processes, but in that sane equipoise of the faculties, during which the feelings are representative of all past experience, – not of the individual only, but of all those by whom she has been educated, and their predecessors even up to the first mother that lived. Shakespeare saw that the want of prominence, which Pope notices for sarcasm, was the blessed beauty of the woman's character, and knew that it arose not from any deficiency, but from the more exquisite harmony of all the parts of the moral being constituting one living total of head and heart. He has drawn it, indeed, in all its distinctive energies of faith, patience, constancy, fortitude, – shown in all of them as following the heart, which gives its results by a nice tact and happy intuition, without the intervention of the discursive faculty, – sees all things in and by the light of the affections, and errs, if it ever err, in the exaggerations of love alone. In all the Shakespearian women there is essentially the same foundation and principle; the distinct individuality and variety are merely the result of the modification of circumstances, whether in Miranda the maiden, in Imogen the wife, or in Katharine the queen.

But to return. The appearance and characters of the super or ultra-natural servants are finely contrasted. Ariel has in every thing the airy tint which gives the name; and it is worthy of remark that Miranda is never directly brought into comparison with Ariel, lest the natural and human of the one and the supernatural of the other should tend to neutralize each other; Caliban, on the other hand, is all earth, all condensed and gross in feelings and images; he has the dawnings of understanding without reason or the moral sense, and in him, as in some brute animals, this advance to the intellectual faculties, without the moral sense, is marked by the appearance of vice. For it is in the primacy of the moral being only that man is truly human; in his intellectual powers he is certainly approached by the brutes, and, man's whole system duly considered, those powers cannot be considered other than means to an end, that is, to morality.

In this scene, as it proceeds, is displayed the impression made by Ferdinand and Miranda on each other; it is love at first sight;–

> at the first sight
> They have changed eyes:–

and it appears to me, that in all cases of real love, it is at one moment that it takes place. That moment may have been prepared by previous esteem, admiration, or even affection, – yet love seems to require a momentary act of volition, by which a tacit bond of devotion is imposed, – a bond not to be thereafter broken without violating what should be sacred in our nature. How finely is the true Shakespearian scene contrasted with Dryden's vulgar alteration of it, in which a mere ludicrous psychological experiment, as it were, is tried – displaying nothing but indelicacy without passion. Prospero's interruption of the courtship has often seemed to me to have no sufficient motive; still his alleged reason –

> lest too light winning
> Make the prize light –

is enough for the ethereal connexions of the romantic imagination, although it would not be so for the historical. The whole courting scene, indeed, in the beginning of the third act, between the lovers is a masterpiece; and the first dawn of disobedience in the mind of Miranda to the command of her father is very finely drawn, so as to seem the working of the Scriptural command, *Thou shalt leave father and mother,* &c. O! with what exquisite purity this scene is conceived and executed! Shakespeare may sometimes be gross, but I boldly say that he is always moral and modest. Alas! in this our day decency of manners is preserved at the expense of morality of heart, and delicacies for vice are allowed, whilst grossness against it is hypocritically, or at least morbidly, condemned.

In this play are admirably sketched the vices generally accompanying a low degree of civilization; and in the first scene of the second act Shakespeare has, as in many other places, shown the tendency in bad men to indulge in scorn and contemptuous expressions, as a mode of getting rid of their own uneasy feelings of inferiority to the good, and also, by making the good ridiculous, of rendering the transition of others to wickedness easy. Shakespeare never puts habitual scorn into the mouths of other than bad men, as here in the instances of Antonio and Sebastian. The scene of the intended assassination of Alonzo and Gonzalo is an exact counterpart of the scene between Macbeth and his lady, only pitched in a lower key throughout, as designed to be frustrated and concealed, and exhibiting the same profound management in the manner of familiarizing a mind, not immediately recipient, to the suggestion of guilt, by associating the proposed crime with something ludicrous or out of place, – something not habitually matter of reverence. By this kind of sophistry the imagination and fancy are first bribed to contemplate the suggested act, and at length to become acquainted with it. Observe how the effect of this scene is heightened by contrast with another counterpart of it in low life, – that between the conspirators Stephano, Caliban, and Trinculo in the second scene of the third act, in which there are the same essential characteristics.

In this play and in this scene of it are also shown the springs of the vulgar in politics, – of that kind of politics which is inwoven with human nature. In his treatment of this subject, wherever it occurs, Shakespeare is quite peculiar. In other writers we find the particular opinions of the individual; in Massinger it is rank republicanism; in Beaumont and Fletcher even *jure divino* principles are carried to excess; – but Shakespeare never promulgates any party tenets. He is always the philosopher and the moralist, but at the same time with a profound veneration for all the established institutions of society, and for those classes which form the permanent elements of the state – especially never introducing a professional character, as such, otherwise than as respectable. If he must have any name, he should be styled a philosophical aristocrat, delighting in those hereditary institutions which have a tendency to bind one age to another, and in that distinction of ranks, of which, although few may be in possession, all enjoy the advantages. Hence, again, you will observe the good nature with which he seems always to make sport with the passions and follies of a mob, as with an irrational animal. He is never angry with it, but hugely content with holding up its absurdities to its face; and sometimes you may trace a tone of almost affectionate superiority, something like that in which a father speaks of the rogueries of a child. See the good-humoured way in which he describes Stephano passing from the most licentious freedom to absolute despotism over Trinculo and Caliban. The truth is, Shakespeare's characters are all *genera* intensely individualized; the results of meditation, of which observation supplied the drapery and the colors necessary to combine them with each other. He had virtually surveyed all the great component powers and impulses of human nature, – had seen that their different combinations and subordinations were in fact the individualizers of men, and showed how their harmony was produced by reciprocal disproportions of excess or deficiency. The language in which these truths are expressed was not drawn from any set fashion, but from the profoundest depths of his moral being, and is therefore for all ages.

William Hazlitt Unity and Variety in Shakespeare's Design (1817)

The Tempest is one of the most original and perfect of Shakespeare's productions, and he has shewn in it all the variety of his powers. It is full of grace and grandeur. The human and imaginary characters, the dramatic and the grotesque, are blended together with the greatest art, and without any appearance of it. Though he has here given 'to airy nothing a local habitation and a name', yet that part which is only the fantastic creation of his mind, has the same palpable texture, and coheres 'semblably' with the rest. As the preternatural part has the air of reality, and almost haunts the imagination with a sense of truth, the real characters and events partake of the wildness of a dream. The stately magician, Prospero, driven from his dukedom, but around whom (so potent is his art) airy spirits throng numberless to do his bidding; his daughter Miranda ('worthy of that name') to whom all the power of his art points, and who seems the goddess of the isle; the princely

Ferdinand, cast by fate upon the haven of his happiness in this idol of his love; the delicate Ariel; the savage Caliban, half brute, half demon; the drunken ship's crew – are all connected parts of the story, and can hardly be spared from the place they fill. Even the local scenery is of a piece and character with the subject. Prospero's enchanted island seems to have risen up out of the sea; the airy music, the tempest-tost vessel, the turbulent waves, all have the effect of the landscape background of some fine picture. Shakespear's pencil is (to use an allusion of his own) 'like the dyer's hand, subdued to what it works in'. Every thing in him, though it partakes of 'the liberty of wit', is also subjected to 'the law' of the understanding. For instance, even the drunken sailors, who are made reeling-ripe, share, in the disorder of their minds and bodies, in the tumult of the elements, and seem on shore to be as much at the mercy of chance as they were before at the mercy of the winds and waves. These fellows with their sea-wit are the least to our taste of any part of the play: but they are as like drunken sailors as they can be, and are an indirect foil to Caliban, whose figure acquires a classical dignity in the comparison. The character of Caliban is generally thought (and justly so) to be one of the author's masterpieces. It is not indeed pleasant to see this character on the stage any more than it is to see the god Pan personated there. But in itself it is one of the wildest and most abstracted of all Shakespear's characters, whose deformity whether of body or mind is redeemed by the power and truth of the imagination displayed in it. It is the essence of grossness, but there is not a particle of vulgarity in it. Shakespear has described the brutal mind of Caliban in contact with the pure and original forms of nature; the character grows out of the soil where it is rooted, uncontrouled, uncouth and wild, uncramped by any of the meannesses of custom. It is 'of the earth, earthy'. It seems almost to have been dug out of the ground, with a soul instinctively superadded to it answering to its wants and origin. Vulgarity is not natural coarseness, but conventional coarseness, learnt from others, contrary to, or without an entire conformity of natural power and disposition; as fashion is the common-place affectation of what is elegant and refined without any feeling of the essence of it. Schlegel, the admirable German critic on Shakespear, observes that Caliban is a poetical character, and 'always speaks in blank verse'. He first comes in thus:

Caliban. As wicked dew as e'er my mother brush'd
With raven's feather from unwholesome fen,
Drop on you both: a south-west blow on ye,
And blister you all o'er!
Prospero. For this, be sure, to-night thou shalt have cramps,
Side-stitches that shall pen thy breath up; urchins
Shall, for that vast of night that they may work
All exercise on thee: thou shalt be pinched
As thick as honey-combs, each pinch more stinging
Than bees that made them.
Caliban. I must eat my dinner.
This island's mine by Sycorax my mother,
Which thou tak'st from me. When thou camest first,
Thou stroak'dst me, and mad'st much of me; would'st give me
Water with berries in't; and teach me how
To name the bigger light and how the less
That burn by day and night; and then I lov'd thee,
And shew'd thee all the qualities o' th' isle,
The fresh springs, brine-pits, barren place and fertile:
Curs'd be I that I did so! All the charms
Of Sycorax, toads, beetles, bats, light on you!
For I am all the subjects that you have,
Who first was mine own king; and here you sty me
In this hard rock, whiles you do keep from me
The rest o' th' island.

And again, he promises Trinculo his services thus, if he will free him from his drudgery.

I'll shew thee the best springs; I'll pluck thee berries,
I'll fish for thee, and get thee wood enough.
I pr'ythee let me bring thee where crabs grow,
And I with my long nails will dig thee pig-nuts:
Shew thee a jay's nest, and instruct thee how
To snare the nimble marmozet: I'll bring thee
To clust'ring filberds; and sometimes I'll get thee
Young sea-mells from the rock.

In conducting Stephano and Trinculo to Prospero's cell, Caliban shews the superiority of natural capacity over greater knowledge and greater folly; and in a former scene, when Ariel frightens them with his music, Caliban to encourage them accounts for it in the eloquent poetry of the senses.

– Be not afraid, the isle is full of noises,
Sounds, and sweet airs, that give delight and hurt not.

Sometimes a thousand twanging instruments
Will hum about mine ears, and sometimes voices,
That if I then had waked after long sleep,
Would make me sleep again; and then in dreaming,
The clouds methought would open, and shew riches
Ready to drop upon me: when I wak'd,
I cried to dream again.

This is not more beautiful than it is true. The poet here shews us the savage with the simplicity of a child, and makes the strange monster amiable. Shakespear had to paint the human animal rude and without choice in its pleasures, but not without the sense of pleasure or some germ of the affections. Master Barnardine in *Measure for Measure*, the savage of civilized life, is an admirable philosophical counterpart to Caliban.

Shakespear has, as it were by design, drawn off from Caliban the elements of whatever is ethereal and refined, to compound them in the unearthly mould of Ariel. Nothing was ever more finely conceived than this contrast between the material and the spiritual, the gross and delicate. Ariel is imaginary power, the swiftness of thought personified. When told to make good speed by Prospero, he says, 'I drink the air before me'. This is something like Puck's boast on a similar occasion, 'I'll put a girdle round about the earth in forty minutes.' But Ariel differs from Puck in having a fellow feeling in the interests of those he is employed about. How exquisite is the following dialogue between him and Prospero!

Ariel. Your charm so strongly works them,
That if you now beheld them, your affections
Would become tender.
Prospero. Dost thou think so, spirit?
Ariel. Mine would, sir, were I human.
Prospero. And mine shall.
Hast thou, which art but air, a touch, a feeling
Of their afflictions, and shall not myself,
One of their kind, that relish all as sharply,
Passion'd as they, be kindlier moved than thou art?

It has been observed that there is a peculiar charm in the songs introduced in Shakespear, which, without conveying any distinct images, seem to recall all the feelings connected with them, like snatches of half-forgotten music heard indistinctly and at intervals. There is this effect produced by Ariel's songs, which (as we are told) seem to sound in the air, and as if the person playing them were invisible.

Edward Dowden The Serenity of *The Tempest* (1875)

Over the beauty of youth and the love of youth, there is shed, in these plays of Shakspere's final period, a clear yet tender luminousness, not elsewhere to be perceived in his writings. In his earlier plays, Shakspere writes concerning young men and maidens, their loves, their mirth, their griefs, as one who is among them, who has a lively, personal interest in their concerns, who can make merry with them, treat them familiarly, and, if need be, can mock them into good sense. There is nothing in these early plays wonderful, strangely beautiful, pathetic about youth and its joys and sorrows. In the histories and tragedies, as was to be expected, more massive, broader, or more profound objects of interest engaged the poet's imagination. But in these latest plays, the beautiful pathetic light is always present. There are the sufferers, aged, experienced, tried – Queen Katharine, Prospero, Hermione. And over against these there are the children absorbed in their happy and exquisite egoism, – Perdita and Miranda, Florizel and Ferdinand, and the boys of old Belarius.

The same means to secure ideality for these figures, so young and beautiful, is in each case (instinctively perhaps rather than deliberately) resorted to. They are lost children, – princes or a princess, removed from the court, and its conventional surroundings, into some scene of rare, natural beauty. There are the lost princes – Arviragus and Guiderius, among the mountains of Wales, drinking the free air, and offering their salutations to the risen sun. There is Perdita, the shepherdess-princess, 'queen of curds and cream', sharing with old and young her flowers, lovelier and more undying than those that Proserpina let fall from Dis's waggon. There is Miranda, (whose very name is significant of wonder), made up of beauty, and love, and womanly pity, neither courtly nor rustic, with the breeding of an island of enchantment, where Prospero is her tutor and protector, and Caliban her servant, and the Prince of Naples her lover. In each of these plays we can see Shakspere, as it were, tenderly bending over the joys and sorrows of youth. We recognise this rather through the total characterization, and through a feeling and a presence, than through definite incident or statement. But some of this feeling escapes in the disinterested joy and admiration of old Belarius when he gazes at the princely youths, and in Camillo's loyalty to Florizel and Perdita; while it obtains more distinct expression in such a word as that which Prospero utters, when from a distance he watches with pleasure Miranda's zeal to relieve Ferdinand from his task of log-bearing: – 'Poor worm, thou art infected'.*

It is not chiefly because Prospero is a great enchanter, now about to break his magic staff, to drown his book deeper than ever plummet sounded, to dismiss his airy spirits, and to return to the practical service of his Dukedom, that we identify Prospero in some measure with Shakspere himself. It is rather because the temper of Prospero, the grave harmony of his character, his self-mastery, his calm validity of will, his sensitiveness to wrong, his unfaltering justice, and with these, a certain abandonment, a remoteness from the common joys and sorrows of the world, are characteristic of Shakspere as discovered to us in all his latest plays. Prospero is a harmonious and fully developed *will.* In the earlier play of fairy enchantments, *A Midsummer Night's Dream*, the 'human mortals' wander to and fro in a maze of error, misled by the mischievous frolic of Puck, the jester and clown of Fairyland. But here the spirits of the elements, and Caliban the gross genius of brute-matter, – needful for the service of life, – are brought under subjection to the human will of Prospero.

What is more, Prospero has entered into complete possession of himself. Shakspere has shown us his quick sense of injury, his intellectual impatience, his occasional moment of keen irritability, in order that we may be more deeply aware of his abiding strength and self-possession, and that we may perceive how these have been grafted upon a temperament, not impassive or unexcitable. And Prospero has reached not only the higher levels of moral attainment; he has also reached an altitude of thought from which he can survey the whole of human life, and see how small and yet how great it is. His heart is sensitive, he is profoundly touched by the joy of the

* The same feeling appears in the lines which end ACT III, scene i.

Prospero. So glad of this as they I cannot be,
Who are surprised with all; but my rejoicing
At nothing can be more.

children, with whom in the egoism of their love he passes for a thing of secondary interest; he is deeply moved by the perfidy of his brother. His brain is readily set a-work, and can with difficulty be checked from eager and excessive energizing; he is subject to the access of sudden and agitating thought. But Prospero masters his own sensitiveness, emotional and intellectual: –

> We are such stuff
> As dreams are made on, and our little life
> Is rounded with a sleep. Sir, I am vexed;
> Bear with my weakness; my old brain is troubled:
> Be not disturb'd with my infirmity;
> If you be pleased, retire into my cell
> And there repose; a turn or two I'll walk,
> To still my beating mind.

'Such stuff as dreams are made on.' Nevertheless, in this little life, in this dream, Prospero will maintain his dream rights and fulfil his dream duties. In the dream, he, a Duke, will accomplish Duke's work. Having idealized everything, Shakspere left everything real. Bishop Berkeley's foot was no less able to set a pebble flying than was the lumbering foot of Dr. Johnson. Nevertheless, no material substance intervened between the soul of Berkeley and the immediate presence of the play of Divine power.

A thought which seems to run through the whole of *The Tempest*, appearing here and there like a coloured thread in some web, is the thought that the true freedom of man consists in service. Ariel, untouched by human feeling, is panting for his liberty; in the last words of Prospero are promised his enfranchisement and dismissal to the elements. Ariel reverences his great master, and serves him with bright alacrity; but he is bound by none of our human ties, strong and tender, and he will rejoice when Prospero is to him as though he never were.* To Caliban, a land-fish, with the duller elements of earth and water in his composition, but no portion of the higher elements, air and fire, though he receives dim intimations of a higher world, – a musical humming, or a twangling, or a voice heard

* Ariel is promised his freedom after two days, Act I, scene ii. Why two days? The time of the entire action of the Tempest is only three hours. What was to be the employment of Ariel during two days? To make the winds and seas favourable during the voyage to Naples. Prospero's island therefore was imagined by Shakspere as within two days' quick sail of Naples.

in sleep – to Caliban, service is slavery.* He hates to bear his logs; he fears the incomprehensible power of Prospero, and obeys, and curses. The great master has usurped the rights of the brute-power Caliban. And when Stephano and Trinculo appear, ridiculously impoverished specimens of humanity, with their shallow understandings and vulgar greeds, this poor earth-monster is possessed by a sudden *schwärmerei*, a fanaticism for liberty! –

> 'Ban, 'ban, Ca'-Caliban,
> Has a new master; got a new man.
> Freedom, heyday! heyday, freedom! freedom! freedom, heyday, freedom!

His new master also sings his impassioned hymn of liberty, the *Marseillaise* of the enchanted island:

> Flout 'em and scout 'em,
> And scout 'em and flout 'em;
> Thought is free.

The leaders of the revolution, escaped from the stench and foulness of the horse-pond, King Stephano and his prime minister Trinculo, like too many leaders of the people, bring to an end their great achievement on behalf of liberty by quarrelling over booty, – the trumpery which the providence of Prospero had placed in their way. Caliban, though scarce more truly wise or instructed than before, at least discovers his particular error of the day and hour:

> What a thrice-double ass
> Was I, to take this drunkard for a god,
> And worship this dull fool!

It must be admitted that Shakspere, if not, as Hartley Coleridge asserted, 'a Tory and a gentleman', had within him some of the elements of English conservatism.

But while Ariel and Caliban, each in his own way, is impatient of service, the human actors, in whom we are chiefly interested, are

* The conception of Caliban, the 'servant-monster', 'plain-fish and no doubt marketable', the 'tortoise', 'his fins like arms', with 'a very ancient and fish-like smell', who gabbled until Prospero taught him language – this conception was in Shakspere's mind when he wrote *Troilus and Cressida*. Thersites describes Ajax (III, iii): *'He's grown a very land-fish, languageless, a monster.'*

entering into bonds – bonds of affection, bonds of duty, in which they find their truest freedom. Ferdinand and Miranda emulously contend in the task of bearing the burden which Prospero has imposed upon the prince:

> I am in my condition
> A prince, Miranda; I do think, a king:
> I would, not so! and would no more endure
> This wooden slavery than to suffer
> The flesh-fly blow my mouth. Hear my soul speak:
> The very instant that I saw you, did
> My heart fly to your service; there resides,
> To make me slave to it; and for your sake
> Am I this patient log-man.

And Miranda speaks with the sacred candour from which spring the nobler manners of a world more real and glad than the world of convention and proprieties and pruderies:

> Hence, bashful cunning!
> And prompt me, plain and holy innocence!
> I am your wife, if you will marry me;
> If not, I'll die your maid: to be your fellow
> You may deny me; but I'll be your servant
> Whether you will or no.
> *Fer.* My mistress, dearest;
> And I thus humble ever.
> *Mir.* My husband, then?
> *Fer.* Ay, with a heart as willing
> As bondage e'er of freedom.

In an earlier part of the play, this chord which runs through it had been playfully struck in the description of Gonzalo's imaginary commonwealth, in which man is to be enfranchised from all the laborious necessities of life. Here is the ideal of notional liberty, Shakspere would say, and to attempt to realise it at once lands us in absurdities and self-contradictions:

> For no kind of traffic
> Would I admit: no name of magistrate;
> Letters should not be known: riches, poverty,
> And use of service none; contract, succession,
> Bourn, bound of land, tilth, vineyard, none;
> No use of metal, corn, or wine, or oil;

No occupation; all men idle, all,
And women too, but innocent and pure;
No sovereignty.
Seb. Yet he would be king on't.*

Finally, in the Epilogue, which was written perhaps by Shakspere, perhaps by some one acquainted with his thoughts, Prospero in his character of a man, no longer a potent enchanter, petitions the spectators of the theatre for two things, pardon and freedom. It would be straining matters to discover in this Epilogue profound significances. And yet in its playfulness it curiously falls in with the moral purport of the whole. Prospero, the pardoner, implores pardon. Shakspere was aware – whether such be the significance (aside – for the writer's mind) of this Epilogue or not – that no life is ever lived which does not need to receive as well as to render forgiveness. He knew that every energetic dealer with the world must seek a sincere and liberal pardon for many things. Forgiveness and freedom: these are keynotes of the play. When it was occupying the mind of Shakspere, he was passing from his service as artist to his service as English country gentleman. Had his mind been dwelling on the question of how he should employ his new freedom, and had he been enforcing upon himself the truth that the highest freedom lies in the bonds of duty?†

* Act II, scene i. – The prolonged and dull joking of Sebastian in this scene cannot be meant by Shakspere to be really bright and witty. It is meant to shew that the intellectual poverty of the conspirators is as great as their moral obliquity. They are monsters more ignoble than Caliban. Their laughter is 'the crackling of thorns under a pot'.

† Mr Furnivall, observing that in these later plays breaches of the family bond are dramatically studied, and the reconciliations are domestic reconciliations in *Cymbeline* and *The Winter's Tale*, suggests to me that they were a kind of confession on Shakspere's part that he had inadequately felt the beauty and tenderness of the common relations of father and child, wife and husband; and that he was now quietly resolving to be gentle, and wholly just to his wife and his home. I cannot altogether make this view of the later plays my own, and leave it to the reader to accept and develop as he may be able.

Henry James Introduction to *The Tempest* (1907)

If the effect of the Plays and Poems, taken in their mass, be most of all to appear often to mock our persistent ignorance of so many of the conditions of their birth, and thereby to place on the rack again our strained and aching wonder, this character has always struck me as more particularly kept up for them by *The Tempest*; the production, of the long series, in which the Questions, as the critical reader of Shakespeare must ever comprehensively and ruefully call them and more or less resignedly live with them, hover before us in their most tormenting form. It may seem no very philosophic state of mind, the merely baffled and exasperated view of one of the supreme works of all literature; though I feel, for myself, that to confess to it now and then, by way of relief, is no unworthy tribute to the work. It is not, certainly, the tribute most frequently paid, for the large body of comment and criticism of which this play alone has been the theme abounds much rather in affirmed conclusions, complacencies of conviction, full apprehensions of the meaning and triumphant pointings of the moral. The Questions, in the light of all this wisdom, convert themselves with comparatively small difficulty, into smooth and definite answers; the innumerable dim ghosts that flit, like started game at eventide, through the deep dusk of our speculation, with just form enough to quicken it and no other charity for us at all, bench themselves along the vista as solidly as Falstaff and as vividly as Hotspur. Everything has thus been attributed to the piece before us, and every attribution so made has been in turn brushed away; merely to glance at such a monument to the interest inspired is to recognise a battleground of opposed factions, not a little enveloped in sound and smoke. Of these copious elements, produced for the most part of the best intention, we remain accordingly conscious; so that to approach the general bone of contention, as we can but familiarly name it, for whatever purpose, we have to cross the scene of action at a mortal risk, making the fewest steps of it and trusting to the probable calm at the centre of the storm. There in fact, though there only, we find that serenity; find the subject itself intact and unconscious, seated as unwinking and inscrutable as a divinity in a temple, save for that vague flicker of derision, the only response to our interpretative heat, which adds the last beauty to its face. The divinity never relents – never, like the image of life in *The Winter's Tale*, steps down from its pedestal; it simply leaves us to stare on through the ages, with this fact indeed of having crossed the circle of fire, and so got into the real and right relation to it, for our one comfort.

The position of privilege of *The Tempest* as the latest example, to all appearance, of the author's rarer work, with its distance from us in time thereby shortened to the extent of the precious step or two, was certain to expose it, at whatever final cost, we easily see, to any amount of interpretative zeal. With its first recorded performance that of February 1613, when it was given in honour of the marriage of the Princess Elizabeth, its finished state cannot have preceded his death by more than three years, and we accordingly take it as the finest flower of his experience. Here indeed, as on so many of the Questions, judgments sharply differ, and this use of it as an ornament to the nuptials of the daughter of James I and the young Elector Palatine may have been but a repetition of previous performances; though it is not in such a case supposable that these can have been numerous. They would antedate the play, at the most, by a year or two, and so not throw it essentially further back from us. *The Tempest* speaks to us, somehow, convincingly, as a *pièce de circonstance*, and the suggestion that it was addressed, in its brevity, its rich simplicity, and its free elegance, to court-production, and above all to providing, with a string of other dramas, for the 'intellectual' splendour of a wedding-feast, is, when once entertained, not easily dislodged. A few things fail to fit, but more fit strikingly. I like therefore to think of the piece as of 1613. To refer it, as it is referred by other reckonings, to 1611 is but to thicken that impenetrability of silence in which Shakespeare's latest years enfold him. Written as it must have been on the earlier calculation, before the age of forty-seven, it has that rare value of the richly mature note of a genius who, by our present measure of growth and fulness, was still young enough to have had in him a world of life: we feel behind it the immense procession of its predecessors, while we yet stare wistfully at the plenitude and the majesty, the expression as of something broad-based and ultimate, that were not, in any but a strained sense, to borrow their warrant from the weight of years. Nothing so enlarges the wonder of the whole time-question in Shakespeare's career as the fact of this date, in easy middle life, of his time-climax; which, if we knew less, otherwise, than we do about him, might affect us as an attempt, on the part of treacherous History, to pass him off as one of those monsters of precocity who, fortunately for their probable reputation, the too likely betrayal of short-windedness, are cut off in their comparative prime. The transmuted young rustic who, after a look over London, brief at the best, was ready at the age of thirty to produce *The Merchant of Venice* and *A Midsummer Night's Dream* (and this after the half-dozen splendid prelusive things that had included, at twenty-eight, *Romeo and Juliet*), had been indeed a monster of precocity – which all geniuses of the first order are not; but the day of his paying for it had neither arrived nor, however faintly, announced itself, and the fathomless strangeness of his story, the abrupt stoppage of his pulse after *The Tempest*, is not, in charity, lighted for us by a glimmer of explanation. The explanation by some interposing accident is as absent as any symptom of 'declining powers'.

His powers declined, that is – but declined merely to obey the spring we should have supposed inherent in them; and their possessor's case derives from this, I think, half the secret of its so inestimably mystifying us. He died, for a nature so organized, too lamentably soon; but who knows where we should have been with him if he had not lived long enough so to affirm, with many other mysteries, the mystery of his abrupt and complete cessation? There is that in *The Tempest*, specifically, though almost all indefinably, which seems to show us the artist consciously tasting of the first and rarest of his gifts, that of imaged creative Expression, the instant sense of some copious equivalent of thought for every grain of the grossness of reality; to show him as unresistingly aware, in the depths of his genius, that nothing like it had ever been known, or probably would ever be again known, on earth, and as so given up, more than on other occasions, to the joy of sovereign *science*. There are so many sides from which any page that shows his stamp may be looked at that a handful of reflections can hope for no coherency, in the chain of association immediately formed, unless they happen to bear upon some single truth. Such a truth then, for me, is this comparative – by which one can really but mean this superlative – artistic value of the play seen in the meagre circle of the items of our knowledge about it. Let me say that our knowledge, in the whole connection, is a quantity that shifts, surprisingly, with the measure of a felt need; appearing to some of us, on some sides, adequate, various, large, and appearing to others, on whatever side, a scant beggar's portion. We are concerned, it must be remembered, here – that is for getting *generally* near our author – not only with the number of the mustered facts, but with the kind of fact that each may strike us as being: never unmindful that such matters, when they are few, may go far for us if they be individually but ample and significant; and when they are numerous, on the other hand, may easily fall short enough to break our hearts if they be at the same time but individually small and poor. Three or four stepping-stones across a stream will serve if they are broad slabs, but it will take more than may be counted if they are only pebbles. Beyond all gainsaying then, by many an estimate, is the penury in which even the most advantageous array of the Shakespearean facts still leaves us: strung together with whatever ingenuity they remain, for our discomfiture, as the pebbles across the stream.

To balance, for our occasion, this light scale, however, *The Tempest* affects us, taking its complexity and its perfection together, as the rarest of all examples of literary art. There may be other things as exquisite, other single exhalations of beauty reaching as high a mark and sustained there for a moment, just as there are other deep wells of poetry from which cupfuls as crystalline may, in repeated dips, be drawn; but nothing, surely, of equal length and variety lives so happily and radiantly as a whole: no poetic birth ever took place under a star appointed to blaze upon it so steadily. The felicity enjoyed is enjoyed longer and more intensely, and the art involved, completely revealed, as I suggest, to the master, holds the securest revel. The man himself, in the Plays, we directly touch, to my consciousness, positively nowhere: we are dealing too perpetually with the artist, the monster and magician of a thousand masks, not one of which we feel him drop long enough to gratify with the breath of the interval that strained attention in us which would be yet, so quickened, ready to become deeper still. Here at last the artist is, comparatively speaking, so generalised, so consummate and typical, so frankly amused with himself, that is with his art, with his power, with his theme, that it is as if he came to meet us more than his usual half-way, and as if, thereby, in meeting *him*, and touching him, we were nearer to meeting and touching the man. The man everywhere, in Shakespeare's work, is so effectually locked up and imprisoned in the artist that we but hover at the base of thick walls for a sense of him; while, in addition, the artist is so steeped in the abysmal objectivity of his characters and situations that the great billows of the medium itself play with him, to our vision, very much as, over a ship's side, in certain waters, we catch, through transparent tides, the flash of strange sea-creatures. What we are present at in this fashion is a series of incalculable plunges – the series of those that have taken effect, I mean, after the great primary plunge, made once for all, of the man into the artist: the successive plunges of the artist himself into Romeo and into Juliet, into Shylock, Hamlet, Macbeth, Coriolanus, Cleopatra, Antony, Lear, Othello, Falstaff, Hotspur; immersions during which, though he always ultimately finds his feet, the very violence of the movements involved troubles and distracts our sight. In *The Tempest*, by the supreme felicity I speak of, is no violence; he sinks as deep as we like, but what he sinks into, beyond all else, is the lucid stillness of his style.

One can speak, in these matters, but from the impression determined by one's own inevitable standpoint; again and again, at any rate, such a masterpiece puts before me the very act of the momentous conjunction taking place for the poet, at a given hour, between his charged inspiration and his clarified experience: or, as I should perhaps better express it, between his human curiosity and his aesthetic passion. Then, if he happens to have been, all his career, with his equipment for it, more or less the victim and the slave of the former, he yields, by way of a change, to the impulse of allowing the latter, for a magnificent moment, the upper hand. The human curiosity, as I call it, is always there – with no more need of making provision for it than use in taking precautions against it; the surrender to the luxury of expertness may therefore go forward on its own conditions. I can offer no better description of *The Tempest* as fresh re-perusal lights it for me than as such a surrender, sublimely enjoyed; and I may frankly say that, under this impression of it, there is no refinement of the artistic consciousness that I do not see my way – or feel it, better, perhaps, since we but grope, at the best, in our darkness – to attribute to the author. It is a way that one follows to the end, because it is a road, I repeat, on which one least misses some glimpse of him face to face. If it be true that the thing was concocted to meet a particular demand, that of the master of the King's revels, with his prescription of date, form, tone and length, this, so far from interfering with the Poet's perception of a charming opportunity to taste for *himself*, for himself above all, and as he had almost never so tasted, not even in *A Midsummer Night's Dream*, of the quality of his mind and the virtue of his skill, would have exceedingly favoured the happy case. Innumerable one may always suppose these delicate debates and intimate understandings of an artist with himself. 'How much *taste*, in the world, may I conceive that I have? – and what a charming idea to snatch a moment for finding out! What moment could be better than this – a bridal evening before the Court, with extra candles and the handsomest company – if I can but put my hand on the right "scenario"?' We can catch, across the ages, the searching sigh and the look about; we receive the stirred breath of the ripe, amused genius; and, stretching, as I admit I do at least, for a still closer conception of the beautiful crisis, I find it pictured for me in some such presentment as that of a divine musician who, alone in his room, preludes or improvises at close of day. He sits at the harpsichord, by the open window, in the summer dusk; his hands wander over the keys. They stray far, for his motive, but at last he finds and holds it; then he lets himself go, embroidering and refining: it is the thing for the hour and his mood. The neighbours may gather in the garden, the nightingale be hushed on the bough; it is none the less a private occasion, a concert of one, both performer and auditor, who plays for his own ear, his own hand, his own innermost sense, and for the bliss and capacity of his instrument. Such are the only hours at which the artist *may*, by any measure of his own (too many things, at others, make heavily against it); and their challenge to him is irresistible if he has known, all along, too much compromise and too much sacrifice.

The face that beyond any other, however, I seem to see *The Tempest* turn to us is the side on which it so superlatively speaks of that endowment for Expression, expression as a primary force, a consuming, an independent passion, which was the greatest ever laid upon man. It is for Shakespeare's power of constitutive speech quite as if he had swum into our ken with it from another planet, gathering it up there, in its wealth, as something antecedent to the occasion and the need, and if possible quite in excess of them; something that was to make of our poor world a great flat table for receiving the glitter and clink of outpoured treasure. The idea and the motive are more often than not so smothered in it that they scarce know themselves, and the resources of such a style, the provision of images, emblems, energies of every sort, laid up in advance, affects us as the storehouse of a king before a famine or a siege – which not only, by its scale, braves depletion or exhaustion, but bursts, through mere excess of quantity or presence, out of all doors and windows. It renders the poverties and obscurities of our world, as I say, in the dazzling terms of a richer and better. It constitutes, by a miracle, more than half the author's material; so much more usually does it happen, for the painter or the poet, that life itself, in its appealing, overwhelming crudity, offers itself as the paste to be kneaded. Such a personage works in general in the very elements of experience; whereas we see Shakespeare working predominantly in the terms of expression, *all* in the terms of the artist's specific vision and genius; with a thicker cloud of images to attest his approach, at any point than the comparatively meagre given case ever has to attest its own identity. He points for us as no one else the relation of style to meaning and of manner to motive; a matter on which, right and left, we hear such rank ineptitudes uttered. Unless it be true that these things, on either hand, are inseparable; unless it be true that the phrase, the cluster and order of terms, *is* the object and the sense, in as close a compression as that of body and soul, so that any consideration of them as distinct, from the moment style is an active, applied force, becomes a gross stupidity: unless we recognise this reality the author of *The Tempest* has no lesson for us. It is by his expression of it exactly as the expression stands that the particular thing is created, created as interesting, as beautiful, as strange, droll or terrible – as related, in short, to our understanding or our sensibility; in consequence of which we reduce it to naught when we begin to talk of either of its presented parts as matters by themselves.

All of which considerations indeed take us too far; what it is important to note being simply our Poet's high testimony to this independent, absolute value of Style, and to its need thoroughly to project and seat itself. It had been, as so seating itself, the very home of his mind, for his all too few twenty years; it had been the supreme source to him of the joy of life. It had been in fine his material, his plastic clay; since the more subtly he applied it the more secrets it had to give him, and the more these secrets might appear to him, at every point, one with the lights and shades of the human picture, one with the myriad pulses of the spirit of man. Thus it was that, as he passed from one application of it to another, tone became, for all its suggestions, more and more sovereign to him, and the subtlety of its secrets an exquisite interest. If I see him, at the last, over *The Tempest*, as the composer, at the harpsichord or the violin, extemporising in the summer twilight, it is exactly that he is feeling there for tone and, by the same token, finding it – finding it as *The Tempest*, beyond any register of ours, immortally gives it. This surrender to the highest sincerity of virtuosity, as we nowadays call it, is to my perception *all The Tempest*; with no possible depth or delicacy in it that such an imputed character does not cover and provide for. The subject to be treated was the simple fact (if one may call anything in the matter simple) that refinement, selection, economy, the economy not of poverty, but of wealth a little weary of congestion – the very air of the lone island and the very law of the Court celebration – were here implied and imperative things. Anything was a subject, always, that offered to sight an aperture of size enough for expression and its train to pass in and deploy themselves. If they filled up all the space, none the worse; they occupied it as nothing else could do. The subjects of the Comedies are, without exception, old wives' tales – which we are not too insufferably aware of only because the iridescent veil so perverts their proportions. The subjects of the Histories are no subjects at all; each is but a row of pegs for the hanging of the cloth of gold that is to muffle them. Such a thing as *The Merchant of Venice* declines, for very shame, to be reduced to its elements of witless 'story'; such things as the two Parts of *Henry the Fourth* form no more than a straight convenient channel for the procession of evoked images that is to pour through it like a torrent. Each of these productions is none the less of incomparable splendour; by which splendour we are bewildered till we see how it comes. Then we see that every inch of it is personal tone, or in other words brooding expression raised to the highest energy. Push such energy far enough – far enough if you can! – and, being what it is, it then inevitably provides for Character. Thus we see character, in every form of which the 'story' gives the thinnest hint, marching through the pieces I have named in its habit as it lives, and so filling out the scene that nothing is missed. The 'story' in *The Tempest* is a thing of naught, for any story will provide a remote island, a shipwreck and a coincidence. Prospero and Miranda, awaiting their relatives, are, in the present case, *for* the relatives, the coincidence – just as the relatives are the coincidence for them. Ariel and Caliban, and the island-airs and island-scents, and all the rest of the charm and magic and the ineffable delicacy (a delicacy positively at its highest in the conception and execution of Caliban) are the style handed over to its last disciplined passion of curiosity; a curiosity which flowers, at this pitch, into the freshness of each of the characters.

There are judges for whom the piece is a tissue of symbols; symbols of the facts of State then apparent, of the lights of philosophic and political truth, of the 'deeper meanings of life', above all, of a high crisis in its author's career. At this most relevant of its mystic values only we may glance; the consecrated estimate of Prospero's surrender of his magic robe and staff as a figure for Shakespeare's own self-despoilment, his considered purpose, at this date, of future silence. Dr. George Brandes works out in detail that analogy; the production becomes, on such a supposition, Shakespeare's 'farewell to the stage'; his retirement to Stratford, to end his days in the care of his property and in oblivion of the theatre, was a course for which his arrangements had already been made. The simplest way to put it, since I have likened him to the musician at the piano, is to say that he had decided upon the complete closing of this instrument, and that in fact he was to proceed to lock it with the sharp click that has reverberated through the ages, and to spend what remained to him of life in walking about a small, squalid country-town with his hands in his pockets and an ear for no music now but the chink of the coin they might turn over there. This is indeed in general the accepted, the imposed view of the position he had gained: this freedom to 'elect', as we say, to cease, intellectually, to exist: this ability, exercised at the zenith of his splendour, to shut down the lid, from one day to another, on the most potent aptitude for vivid reflection ever lodged in a human frame and to conduct himself thereafter, in all ease and comfort, not only as if it were not, but as if it had never been. I speak of our 'accepting' the prodigy, but by the established record we have no choice whatever; which is why it is imposed, as I say, on our bewildered credulity. With the impossibility of proving that the author of *The Tempest* did, after the date of that production, ever again press the spring of his fountain, ever again reach for the sacred key or break his heart for an hour over his inconceivable act of sacrifice, we are reduced to behaving as if we understood the strange case; so that any rubbing of our eyes, as under the obsession of a wild dream, has been held a gesture that, for common decency, must mainly take place in private. If I state that my small contribution to any renewed study of the matter can amount, accordingly, but to little more than an irresistible need to rub mine in public, I shall have done the most that the condition of our knowledge admits of. We can 'accept', but we can accept only in stupefaction – a stupefaction that, in presence of *The Tempest*, and of the intimate meaning so imputed to it, must despair of ever subsiding. These things leave us in darkness – in gross darkness about the Man; the case of which they are the warrant is so difficult to embrace. None ever appealed so sharply to some light of knowledge, and nothing could render our actual knowledge more contemptible. What manner of human being was it who *could* so, at a given moment, announce his intention of capping his divine flame with a twopenny extinguisher, and who then, the announcement made, could serenely succeed in carrying it out? Were it a question of a flame spent or burning thin, we might feel a little more possessed of matter for comprehension; the fact being, on the contrary, one can only repeat, that the value of *The Tempest* is, exquisitely, in its refinement of power, its renewed artistic freshness and roundness, its mark as of a distinction unequalled, on the whole (though I admit that we here must take subtle measures), in any predecessor. Prospero has simply waited, to cast his magic ring into the sea, till the jewel set in it shall have begun to burn as never before.

So it is then; and it puts into a nutshell the eternal mystery, the most insoluble that ever was, the complete rupture, for our understanding, between the Poet and the Man. There are moments, I admit, in this age of sound and fury, of connections, in every sense, too maddeningly multiplied, when we are willing to let it pass as a mystery, the most soothing, cooling, consoling too perhaps, that ever was. But there are others when, speaking for myself, its power to torment us intellectually seems scarcely to be borne; and we know these moments best when we hear it proclaimed that a comfortable clearness reigns. I have been for instance reading over Mr. Halliwell-Phillipps, and I find him apparently of the opinion that it is all our fault if everything in our author's story, and above all in this last chapter of it, be not of a primitive simplicity. The complexity arises from our suffering our imagination to meddle with the Man at all; who is quite sufficiently presented to us on the face of the record. For critics of this writer's complexion the only facts we are urgently concerned with are the facts of the Poet, which are abundantly constituted by the Plays and the Sonnets. The Poet is *there*, and the Man is outside: the Man is for instance in such a perfectly definite circumstance as that he could never miss, after *The Tempest*, the key of his piano, as I have called it, since he could play so freely with the key of his cash-box. The supreme master of expression had made, before fifty, all the money he wanted; therefore what was there more to express? This view is admirable if you can get your mind to consent to it. It must ignore any impulse, in presence of Play or Sonnet (whatever vague stir behind either may momentarily act as provocation) to try for a lunge at the figured arras. In front of the tapestry sits the immitigably respectable person whom our little slateful of gathered and numbered items, heaven knows, does amply account for, since there is nothing in him to explain; while the undetermined figure, on the other hand – undetermined whether in the sense of respectability or of anything else – the figure who supremely interests us, remains as unseen of us as our Ariel, on the enchanted island, remains of the bewildered visitors. Mr. Halliwell-Phillipps's theory, as I understand it – and I refer to it but as an advertisement of a hundred others – is that we too are but bewildered visitors, and that the state of mind of the Duke of Naples and his companions is our proper critical portion.

If our knowledge of the greatest of men consists therefore but of the neat and 'proved' addition of two or three dozen common particulars, the rebuke to a morbid and monstrous curiosity is no more than just. We know enough, by such an implication, when we admire enough, and as difficulties would appear to abound on our attempting to push further, this is an obvious lesson to us to stand as still as possible. Not difficulties – those of penetration, exploration, interpretation, those, in the word that says everything, of appreciation – are the approved field of criticism, but the very forefront of the obvious and the palpable, where we may go round and round, like holiday-makers on hobby-horses, at the turning of a crank. Differences of estimate, in this relation, come back, too clearly, let us accordingly say, to differences of view of the character of genius in general – if not, in truth, more exactly stated, to that strangest of all fallacies, the idea of the separateness of a great man's parts. His genius places itself, under this fallacy, on one side of the line and the rest of his identity on the other; the line being that, for instance, which, to Mr. Halliwell-Phillipps's view, divides the author of *Hamlet* and *The Tempest* from the man of exemplary business-method whom alone we may propose to approach at all intimately.

The stumbling-block here is that the boundary exists only in the vision of those able to content themselves with arbitrary marks. A mark becomes arbitrary from the moment we have no authoritative sign of where to place it, no sign of higher warrant than that it smoothes and simplifies the ground. But though smoothing and simplifying, on such terms, may, by restricting our freedom of attention and speculation, make, on behalf of our treatment of the subject, for a livelier effect of business – that business as to a zealous care for which we seem taught that our author must above all serve as our model – it will see us little further on any longer road. The fullest appreciation possible is the high tribute we must offer to greatness, and to make it worthy of its office we must surely know where we are with it. In greatness as much as in mediocrity the man is, under examination, *one*, and the elements of character melt into each other. The genius is a part of the mind, and the mind a part of the behaviour; so that, for the attitude of inquiry, without which appreciation means nothing, where does one of these provinces end and the other begin? We may take the genius first or the behaviour first, but we inevitably proceed from the one to the other; we inevitably encamp, as it were, on the high central table-land that they have in common. How are we to arrive at a relation with the object to be penetrated if we are thus forever met by a locked door flanked with a sentinel who merely invites us to take it for edifying? We take it ourselves for attaching – which is the very essence of mysteries – and profess ourselves doomed forever to hang yearningly about it. An obscurity endured, in fine, one inch further, or in one hour longer, than our necessity truly holds us to, strikes us but as an artificial spectre, a muffled object with waving arms, set up to keep appreciation down.

For it is never to be forgotten that we are here in presence of the human character the most magnificently endowed, in all time, with the sense of the life of man, and with the apparatus for recording it; so that of *him*, inevitably, it goes hardest of all with us to be told that we have nothing, or next to nothing, to do with the effect in him of this gift. If it does not satisfy us that the effect was to make him write *King Lear* and *Othello*, we are verily difficult to please: so it is, meanwhile, that the case for the obscurity is argued. That is sovereign, we reply, so far as it goes; but it tells us nothing of the effect on him of being *able* to write Lear and Othello. No scrap of testimony of what this may have been is offered us; it is the quarter in which our blankness is most blank, and in which we are yet most officiously put off. It is true of the poet in general – in nine examples out of ten – that his life is mainly inward, that its events and revolutions are his great impressions and deep vibrations, and that his 'personality' is all pictured in the publication of his verse. Shakespeare, we essentially feel, is the tenth, is the millionth example; not the sleek bachelor of music, the sensitive harp set once for all in the window to catch the air, but the spirit in hungry quest of every possible experience and adventure of the spirit, and which, betimes, with the boldest of all intellectual movements, was to leap from the window into the street. We are in the street, as it were, for admiration and wonder, when the incarnation alights, and it is of no edification to shrug shoulders at the felt impulse (when made manifest) to follow, to pursue, all breathlessly to track it on its quickly-taken way. Such a quest of imaginative experience, we can only feel, has itself constituted one of the greatest observed adventures of mankind; so that no point of the history of it, however far back seized, is premature for our fond attention. Half our connection with it is our desire to 'assist' at it; so how can we fail of curiosity and sympathy? The answer to which is doubtless again that these impulses are very well, but that as the case stands they can move but in one channel. We are free to assist in the Plays themselves – to assist at whatever we like; so long, that is, as, after the fashion I have noted, we rigidly limit our inductions from them. It is put to us once more that we can make no bricks without straw, and that, rage as we may against our barrier, it none the less stubbornly exists. Granted on behalf of the vaulting spirit all that we claim for it, is still, in the street, as we say – and in spite of the effect we see it as acrobatically producing there – absolutely defies pursuit. Beyond recovery, beyond curiosity, it was to lose itself in the crowd. The crowd, for that matter, the witnesses we must take as astonished and dazzled, has, though itself surviving but in a dozen or two dim, scarce articulate ghosts, been interrogated to the last man and the last distinguishable echo. This has practically elicited nothing – nothing, that is, of a nature to gratify the indiscreetly, the morbidly inquisitive; since we find ourselves not rarely reminded that morbidity may easily become a vice. *He* was notoriously not morbid; he stuck to his business – save when he so strangely gave it up; wherefore his own common sense about things in general is a model for the tone he should properly inspire. 'You speak of his career as a transcendent "adventure," as *the* conspicuously transcendent adventure – even to the sight of his contemporaries – of the mind of man; but no glimmer of any such story, of any such figure or "presence," to use your ambiguous word, as you desire to read into the situation, can be discerned in any quarter. So what is it you propose we should do? What evidence do you suggest that, with this absence of material, we should put together? We have what we have; we are not concerned with what we have not.'

In some such terms as that, one makes out, does the best attainable 'appreciation' appear to invite us to let our great personage, the mighty adventurer, slink past. He slunk past in life: that was good enough for him, the contention appears to be. Why therefore should he not slink past in immortality? One's reply can indeed only be that he evidently must; yes I profess that, even while saying so, our poor point, for which *The Tempest* once more gives occasion, strikes me as still, as always, in its desperate way, worth the making. The question, I hold, will eternally interest the student of letters and of the human understanding, and the envied privilege of our play in particular will be always to keep it before him. *How* did the faculty so radiant there contrive, in such perfection, the arrest of its divine flight? By what inscrutable process was the extinguisher applied and, when once applied, kept in its place to the end? What became of the checked torrent, as a latent, bewildered presence and energy, in the life across which the dam was constructed? What other mills did it set itself turning, or what contiguous country did it – rather indeed did it *not*, in default of these – inevitably ravage? We are referred, for an account of the matter, to recorded circumstances which are only not supremely vulgar because they are supremely dim and few; in which character they but mock, and as if all consciously, as I have said, at our unrest. The one at all large indication they give is that our hero may have died – since he died so soon – of his unnatural effort. Their quality, however, redeems them a little by having for its effect that they throw us back on the work itself with a rebellious renewal of appetite and yearning. The secret that baffles us being the secret of the Man, we know, as I have granted, that we shall never touch the Man *directly* in the Artist. We stake our hopes thus on indirectness, which may contain possibilities; we take that very truth for our counsel of despair, try to look at it as helpful for the Criticism of the future. That of the past has been too often infantile; one has asked one's self how it *could*, on such lines, get at him. The figured tapestry, the long arras that hides him, is always there, with its immensity of surface and its proportionate underside. May it not then be but a question, for the fulness of time, of the finer weapon, the sharper point, the stronger arm, the more extended lunge?

W. H. Auden Caliban to the Audience (1945)

If now, having dismissed your hired impersonators with verdicts ranging from the laudatory orchid to the disgusted and disgusting egg, you ask and, of course, notwithstanding the conscious fact of his irrevocable absence, you instinctively *do* ask for our so good, so great, so dead author to stand before the finally lowered curtain and take his shyly responsible bow for this, his latest, ripest production, it is I – my reluctance is, I can assure you, co-equal with your dismay – who will always loom thus wretchedly into your confused picture, for, in default of the all-wise, all-explaining master you would speak *to*, who else at least can, who else indeed must respond to your bewildered cry, but its very echo, the begged question you would speak to him *about*.

* * *

We must own [*for the present I speak your echo*] to a nervous perplexity not unmixed, frankly, with downright resentment. How *can* we grant the indulgence for which in his epilogue your personified type of the creative so lamely, tamely pleaded? Imprisoned, by you, in the mood doubtful, loaded, by you, with distressing embarrassments, we are, we submit, in no position to set *anyone* free.

Our native Muse, heaven knows and heaven be praised, is not exclusive. Whether out of the innocence of a child-like heart to whom all things are pure, or with the serenity of a status so majestic that the mere keeping up of tones and appearances, the suburban wonder as to what the strait-laced Unities might possibly think, or sad sour Probability possibly say, are questions for which she doesn't because she needn't, she hasn't in her lofty maturity any longer to care a rap, she invited, dear generous-hearted creature that she is, just *tout le monde* to drop in at any time so that her famous, memorable, sought-after evenings present to the speculative eye an ever-shining, never-tarnished proof of her amazing unheard-of power to combine and happily contrast, to make *every* shade of the social and moral palette contribute to the general richness, of the skill, unapproached and unattempted by Grecian aunt or Gaelic sister, with which she can skate full tilt toward the forbidden incoherence and then, in the last split second, on the shuddering edge of the bohemian standardless abyss effect her breathtaking triumphant turn.

No timid segregation by rank or taste for her, no prudent listing into those who will, who might, who certainly would not get on, no nicely graded scale of invitations to heroic formal Tuesdays, young comic Thursdays, al fresco farcical Saturdays. No, the real, the only test of the theatrical as of the gastronomic, her practice confidently wagers, is the mixed perfected brew.

As he looks in on her, so marvellously at home with all her cosy swarm about her, what accents will not assault the new arrival's ear, the magnificent tropes of tragic defiance and despair, the repartee of the high humour, the pun of the very low, cultured drawl and manly illiterate bellow, yet all of them gratefully doing their huge or tiny best to make the party go?

And if, assured by her smiling wave that of course he may, he should presently set out to explore her vast and rambling mansion, to do honour to its dear odd geniuses of local convenience and proportion, its multiplied deities of mysterious stair and interesting alcove, not one of the laughing groups and engrossed warmed couples that he keeps 'surprising' – the never-ending surprise for him is that he doesn't seem to – but affords some sharper instance of relations he would have been the last to guess at, choleric prince at his ease with lymphatic butler, moist hand-taking so to dry, youth getting on quite famously with stingy cold old age, some stranger vision of the large loud liberty violently rocking yet never, he is persuaded, finally upsetting the jolly crowded boat.

What, he may well ask, has the gracious goddess done to all these people that, at her most casual hint, they should so trustingly, so immediately take off those heavy habits one thinks of them as having for their health and happiness day and night to wear, without in this unfamiliar unbuttoned state – the notable absence of the slightest shiver or not-quite-inhibited sneeze is indication positive – for a second feeling the draught? Is there, could there be, *any* miraculous suspension of the wearily historic, the dingily geographic, the dully drearily sensible beyond her faith, her charm, her love, to command? Yes, there could be, yes, alas, indeed yes, O there is, right here, right now before us, the situation present.

How *could* you, you who are one of the oldest habitués at these delightful functions, one, possibly the closest, of her trusted inner circle, how could you be guilty of the incredible unpardonable treachery of bringing along the one creature, as you above all men must have known, whom she cannot and will not under any circumstances stand, the solitary exception she is not at any hour of the day or night at home to, the unique case that her attendant spirits have absolute instructions never, neither at the front door nor at the back, to admit?

At Him and at Him only does she draw the line, not because there are any limits to her sympathy but precisely because there are none. Just because of all she is and all she means to be, she cannot conceivably tolerate in her presence the represented principle of *not* sympathizing, *not* associating, *not* amusing, the only child of her Awful Enemy, the rival whose real name she will never sully her lips with – 'that envious witch' is sign sufficient – who does not rule but defiantly is the unrectored chaos.

All along and only too well she has known what would happen if, by any careless mischance – of conscious malice she never dreamed till now – He should ever manage to get in. She foresaw what He would do to the conversation, lying in wait for its vision of private love or public justice to warm to an Egyptian brilliance and then with some fish-like odour or *bruit insolite* snatching the visionaries back tongue-tied and blushing to the here and now; she foresaw what He would do to the arrangements, breaking, by a refusal to keep in step, the excellent order of the dancing ring, and ruining supper by knocking over the loaded appetizing tray; worst of all, she foresaw, she dreaded what He would end up by doing to her, that, not content with upsetting her guests, with spoiling their fun, His progress from outrage to outrage would not relent before the gross climax of His making, horror unspeakable, a pass at her virgin self.

Let us suppose, even, that in your eyes she is by no means as we have always fondly imagined, your dear friend, that what we have just witnessed was not what it seemed to us, the inexplicable betrayal of a life-long sacred loyalty, but your long-premeditated just revenge, the final evening up of some ancient never-forgotten score, then even so, why make us suffer who have never, in all conscience, done you harm? Surely the theatrical relation, no less than the marital, is governed by the sanely decent general law that, before visitors, in front of the children or the servants, there shall be no indiscreet revelation of animosity, no 'scenes', that, no matter to what intolerable degrees of internal temperature and pressure restraint may raise both the injured and the guilty, nevertheless such restraint is applied to tones and topics, the exhibited picture must be still as always the calm and smiling one of the most malicious observer can see nothing wrong with, and not until the last of those whom manifested anger or mistrust would embarrass or amuse or not be good for have gone away or out or up, is the voice raised, the table thumped, the suspicious letter snatched at or the outrageous bill furiously waved.

For we, after all – you cannot have forgotten this – are strangers to her. We have never claimed her acquaintance, knowing as well as she that we do not and never could belong on her side of the curtain. All we have ever asked for is that for a few hours the curtain should be left undrawn, so as to allow our humble ragged selves the privilege of craning and gaping at the splendid goings-on inside. We most emphatically do *not* ask that she should speak to us, or try to understand us; on the contrary our one desire has always been that she should preserve for ever her old high strangeness, for what delights us about her world is just that it neither is nor possibly could become one in which we could breathe or behave, that in her house the right of innocent passage should remain so universal that the same neutral space accommodates the conspirator and his victim; the generals of both armies, the chorus of patriots and the choir of nuns, palace and farmyard, cathedral and smugglers' cave, that time should never revert to that intransigent element we are so ineluctably and only too familiarly in, but remain the passive good-natured creature she and her friends can by common consent do anything they like with – (it is not surprising that they should take advantage of their strange power and so frequently skip hours and days and even years: the dramatic mystery is that they should always so unanimously agree upon exactly how many hours and days and years to skip) – that upon their special constitutions the moral law should continue to operate so exactly that the timid not only deserve but actually win the fair, and it is the socially and physically unemphatic David who lays low the gorilla-chested Goliath with one well-aimed custard pie, that in their blessed climate, the manifestation of the inner life should always remain so easy and habitual that a sudden eruption of musical and metaphorical power is instantly recognized as standing for grief and disgust, an elegant *contrapposto* for violent death, and that consequently the picture which they in there present to us out here is always that of the perfectly tidiable case of disorder, the beautiful and serious problem exquisitely set without a single superfluous datum and insoluble with less, the expert landing of all the passengers with all their luggage safe and sound in the best of health and spirits and without so much as a scratch or a bruise.

Into that world of freedom without anxiety, sincerity without loss of vigour, feeling that loosens rather than ties the tongue, we are not, we reiterate, so blinded by presumption to our proper status and interest as to expect or even wish at any time to enter, far less to dwell there.

Must we – it seems oddly that we must – remind you that our existence does not, like hers, enjoy an infinitely indicative mood, an eternally present tense, a limitlessly active voice, for in our shambling, slovenly makeshift world any two persons, whether domestic first or neighbourly second, require and necessarily presuppose in both their numbers and in all their cases, the whole inflected gamut of an alien third since, without a despised or dreaded Them to turn the back *on*, there could be no intimate or affectionate Us to turn the eye *to*; that, *chez nous*, space to never the whole uninhabited circle but always some segment, its eminent domain upheld by two coordinates. There always has been and always will be not only the vertical boundary, the river on this side of which initiative and honesty stroll arm in arm wearing sensible clothes, and beyond which is a savage elsewhere swarming with contagious diseases, but also its horizontal counterpart, the railroad above which houses stand in their own grounds, each equipped with a garage and a beautiful woman, sometimes with several, and below which huddled shacks provide a squeezing shelter to collarless herds who eat blancmange and have never said anything witty. Make the case as special as you please; take the tamest congregation or the wildest faction; take, say, a college. What river and railroad did for the grosser instance, lawn and corridor do for the more refined, dividing the tender who value from the tough who measure, the superstitious who still sacrifice to causation from the heretics who have already reduced the worship of truth to bare description, and so creating the academic fields to be guarded with umbrella and learned periodical against the trespass of any unqualified stranger, not a whit less jealously than the game-preserve is protected from the poacher by the unamiable shot-gun. For without these prohibitive frontiers we should never know who we were or what we wanted. It is they who donate to neighbourhood all its accuracy and vehemence. It is thanks to them that we do know with whom to associate, make love, exchange recipes and jokes, go mountain climbing or sit side by side fishing from piers. It is thanks to them, too, that we know against whom to rebel. We *can* shock our parents by visiting the dives below the railroad tracks, we *can* amuse ourselves on what would otherwise have been a very dull evening indeed, in plotting to seize the post office across the river.

Of course these several private regions must together comprise one public whole – we would never deny that logic and instinct require that – of course. We and They are united in the candid glare of the same commercial hope by day, and the soft refulgence of the same erotic nostalgia by night – and this is our point – without our privacies of situation, our local idioms of triumph and mishap, our different doctrines concerning the transubstantiation of the larger pinker bun on the terrestrial dish for which the mature sense may reasonably water and the adult fingers furtively or unabashedly go for, our specific choices of which hill it would be romantic to fly away over or what sea it would be exciting to run away to, our peculiar visions of the absolute stranger with a spontaneous longing for the lost who will adopt our misery not out of desire but pure compassion, without, in short, our devoted pungent expression of the partial and contrasted, the Whole would have no importance and its Day and Night no interest.

So, too, with Time who, in our auditorium, is not the dear old buffer so anxious to please everybody, but a prim magistrate whose court never adjourns, and from whose decisions, as he laconically sentences one to loss of hair and talent, another to seven days' chastity, and a third to boredom for life, there is no appeal. We should not be sitting here now, washed, warm, well-fed, in seats we have paid for, unless there were others who are not here; our liveliness and good-humour, such as they are, are those of survivors, conscious that there are others who have not been so fortunate, others who did not succeed in navigating the narrow passage or to whom the natives were not friendly, others whose streets were chosen by the explosion or through whose country the famine turned aside from ours to go, others who failed to repel the invasion of bacteria or to crush the insurrection of their bowels, others who lost their suit against their parents or were ruined by wishes they could not adjust or murdered by resentments they could not control; aware of some who were better and bigger but from whom, only the other day, Fortune withdrew her hand in sudden disgust, now nervously playing chess with drunken sea-captains in sordid cafés on the equator or the Arctic Circle, or lying, only a few blocks away, strapped and screaming on iron beds or dropping to naked pieces in damp graves. And shouldn't you too, dear master, reflect – forgive us for mentioning it – that we might very well not have been attending a production of yours this evening, had not some other and maybe – who can tell? – brighter talent married a barmaid or turned religious and shy or gone down in a liner with all his manuscripts, the loss recorded only in the corner of some country newspaper below A Poultry Lover's Jottings?

You yourself, we seem to remember, have spoken of the conjured spectacle as 'a mirror held up to nature', a phrase misleading in its aphoristic sweep but indicative at least of one aspect of the relations between the real and the imagined, their mutual reversal of value, for isn't the essential artistic strangeness to which your citation of the sinisterly biased image would point just this: that on the far side of the mirror the general will to compose, to form at all costs a felicitous pattern, becomes the *necessary cause* of any particular effort to live or act or love or triumph or vary, instead of being as, in so far as it emerges at all, it is on this side, their *accidental effect*?

Does Ariel – to nominate the spirit of reflection in your terms – call for manifestation? Then neither modesty nor fear of reprisals excuses the one so called on from publicly confessing that she cheated at croquet or that he committed incest in a dream. Does He demand concealment? Then their nearest and dearest must be deceived by disguises of sex and age which anywhere else would at once attract the attentions of the police or the derisive whistle of the awful schoolboy. That is the price asked, and how promptly and gladly paid, for universal reconciliation and peace, for the privilege of all galloping together past the finishing post neck and neck.

How then, we continue to wonder, knowing all this, could you act as if you did not, as if you did not realize that the embarrassing compresence of the absolutely natural, incorrigibly right-handed, and, to any request for co-operation, utterly negative, with the enthusiastically self-effacing would be a simultaneous violation of both worlds, as if you were not perfectly well aware that the magical musical condition, the orphic spell that turns the fierce dumb greedy beasts into grateful guides and oracles who will gladly take one anywhere and tell one everything free of charge, is precisely and simply that of his finite immediate note *not*, under any circumstances, being struck, of its not being tentatively whispered, far less positively banged.

Are we not bound to conclude, then, that, whatever snub to the poetic you may have intended incidentally to administer, your profounder motive in so introducing Him to them among whom, because He doesn't belong, He couldn't appear as anything but His distorted parody, a deformed and savage slave, was to deal with a mortal face-slapping insult to us among whom He does and is, moreover, all grossness turned to glory, no less a person than the nude august elated archer of our heaven, the darling single son of Her who, in her right milieu, is certainly no witch but the most sensible of all the gods, whose influence is as sound as it is pandemic, on the race-track no less than in the sleeping cars of the Orient Express, our great white Queen of Love herself?

But even that is not the worst we suspect you of. If your words have not buttered any parsnips, neither have they broken any bones.

He, after all, can come back to us now to be comforted and respected, perhaps, after the experience of finding himself for a few hours and for the first time in His life not wanted, more fully and freshly appreciative of our affection than He has always been in the past; as for His dear mother, She is far too grand and far too busy to hear or care what you say or think. If only we were certain that your malice was confined to the verbal affront, we should long ago have demanded our money back and gone whistling home to bed. Alas, in addition to resenting what you have openly said, we fear even more what you may secretly have done. Is it possible that, not content with inveigling Caliban into Ariel's kingdom, you have also let loose Ariel in Caliban's? We note with alarm that when the other members of the final tableau were dismissed, He was not returned to His arboreal confinement as He should have been. Where is He now? For if the intrusion of the real has disconcerted and incommoded the poetic, that is a mere bagatelle compared to the damage which the poetic would inflict if it ever succeeded in intruding upon the real. We want no Ariel here, breaking down our picket fences in the name of fraternity, seducing our wives in the name of romance, and robbing us of our sacred pecuniary deposits in the name of justice. Where is Ariel? What have you done with Him? For we won't, we daren't leave until you give us a satisfactory answer.

PART TWO

Recent Studies

J. Middleton Murry Shakespeare's Dream (1936)

In *The Tempest* this 'sensation' of the final Shakespeare achieves its perfect dramatic form. The relation between it and its predecessors is made sensible by Alonso's question to Prospero:

When did you lose your daughter?
Pros. In this last tempest. (v i 152–3)

Marina was lost in an actual tempest; Perdita, first, in the tempest of her father's jealousy, and then exposed in an actual tempest: but Miranda is not involved in a tempest at all. Her tempest is one in which others are overwhelmed, wherein she is engulfed by her imagination alone:

O, I have suffered
With those that I saw suffer: a brave vessel
Who had, no doubt, some noble creature in her,
Dash'd all to pieces. O, the cry did knock
Against my very heart. (I ii 5–9)

And, when the noble creature emerges, it is in love of him that she is lost. Miranda sees Ferdinand first, by Prospero's art. It was needed to safeguard her; for when at last she sees the others of the company before her, she cries:

O wonder!
How many goodly creatures are there here!
How beauteous mankind is! O brave new world
That has such people in it! (v i 181–4)

And Prospero's wise-sad answer to her ecstasy is simply: ''Tis new to thee'. Of the four chief actors who are before her eyes, three are evil; or, more truly, were evil. The one untainted is Gonzalo, whose loving-kindness had saved Prospero from death, and steaded him with the means of life, and more:

Knowing I loved my books, he furnish'd me
From mine own library with volumes that
I prize above my dukedom. (I ii 166–8)

From Prospero's study of these volumes comes his power. He is the votary of wisdom. Because he had been so 'transported and rapt in secret studies', he had fallen a victim to the machinations of his brother and lost his dukedom.

Because I am by temperament averse to reading Shakespeare as allegory I am struck by my own impression that *The Tempest* is more nearly symbolical than any of his plays. I find it impossible to deny that Prospero is, to some extent, an imaginative paradigm of Shakespeare himself in his function as poet; and that he does in part embody Shakespeare's self-awareness at the conclusion of his poetic career.

To this conclusion I am forced by many considerations. The simplest and weightiest of them all is this. That there is a final period in Shakespeare's work, which exists in reality and is as subtly homogeneous as a living thing, is to me indubitable. It is equally certain that *The Tempest* is, artistically, imaginatively and 'sensationally', the culmination of that period. And, finally, it is certain that Prospero's function in the drama of *The Tempest* is altogether peculiar. He is its prime mover; he governs and directs it from the beginning to the end; he stands clean apart from all Shakespeare's characters in this, or any other period of his work. He is the quintessence of a quintessence of a quintessence.

To what extent Prospero is Shakespeare, I do not seek to determine. I have no faith in allegorical interpretation, because I am certain that allegory was alien to Shakespeare's mind. I can conceive innumerable interpretations of Prospero beginning thus: 'It is through his dedication to the pursuit of secret wisdom that he loses his dukedom; so Shakespeare, through his dedication to the mystery of Poetry, forwent the worldly eminence which his genius could have achieved.' That kind of thing means nothing to me, and I find no trace of it in the length and breadth of Shakespeare's work. When I reach the conclusion that Prospero is, in some sense, Shakespeare, I mean no more than that, being what he is, fulfilling his unique function in a Shakespeare play, and that in all probability Shakespeare's last, it was inevitable that Prospero should be, as it were, uniquely 'shot with' Shakespeare. I mean no more than that it is remarkable and impressive that Shakespeare should have given his last play this particular form, which carried with it this particular necessity: which is no other than that of coming as near to projecting the last phase of his own creative imagination into the figure of a single character as Shakespeare could do without shattering his own dramatic method. But, in saying this, I do not mean that Shakespeare deliberately contrived *The Tempest* to this end. He wanted, simply, to write a play that would satisfy himself, by expressing something, or many things, that still were unexpressed. For this purpose, a Prospero was necessary.

He was necessary to make accident into design. *The Winter's Tale* is a lovely story, but it is in substance (though not in essence) a simple tale, a sequence of chances. There is no chance in *The Tempest*; everything is foreordained. Of course, this is appearance only. The events of *The Winter's Tale* are no less foreordained than those of *The Tempest*; both are foreordained by Shakespeare. But in *The Tempest*, Shakespeare employs a visible agent to do the work. That is the point. For it follows, first, that the visible agent of Shakespeare's poetic mind must be one endowed with supernatural powers, a 'magician'; and, second, that what he foreordains must be, in some quintessential way, human and humane. Once grant a character such powers, their use must satisfy us wholly. Chance may be responsible for the loss and saving of Perdita, and the long severance of Hermione and Leontes, but not humane omnipotence.

It may be said that this is to put the cart before the horse, and that Shakespeare was concerned primarily with the solution of a 'technical' problem. It may be that his central 'idea' was the obliteration of the evil done and suffered by one generation through the love of the next, and that his problem was to represent that 'idea' with the same perfection as he had in the past represented the tragedy of the evil done and suffered. (Though to call this a merely technical problem is fantastic: a whole religion is implicit in it.) In *The Winter's Tale* he had pretty completely humanized the crude story of *Pericles*: but Leontes' jealousy was extravagant, Antigonus' dispatch a joke, the oracle clumsy, and Hermione's disguise as statue a theatrical trick. The machinery was unworthy of the theme. It stood in the way of the theme's significance.

We are driven back to the same conclusion. In order to precipitate the significance of the theme out of a condition of solution, a palpable directing intelligence was required. What seemed to be accident must now be felt as design. There is but one accident in *The Tempest*, the accident which brings the ship to the island. And Shakespeare is emphatic that this is accident:

> *Mir.* And now, I pray you, sir,
> For still 'tis beating in my mind, your reason
> For raising this sea-storm?
> *Pros.* Know thus far forth,
> By accident most strange, bountiful Fortune,
> Now my dear lady, hath mine enemies
> Brought to this shore; and by my prescience
> I find my zenith doth depend upon
> A most auspicious star, whose influence
> If now I court not but omit, my fortunes
> Will ever after droop. (I ii 175–83)

Initial accident there must be. If Prospero's power extended to the world beyond the Island, so that he could compel the voyage thither, the drama would be gone. Prospero would be omnipotent indeed; and the presence of evil and wrong in the world he controlled would be evidence of devilishness in his nature. *The Tempest* implies a tremendous criticism of vulgar religion. I do not think that Shakespeare intended this deliberately; it was the spontaneous outcome of the working of his imagination. But I think there was a moment in the writing of his drama when he was deeply disturbed by the implications of the method to which he had been brought by the natural effort towards complete utterance of his 'sensation'.

The Island is a realm where God is Good, where true Reason rules; it is what would be if Humanity – the best in man – controlled the life of man. And Prospero is a man in whom the best in man has won the victory: not without a struggle, of which we witness the reverberation:

> *Ari.* Your charm so strongly works them
> That if you now beheld them, your affections
> Would become tender.
> *Pros.* Dost thou think so, spirit?
> *Ari.* Mine would, sir, were I human.
> *Pros.* And mine shall.
> Hast thou, which art but air, a touch, a feeling
> Of their afflictions, and shall not myself,
> One of their kind, that relish all as sharply,
> Passion as they, be kindlier moved than thou art?
> Though with their high wrongs I am struck to the quick,
> Yet with my nobler reason 'gainst my fury
> Do I take part: the rarer action is

In virtue than in vengeance; they being penitent,
The sole drift of my purpose doth extend
Not a frown further. Go, release them, Ariel:
My charms I'll break, their senses I'll restore,
And they shall be themselves. (v i 17–32)

'Themselves' – not what they were, but what they should be. This is no stretch of interpretation. Gonzalo drives it home afterwards. 'All of us found ourselves, when no man was his own.'

The Island is a realm, then; controlled by a man who has become himself, and has the desire, the will and the power to make other men themselves. Miranda is what she is because she has been his pupil:

Here
Have I, thy schoolmaster, made thee more profit
Than other princess' can that have more time
For vainer hours; and tutors not so careful. (I ii 171–4)

Here is a difference between Miranda and Perdita; and an important one, for it belongs, as we shall see, to the essence of Shakespeare's thinking. It is not a difference in the imaginative substance of those lovely creatures. We must not say that Perdita is the child of nature, and Miranda the child of art. They are creatures of the same kind. The difference is only that in *The Tempest* Shakespeare wants to make clear what he means: that men and women do not become their true selves by Nature merely, but by Nurture. So it is that, for all his power, Prospero cannot transmute Caliban, for he is one

on whose nature
Nurture can never stick; on whom my pains
Humanely taken, all, all lost, quite lost. (IV i 188–91)

The thought is vital to *The Tempest*. The Island is a realm where by Art or Nurture Prospero transforms man's Nature to true Human Nature. The process, in the case of the evil-doers, must by dramatic necessity be sudden, and as it were magical; but we must understand its import. For this process is the meaning of Prospero.

We can approach Prospero by way of Gonzalo, who was, to the limit of his power, Prospero's loyal and understanding friend in the evil past. Gonzalo has his own dream. After the shipwreck, he looks upon the beauty and richness of the enchanted island. 'Had I plantation of this isle, my lord' – if it were his to colonize and rule – 'what would I do?' And he answers; or rather Shakespeare answers for him. It is significant that Shakespeare takes his words from Montaigne. We have a choice: either the passage from Montaigne's essay 'Of the Caniballes' was so familiar to Shakespeare that he knew it by heart, or he wrote Gonzalo's words with the passage from Florio's Montaigne before his eyes. Other solution there is none. This is not reminiscence, but direct copying. I am sorry, says Montaigne, that the 'cannibals' were not discovered long ago, when there were living men who could have appreciated their significance:

> I am sorie, *Lycurgus* and *Plato* had it not: for me seemeth that what in those nations we see by experience, doth not only exceed all the pictures wherewith licentious Poesie hath proudly imbellished the golden age, and all her quaint inventions to faine a happy condition of man, but also the conception and desire of Philosophy. They could not imagine a genuitie so pure and simple, as we see it by experience; nor ever beleeve our societie might be maintained with so little art and humane combination.

The words are worth the scrutiny. We know that Shakespeare read and studied them while he was writing *The Tempest*. There are very few passages, outside North's Plutarch, of which we can certainly say so much: and assuredly no passage of the few we know that Shakespeare studied bears so nearly upon the heart of his final theme as this one.

Montaigne says that he regrets that Plato and Lycurgus did not know of the 'cannibals'. Those great lawmakers – one the legislator of an actual, the other of an ideal society – would have seen in the society of the South American savages something that exceeded 'the conception and desire of philosophy'. They could never have believed that a society of men might be maintained with so little art and humane combination – that is to say, with so little artifice and contrivance. Montaigne is saying that the life of the South American Indians proves that mankind is capable of living peacefully, happily and humanely without the constraint of law, or the institution of private property:

> It is a nation, would I answer Plato, that hath no kinde of traffike, no knowledge of Letters, no intelligence of numbers, no name of magistrate, nor of politike superioritie; no use of service, of riches or of povertie; no

contracts, no successions, no partitions, no occupation but idle: no respect of kindred, but common, no apparel but naturall, no manuring of lands, no use of wine, corne, or mettle. The very words that import lying, falsehood, treason, dissimulations, covetousnes, envie, detraction, and pardon, were never heard of amongst them. How dissonant would hee finde his imaginarie commonwealth from this perfection!

Gonzalo imagines that he has the empty island to colonize. What would I do? he says:

> I' the commonwealth I would by contraries
> Execute all things: for no kind of traffic
> Would I admit; no name of magistrate;
> Letters should not be known; riches, poverty
> And use of service, none; contract, succession,
> Bourne, bound of land, tilth, vineyard, none;
> No use of metal, corn, or wine, or oil;
> No occupation; all men idle, all;
> And women, too, but innocent and pure;
> No sovereignty . . .
> All things in common nature should produce
> Without sweat or endeavour: treason, felony,
> Sword, pike, knife, gun, or need of any engine
> Would I not have; but nature should bring forth,
> Of its own kind, all foison, all abundance,
> To feed my innocent people. (II i 143–60)

What Shakespeare has done is singular, and revealing. Montaigne, true sceptic that he was, had pitted the savage against the civilized. Shakespeare omits from Montaigne's picture the incessant fighting, the plurality of wives, the cannibalism itself, and puts his words in Gonzalo's mouth as a description of the ideal; and at the same time he sets before us, in Caliban, his own imagination of the savage, in which brutality and beauty are astonishingly one nature. So Shakespeare makes clear his conviction that it is not by a return to the primitive that mankind must advance. Yet he is as critical as Montaigne himself of the world of men. The wise Gonzalo when he looks upon the 'strange shapes' who bring in the unsubstantial banquet and 'dance about it with gentle actions of salutation, inviting the king to eat', says:

> If in Naples
> I should report this now, would they believe me?
> If I should say, I saw such islanders –

> For, certes, these are people of the island –
> Who, though they are of monstrous shape, yet, note
> Their manners are more gentle-kind than of
> Our human generation you shall find
> Many, nay almost any. (III iii 27–34)

But these are not savages; they are Prospero's spirits.

This reaction to Montaigne, this subtle change of Montaigne, might be put down to a purely instinctive motion in Shakespeare, were it not for the fact that Shakespeare had used this essay of Montaigne before. He had been reading it at the time he was writing *The Winter's Tale*, for Polixenes' memorable defence of the Art which mends Nature, and is therefore itself Nature, is a reply to the passage in Montaigne's essay which immediately precedes those we have quoted. Montaigne begins by declaring that there is nothing in the Indians – head-hunting, cannibalism, incessant warfare, and community of wives, included – that is either barbarous or savage 'unless men call that barbarisme which is not common to them'. He is, of course, turning it all to the account of his ethical scepticism: truth this side of the Alps, falsehood the other. He goes on:

> They are even savage, as we call those fruits wilde, which nature of her selfe, and of her ordinarie progresse hath produced: whereas indeed they are those which our selves have altered by our artificiall devices, and diverted from their common order, we should rather terme savage. In those are the true and most profitable vertues, and naturall properties most lively and vigorous, which in these we have bastardized, applying them to the pleasure of our corrupted taste. And if notwithstanding, in divers fruits of those countries that were never tilled, we shall finde, that in respect of ours they are most excellent, and as delicate unto our taste; there is no reason, art should gaine the point of honour of our great and puissant mother Nature . . . Those nations seem therefore so barbarous to me because they have received very little fashion from humane wit, and are yet neere their originall naturalitie. The lawes of nature do yet commande them, which are but little bastardized by ours . . .

Precisely so did Perdita exclude 'carnations and streaked gillyvors' from her garden, because they are called 'nature's bastards', because

> There is an art which in their piedness shares
> With great creating nature.

Shakespeare will have nothing to do with that false antithesis between Art and Nature. Says Polixenes: 'Nature is made better by no mean but Nature makes that mean'. The Art that makes Nature better is Nature's Art. That is the true distinction, between Nature's art and man's, and it has perhaps never been more simply or subtly formulated. Where man's art improves nature, it is nature's art in man; where it makes nature worse, it is man's art alone. In *The Winter's Tale*, we have first, Shakespeare's casual, in *The Tempest* his deliberate reply to the scepticism of Montaigne.

And thus it is that Shakespeare, in Gonzalo's words, with splendid irony changes Montaigne's report of the Indians, from mere nature, to a picture of nature's art in man, working on man. He discards the savagery, and retains only what belongs to the ideal and human. It is the innocence not of the primitive, but of the ultimate, which he seeks to embody. And that is manifest from the very structure of *The Tempest*. Caliban is the primitive; but Miranda and Ferdinand are the ultimate. There is no confusion possible between them, and the sophistry of Montaigne is exorcised by a wave of the wand. Nature and Nurture alone can make human Nature. But the nurture that is Nature's own is hard to find.

In *The Tempest* there is Prospero to govern the process, and to work the miracle of a new creation. Poised between Caliban, the creature of the baser elements – earth and water – and Ariel, the creature of the finer – fire and air – is the work of Prospero's alchemy: the loving humanity of Ferdinand and Miranda. Miranda is a new creature; but Ferdinand must be made new. He is made new by the spell of Ariel's music.

Sitting on a bank,
Weeping again the king my father's wreck,
This music crept by me upon the waters,
Allaying both their fury and my passion
With its sweet air: thence I have follow'd it,
Or it hath drawn me rather. But 'tis gone.
No, it begins again.

ARIEL *sings*

Full fathom five thy father lies;
Of his bones are coral made;
Those are pearls that were his eyes:
Nothing of him that doth fade
But doth suffer a sea-change

Into something rich and strange.
Sea-nymphs hourly ring his knell:
Burthen. Ding-dong!
Hark, now I hear them – Ding-dong, bell.
(I ii 392–407)

From the ecstasy of that transforming music, Ferdinand awakes to behold Miranda, and Miranda beholds him. *Jam nova progenies* . . .

Beneath a like transforming spell, eventually all the company pass – Alonzo, the false brother, Sebastian and Antonio, the traitors. In the men of sin it works madness, or what seems like madness, but is a desperation wrought by the dreadful echoing of the voice of conscience by the elements:

Gon. I' the name of something holy, sir, why stand you
In this strange stare?
Alon. O, it is monstrous, monstrous!
Methought the billows spoke, and told me of it;
The winds did sing it to me; and the thunder,
That deep and dreadful organ-pipe, pronounced
The name of Prosper; it did bass my trespass.
Therefore my son i' the ooze is bedded, and
I'll seek him deeper than e'er plummet sounded,
And with him there lie mudded. [*Exit*
Seb. But one fiend at a time!
I'll fight their legions o'er.
Ant. I'll be thy second. [*Exeunt* SEB. *and* ANT.
Gon. All three of them are desperate: their great guilt,
Like poison given to work a great time after,
Now 'gins to bite the spirits. (III iii 94–106)

That which Christian theology imposes on evil men at the Judgment-Day – 'The tortures of the damned' – by Prospero's art they experience in life. They are rapt out of time by his spells. To Gonzalo, whose life is clear, it brings only such change as that which Ariel's music works upon Ferdinand. But by these different paths, they reach the condition which Gonzalo describes: 'All of us found ourselves, when no man was his own.'

So that when Miranda looks upon them, and cries for joy at 'the brave new world that has such creatures in it', they really are new creatures that she sees. They have suffered a sea-change. And Prospero's wise-sad word: ''Tis new to thee', if we were to take it precisely, applies only to the world beyond the island, not to those of its creatures he has transformed. But it is not the word of Prospero;

it is of Prospero 'shot by' Shakespeare, who knows it is not so easy to transform men, still less a world.

And it is a sudden pang of this awareness which works in the strange conclusion of the lovely masque which Prospero sets before Ferdinand and Miranda, to celebrate their betrothal. He has promised to bestow on them 'some vanity of mine art'. It is the kind of lovely thing that Shakespeare found it natural to write: a vision of Nature's beauty, ministering to the natural beauty of Ferdinand's and Miranda's love. Ferdinand, enchanted, cries:

Let me live here ever:
So rare a wonder'd father and a wise
Make this place Paradise. (IV i 122–4)

Suddenly, towards the end of the concluding dance, Prospero remembers the clumsy plot of Caliban and Stephano against his life. He is in no danger, nor could he be conceived to be in danger. Yet he is profoundly disturbed, strangely disturbed, and the strangeness of the disturbance is strangely insisted on.

Fer. This is strange: your father's in some passion
That works him strongly.
Mir. Never till this day
Saw I him touch'd with anger so distemper'd.
Pros. You do look, my son, in a moved sort,
As if you were dismay'd: be cheerful, sir.
Our revels now are ended. These our actors,
As I foretold you, were all spirits and
Are melted into air, into thin air:
And, like the baseless fabric of this vision,
The cloud-capp'd towers, the gorgeous palaces,
The solemn temples, the great globe itself,
Yea, all which it inherit, shall dissolve
And, like this unsubstantial pageant faded,
Leave not a rack behind. We are such stuff
As dreams are made on, and our little life
Is rounded with a sleep. Sir, I am vex'd;
Bear with my weakness; my old brain is troubled:
Be not disturb'd with my infirmity:
If you be pleased, retire into my cell
And there repose: a turn or two I'll walk
To still my beating mind.
Fer. Mir. We wish your peace. (IV i 143–63)

It is not the plot against his life which has produced this disturbance. It is the thought of what the plot means: the Nature on which Nurture will never stick. The disturbance and the thought come from beyond the visible action of the drama itself.

What Prospero seems to be thinking concerning the vanity of his art, has been disturbed and magnified by what Shakespeare is thinking concerning the vanity of his. He has imagined a mankind redeemed, transformed, re-born; the jewel of the wood become the jewel of the world. As the recollection of Caliban's evil purpose seems to wake Prospero, so does the recollection of the world of reality wake Shakespeare: and these two awakings are mingled with one another. In *The Tempest* Shakespeare had embodied his final dream – of a world created anew, a new race of men and women. Was it also *only* a dream?

E. M. W. Tillyard The Tragic Pattern (1938)

It is a common notion that *Cymbeline* and *The Winter's Tale* are experiments leading to the final success of *The Tempest*. I think it quite untrue of *The Winter's Tale*, which, in some ways though not in others, deals with the tragic pattern more adequately than the later play. Certainly it deals with the destructive portion more directly and fully. On the other hand, *The Tempest*, by keeping this destructive portion largely in the background and dealing mainly with regeneration, avoids the juxtaposition of the two themes, which some people (of whom I am not one) find awkward in *The Winter's Tale*. The simple truth is, that if you cram a trilogy into a single play something has to be sacrificed. Shakespeare chose to make a different sacrifice in each of his two successful renderings of the complete tragic pattern: unity in *The Winter's Tale*, present rendering of the destructive part of the tragic pattern in *The Tempest*.

Many readers, drugged by the heavy enchantments of Prospero's island, may demur at my admitting the tragic element to the play at all. I can cite in support one of the latest studies of the play, Dover Wilson's[1] (although I differ somewhat in the way I think the tragic element is worked out). Of the storm scene he writes:

It is as if Shakespeare had packed his whole tragic vision of life into one brief scene before bestowing his new vision upon us.

But one has only to look at the total plot to see that in its main lines it closely follows those of *Cymbeline* and *The Winter's Tale*, and that tragedy is an organic part of it. Prospero, when one first hears of him, was the ruler of an independent state and beloved of his subjects. But all is not well, because the King of Naples is his enemy. Like Basilius in Sidney's *Arcadia*, he commits the error of not attending carefully enough to affairs of state. The reason for this error, his Aristotelian *ἁμαρτία*, is his love of study. He hands over the government to his brother Antonio, who proceeds to call in the King of Naples to turn Prospero out of his kingdom. Fearing the people, Antonio refrains from murdering Prospero and his infant daughter, but sets them adrift in a boat. Now, except for this last item, the plot is entirely typical of Elizabethan revenge tragedy. Allow Prospero to be put to death, give him a son instead of a daughter to live and to avenge him, and your tragic plot is complete. Such are the affinities of the actual plot of *The Tempest*. And in the abstract it is more typically tragic in the fashion of its age than *The Winter's Tale*, with its debt to the Greek romances.

In handling the theme of regeneration, Shakespeare in one way alters his method. Although a royal person had previously been the protagonist, it had been only in name. Cymbeline had indeed resembled Prospero in having his enemies at his mercy and in forgiving them, but he owed his power not to himself, but to fortune and the efforts of others. As for Leontes, he has little to do with his own regeneration; for it would be perverse to make too much of his generosity in sheltering Florizel and Perdita from the anger of Polixenes. But Prospero is the agent of his own regeneration, the parent and tutor of Miranda; and through her and through his own works he changes the minds of his enemies. It was by this centring of motives in Prospero as well as by subordinating the theme of destruction that Shakespeare gave *The Tempest* its unified structure.

In executing his work, Shakespeare chose a method new to himself but repeated by Milton in *Samson Agonistes*. He began his action at a point in the story so late that the story was virtually over; and he included the total story either by narrating the past or by re-enacting samples of it: a complete reaction from the method of frontal attack used in *The Winter's Tale*.

For the re-enactment of tragedy it is possible to think with Dover Wilson that the storm scene does this. But it does nothing to re-enact the specific tragic plot in the play, the fall of Prospero; and one of its aims is to sketch (as it does with incomparable swiftness) the characters of the ship's company. The true re-enactment is in the long first scene of the second act where Antonio, in persuading Sebastian to murder Alonso, personates his own earlier action in plotting against Prospero, thus drawing it out of the past and placing it before us in the present. This long scene, showing the shipwrecked King and courtiers and the conspiracy, has not had sufficient praise nor sufficient attention. Antonio's transformation from the cynical and lazy badgerer of Gonzalo's loquacity to the brilliantly swift and unscrupulous man of action is a thrilling affair. Just so Iago awakes from his churlish 'honesty' to his brilliant machinations. Antonio is indeed one of Shakespeare's major villains:

Ant. Will you grant with me
  That Ferdinand is drown'd?
Seb. He's gone.
Ant. Then, tell me,
  Who's the next heir to Naples?
Seb. Claribel.
Ant. She that is queen of Tunis; she that dwells
  Ten leagues beyond man's life; she that from Naples
  Can have no note, unless the sun were post –
  The man i' the moon's too slow – till new-born chins
  Be rough and razorable; she that from whom
  We all were sea-swallow'd, though some cast again,
  And by that destiny, to perform an act
  Whereof what's past is prologue, what to come,
  In yours and my discharge.
Seb. What stuff is this! how say you?
  'Tis true my brother's daughter's queen of Tunis;
  So is she heir of Naples; 'twixt which regions
  There is some space.
Ant. A space whose every cubit
  Seems to cry out, 'How shall that Claribel
  Measure us back to Naples? Keep in Tunis,
  And let Sebastian wake.' Say this were death
  That now hath seized them; why, they were no worse
  Than now they are. There be that can rule Naples
  As well as he that sleeps; lords that can prate
  As amply and unnecessarily
  As this Gonzalo; I myself could make

A chough of as deep chat. O, that you bore
The mind that I do! What a sleep were this
For your advancement! Do you understand me?

We should do wrong to take the conspiracy very seriously in itself. We know Prospero's power, and when Ariel enters and wakes the intended victims we have no fears for their future safety. But all the more weight should the scene assume as recalling the past.

Dover Wilson[2] greatly contributes to a right understanding of the play by stressing the first lines of the fifth act, when Prospero declares to Ariel that he will pardon his enemies, now quite at his mercy:

Ari. Your charm so strongly works 'em
That if you now beheld them, your affections
Would become tender.
Pros. Dost thou think so, spirit?
Ari. Mine would, sir, were I human.
Pros. And mine shall.
Hast thou, which art but air, a touch, a feeling
Of their afflictions, and shall not myself,
One of their kind, that relish all as sharply,
Passion as they, be kindlier moved than thou art?
Though with their high wrongs I am struck to the quick,
Yet with my nobler reason 'gainst my fury
Do I take part: the rarer action is
In virtue than in vengeance: they being penitent,
The sole drift of my purpose doth extend
Not a frown further.

But when Dover Wilson would have this to represent Prospero's sudden conversion from a previously intended vengeance, I cannot follow him. It is true that Prospero shows a certain haste of temper up to that point of the play, and that he punishes Caliban and the two other conspirators against his life with some asperity; but his comments on them, after his supposed conversion, have for me the old ring:

Mark but the badges of these men, my lords,
Then say if they be true. This mis-shapen knave,
His mother was a witch, and one so strong
That could control the moon, make flows and ebbs,
And deal in her command without her power.
These three have robb'd me; and this demi-devil –

For he's a bastard one – had plotted with them
To take my life. Two of these fellows you
Must know and own; this thing of darkness I
Acknowledge mine.

The last words express all Prospero's old bitterness that Caliban has resisted him and refused to respond to his nurture.[3] Indeed, Prospero does not change fundamentally during the play, though, like Samson's, his own accomplished regeneration is put to the test. If he had seriously intended vengeance, why should he have stopped Sebastian and Antonio murdering Alonso? That he did stop them is proof of his already achieved regeneration from vengeance to mercy. This act, and his talk to Ariel of taking part with his reason against his fury, are once again a re-enactment of a process now past, perhaps extending over a period of many years. I do not wish to imply that the re-enactment is weak or that the temptation to vengeance was not there all the time. Prospero's fury at the thought of Caliban's conspiracy, which interrupts the masque, must be allowed full weight. It is not for nothing that Miranda says that –

never till this day
Saw I him touch'd with anger so distemper'd.

We must believe that Prospero felt thus, partly because Caliban's conspiracy typifies all the evil of the world which has so perplexed him, and partly because he is still tempted to be revenged on Alonso and Antonio. He means to pardon them, and he will pardon them. But beneath his reason's sway is this anger against them, which, like Satan's before the sun in *Paradise Lost*, disfigures his face. When Dover Wilson calls Prospero 'a terrible old man, almost as tyrannical and irascible as Lear at the opening of his play', he makes a valuable comparison, but it should concern Prospero as he once was, not the character who meets us in the play, in whom these traits are mere survivals.

The advantage of this technique of re-enactment was economy, its drawback an inevitable blurring of the sharp outline. The theme of destruction, though exquisitely blended in the whole, is less vivid than it is in *The Winter's Tale*. Having made it so vivid in that play, Shakespeare was probably well content to put the stress on the theme of re-creation. And here he did not work solely by re-enactment. He strengthened Prospero's re-enacted regeneration by the figures of Ferdinand and Miranda. I argued above that, in view of his background of Elizabethan chivalrous convention, Ferdinand need not have been as insignificant as he is usually supposed. Similarly, Miranda's character has been unduly diminished in recent years. To-day, under the stress of the new psychology, men have become nervous lest they should be caught illicitly attaching their daydreams of the perfect woman to a character in fiction. They laugh at the Victorians for falling unawares into this error, and Miranda may have been one of the most popular victims. Hence the anxiety not to admire her too much. E. K. Chambers has written:

> Unless you are sentimentalist inveterate, your emotions will not be more than faintly stirred by the blameless loves at first sight of Ferdinand and Miranda.

Schücking goes further and considers Miranda a poor imitation of Beaumont and Fletcher's idea of the chaste female, an idea that could be dwelt on so lovingly and emphatically only in a lascivious age. In depicting her with her talk of 'modesty, the jewel in my dower' and her protests that if Ferdinand will not marry her, 'I'll die your maid', and in making Prospero so insistent that she should not lose her maidenhead before marriage, Shakespeare, according to Schücking, is yielding to the demands of his age against his own better judgment. But Miranda is sufficiently successful a symbolic figure for it to matter little if she makes conventional and, in her, unnatural remarks. And even this defence may be superfluous. Since Miranda had never seen a young man, it might reasonably be doubted whether she would behave herself with entire propriety when she did. Prospero, too, had made enough mistakes in his life to be very careful to make no more. Further, Miranda was the heiress to the Duchy of Milan and her father hoped she would be Queen of Naples. What most strikingly emerged from the abdication of our late King was the strong 'anthropological' feeling of the masses of the people concerning the importance of virginity in a King's consort. The Elizabethans were not less superstitious than ourselves and would have sympathised with Prospero's anxiety that the future Queen of Naples should keep her maidenhead till marriage: otherwise ill luck would be sure to follow.

To revert to Miranda's character, like Perdita she is both symbol and human being, yet in both capacities somewhat weaker. She is the symbol of 'original virtue,' like Perdita, and should be set against the devilish figure of Antonio. She is the complete embodiment of sympathy with the men she thinks have been drowned: and her instincts are to create, to mend the work of destruction she has witnessed. She is – again like Perdita, though less clearly – a symbol of fertility. Stephano asks of Caliban, 'Is it so brave a lass?' and Caliban answers,

> Ay, lord; she will become thy bed, I warrant,
> And bring thee forth brave brood.

Even if *The Tempest* was written for some great wedding, it need not be assumed that the masque was inserted merely to fit the occasion. Like the goddesses in Perdita's speeches about the flowers, Juno and Ceres and the song they sing may be taken to reinforce the fertility symbolism embodied in Miranda:

> *Juno*. Honour, riches, marriage-blessing,
> Long continuance, and increasing,
> Hourly joys be still upon you!
> Juno sings her blessings on you.
> *Cer*. Earthë's increase, foison plenty,
> Barns and garners never empty,
> Vines with clustering bunches growing,
> Plants with goodly burthen bowing;
> Spring come to you at the farthest
> In the very end of harvest!
> Scarcity and want shall shun you;
> Ceres' blessing so is on you.

The touches of ordinary humanity in Miranda – her siding with Ferdinand against a supposedly hostile father, for instance – are too well known to need recalling. They do not amount to a very great deal and leave her vaguer as a human being than as a symbol. Middleton Murry is not at his happiest when he says that 'they are so terribly, so agonizingly real, these women of Shakespeare's last imagination.' As far as Miranda is concerned, any agonizing sense of her reality derives from the critic and not from the play. But this does not mean that, judged by the play's requirements (which are not those of brilliant realism), Miranda is not perfection. Had she been more weakly drawn, she would have been insignificant, had she been more strongly, she would have interfered with the unifying dominance of Prospero.

Not only do Ferdinand and Miranda sustain Prospero in representing a new order of things that has evolved out of destruction;

they also vouch for its continuation. At the end of the play Alonso and Prospero are old and worn men. A younger and happier generation is needed to secure the new state to which Prospero has so painfully brought himself, his friends, and all his enemies save Caliban.

NOTES

1. *The Meaning of the Tempest*, the Robert Spence Watson Memorial Lecture for 1936, delivered before the Literary and Philosophical Society of Newcastle upon Tyne, on 5 Oct 1936.
2. Op. cit., pp. 14–18.
3. See the admirable discussion of 'nature' and 'nurture' in *The Tempest* in Middleton Murry's *Shakespeare* (1936) pp. 396 ff. (reproduced on pp. 97–101 above).

G. Wilson Knight The Shakespearian Superman (1947)

As Zarathustra thus discoursed he stood nigh unto the entrance of his cave; but with the final words he slipped away from his guests and fled for a brief while into the open air.

O clean odours around me! he cried. O blessed stillness around me! But where are my beasts? Draw nigh, mine Eagle and my Serpent!

Tell me, my beasts – all these Higher men, smell they, perchance, not sweet? O clean odours around me! Now only do I know and feel how I love you, my beasts!

Thus Spake Zarathustra, The Song of Melancholy

We have seen how these final plays tend to refashion old imagery into some surprising dramatic incident; of which the most striking examples are the jewel-thrown-into-the-sea, Thaisa in her casket-coffin; Pericles on board his storm-tossed ship; the co-presence of actual storm and bear, an old poetic association, in *The Winter's Tale*; the appearance of Jupiter the Thunderer in *Cymbeline*. In these we find a variation of a normal Shakespearian process; for Shakespeare is continually at work splitting up and recombining already used plots, persons, and themes, weaving something 'new and strange' from old material. Much of his later tragedy and history is contained in *Titus Andronicus* and *Henry VI*; much of later comedy in *Love's Labour's Lost* and *The Two Gentlemen of Verona*. The opposition of cynic and romantic in *Romeo and Juliet* gives us Mercutio and Romeo; the same opposition – with what a difference! – becomes Iago and Othello; and again, Enobarbus and Antony. Prince Hal and Hotspur together make Henry V; and as for Falstaff, his massive bulk contains in embryo much of the later tragedies in their nihilistic, king-shattering, impact; though, as comedian, he stands between Sir Toby and Autolycus. One could go on, and on.

The last plays are peculiar in their seizing on poetry itself, as it were, for their dominating effects; and in doing this also find themselves often reversing the logic of life as we know it, redeveloping the discoveries and recognitions of old comedy into more purposeful conclusions, impregnated with a far higher order of dramatic belief. The finding of Aemilia as an abbess in *The Comedy of Errors* forecasts the finding of Thaisa as priestess of Diana in *Pericles*; the recovery of Hero, supposed dead, in *Much Ado about Nothing* that of Hermione; Juliet and Imogen endure each a living death after use of similar potions. What is first subsidiary, or hinted by the poetry itself, as when Romeo or Cleopatra dream of reunion beyond, or within, death (*Romeo and Juliet* V i 1–9; *Antony and Cleopatra* V ii 75–100), is rendered convincing later.

This tendency *The Tempest* drives to the limit. For once, Shakespeare has no objective story before him from which to create. He spins his plot from his own poetic world entirely, simplifying the main issues of his total work – plot, poetry, persons; whittling off the non-essential and leaving the naked truth exposed. *The Tempest*, patterned of storm and music, is thus an interpretation of Shakespeare's world.

Its originating action is constructed, roughly, on the pattern of *The Comedy of Errors* and *Twelfth Night*, wherein wreck in tempest leads to separation of certain persons and their reunion on a strange shore; the plots being entwined with magic and amazement, as in Antipholus of Syracuse's comment on Ephesus as a land of 'Lapland sorcerers' (*The Comedy of Errors* IV iii II), and Sebastian's amazement at Olivia's welcome (*Twelfth Night* IV iii 1–21; see also Viola's pun on Illyria and Elysium at I ii 2–3). There is an obvious further relation of *The Tempest* to *A Midsummer Night's Dream*, both plays showing a fairy texture, with Puck and Ariel, on first acquaintance, appearing as blood-brethren, though the differences are great. The balance of tempests and music, not only in imagery but in plot too, throughout the Comedies (including *A Midsummer Night's Dream* and *The Merchant of Venice*) here reaches its consummation; but the Tragedies, wherein tempests and music are yet more profoundly important, are also at work within our new pattern of shipwreck and survival.

Prospero is a composite of many Shakespearian heroes; not in 'character', since there is no one quite like him elsewhere, but rather in his fortunes and the part he plays. As a sovereign wrongfully dethroned he carries the overtones of tragic royalty enjoyed by Richard II. Ejected from his dukedom by a wicked brother – 'That a brother should be so perfidious' (I ii 67) – he is placed, too, like the unfortunate Duke in *As You Like It* and as Don Pedro might have been placed had Don John's rebellion succeeded in *Much Ado about Nothing*. Clarence, Orlando and Edgar suffer from similar betrayals.

Now Prospero's reaction is one of horror at such betrayal of a 'trust' and a 'confidence sans bound' (I ii 96) by 'one whom', as he tells Miranda, 'next thyself of all the world I lov'd' (I ii 69). So Valentine suffers from Proteus' betrayal in *The Two Gentlemen of Verona* and Antonio, as he thinks, from Sebastian's in *Twelfth Night*. King Henry treats the faithless lords in *Henry V* to a long tirade of withering blank-verse on ingratitude and betrayal comparable with Richard II's scathing denunciation of his betrayers. Ingratitude generally is basic to the emotions, speeches, and songs of *As You Like It*; and in *King Lear* we have a 'filial ingratitude' (III iv 14), corresponding to Prospero's viewing of himself as 'a good parent', too kindly begetting in his child (meaning his brother) a corresponding 'falsehood' (I ii 94; cp. *King Lear*, 'Your old kind father whose frank heart gave all' at III iv 20). Loyalty to king, master, friend, wife, husband, is a continual theme. It is basic in *Julius Caesar*, in Brutus' relation to Caesar, in Portia's to Brutus, in the friendship of Brutus and Cassius: it vitalizes the whole of *Antony and Cleopatra*, with the subtly defined, personal, tragedy of Enobarbus – 'a master-leaver and a fugitive' (IV ix 22). There are the loyal friends: Antonio to Sebastian; Horatio to Hamlet; or servants – the Bastard in *King John*, Adam, Kent; Gonzalo here winning a corresponding honour. The extensions into sexual jealousy are equally, or more, important;

as in *The Merry Wives of Windsor, Much Ado about Nothing, Troilus and Cressida, Hamlet* (felt on the father's behalf by the son), *Othello, Antony and Cleopatra, The Winter's Tale, Cymbeline.*

There is a recurring sense of desertion, of betrayal, very strong in *Troilus and Cressida*; and also in *King Lear*, the old man's age underlining his helplessness. In *King Lear*, and often elsewhere, the result is a general nausea at human falsity; the poet continually driving home a distinction of falsehood, and especially flattery, and true, unspectacular, devotion (as in Theseus' words to Hippolyta, *A Midsummer Night's Dream* V i 89–105). This disgust tends to project the action into wild nature, conceived, as in *The Two Gentlemen of Verona, As You Like It*, and *King Lear*, as an improvement on the falsities of civilization. In *King Lear* the return to nature is acted by Edgar and endured, for his purgation, by Lear on the tempest-torn heath; while many variations are played throughout on the comparison and contrast of human evil with the beasts and elemental forces. The pattern of *The Winter's Tale* shows a similar movement from falsehood through rugged nature to an idealized rusticity. Of all this the great prototype, or archetype, is *Timon of Athens*, where the princely hero, conceived as a sublime patron and lover of humanity, is so thunder-struck by discovery of falsehood and ingratitude that he rejects man and all his works and in uncompromising bitterness retires in nakedness to a cave by the sea-shore, where he denounces to all who visit him the vices of civilization and communes, in savage solitude, with all of nature that is vast and eternal; his story finally fading into the ocean surge. *The Tempest* shows a similar movement. Prospero, like Timon and Belarius – for Belarius is another, driven to the mountains by the ingratitude of Cymbeline – lives (presumably) in a cave; like Timon, by the sea.

He is akin, too, to all princes whose depth of understanding accompanies or succeeds political failure: to Hamlet, Brutus, Richard II, Henry VI. Hamlet, like Timon, is an archetypal figure, being a complex of many heroes. He is out of joint with a society of which he clearly sees the decadence and evil. Through his ghostly converse and consequent profundity of spiritual disturbance, he is unfitted for direct action, while nevertheless doing much to control the other persons, indeed dominating them, half magically, from within. Hamlet is a student and scholar; and in this too, as in his surface (though not actual) ineffectuality and his revulsion from an evil society, he forecasts the learned Prospero, whose dukedom was

reputed
In dignity, and for the liberal arts,
Without a parallel. (I ii 72)

Such enlightenment was bought at a cost:

these being all my study,
The government I cast upon my brother,
And to my state grew stranger, being transported
And rapt in secret studies. (I ii 74)

Prospero is in straight descent from those other impractical governors, Agamemnon in *Troilus and Cressida*, whose philosophic attitude to his army's disaster (I iii 1–30) calls forth Ulysses' famous speech on order; and Vincentio, Duke of Vienna, in *Measure for Measure*, whose depth of study and psychological insight make execution of justice impossible. All these are in Prospero; while the surrounding action, both serious and comic, condenses the whole of Shakespeare's political wisdom.

He is also a recreation of Cerimon in *Pericles*. Listen to Cerimon:

I hold it ever
Virtue and cunning were endowments greater
Than nobleness or riches; careless heirs
May the two latter darken and expend;
But immortality attends the former,
Making a man a god. (*Pericles*, III ii 26)

And to Prospero:

I, thus neglecting worldly ends, all dedicated
To closeness and the bettering of my mind
With that which, but by being so retir'd,
O'erpriz'd all popular rate . . . (I ii 89)

The lines set the disadvantage of the monastic life against the supreme end it pursues. Duke Prospero was, like Lord Cerimon (also a nobleman), a religious recluse on the brink of magical power; and may be compared with those earlier religious persons, Friar Laurence in *Romeo and Juliet*, whose magic arts control the action (and who speaks, like Prospero, of his 'cell'), and Friar Francis in *Much Ado about Nothing*, who negotiates Hero's death and reappearance. These are people of spiritual rather than practical efficiency; like Duke Vincentio and Hamlet (who so mysteriously dominates his society, by play-production and otherwise), they are plot-controllers; Duke Vincentio, disguised as a Friar, organizing the whole action, and being directly suggestive of 'power divine' (*Measure for Measure* V i 370). So, too, Prospero manipulates his own plot like a god. He is a blend of Theseus and Oberon.

Prospero is a matured and fully self-conscious embodiment of those moments of fifth-act transcendental speculation to which earlier tragic heroes, including Macbeth, were unwillingly forced. He cannot be expected to do more than typify; there is not time; and, as a person, he is, no doubt, less warm, less richly human, than most of his poetic ancestors. But only if we recognize his inclusiveness, his summing of nearly all Shakespeare's more eminent persons, shall we understand clearly what he is about. He, like others, Vincentio and Oberon pre-eminently, is controlling our plot, composing it before our eyes; but, since the plot is, as we shall see, so inclusive an interpretation of Shakespeare's life-work, Prospero is controlling, not merely a Shakespearian play, but the Shakespearian world. He is thus automatically in the position of Shakespeare himself, and it is accordingly inevitable that he should often speak as with Shakespeare's voice.

Ariel incorporates all those strong picturizations of angels aerially riding observed in our recent analysis of the Vision in *Cymbeline*.[1] To these we may add the Dauphin's humorous but poetically revealing comparison of his horse to a Pegasus in *Henry V*:

> When I bestride him, I soar, I am a hawk: he trots in the air; the earth sings when he touches it; the basest horn of his hoof is more musical than the pipe of Hermes. . . . It is a beast for Perseus; he is pure air and fire; and the dull elements of earth and water never appear in him but only in patient stillness while his rider mounts him; he is indeed a horse. . . . It is a theme as fluent as the sea. (III vii 11–44)

Precisely from this complex of air, fire, music and lightly apprehended sea in contrast to the duller Caliban-elements of earth and water Ariel is compounded. He personifies all Shakespeare's more volatile and aerial impressionism (he is called a 'bird' at IV i 184, 'chick' at V i 316, and 'an airy spirit' in the *dramatis personae*), especially those images or phrases involving 'swift' (i.e. either intuitional or emotional) thought (a vein of poetry discussed in *The Shakespearian Tempest*, Appendix A, particularly pp. 308–11). A good example occurs in the association of thought's swiftness and 'feathered Mercury' at *King John* IV ii 174. Ariel is mercurial and implicit in both the agile wit and Queen Mab fantasies of the aptly-named Mercutio; compare his definition of dreams, 'as thin of substance as the air' (*Romeo and Juliet* I iv 100), with Prospero's 'thou, which art but air' (V i 21), addressed to Ariel. Ariel is implicit often in Shakespeare's love-poetry: though he is not an Eros-personification, yet, wherever we find emphasis on love's lightning passage, as at *Romeo and Juliet* II ii 118–20 or *A Midsummer Night's Dream* I i 141–9; on its uncapturable perfection, as throughout *Troilus and Cressida* (with strong emphasis on volatility and speed at III ii 8–15 and IV ii 14); on its spiritual powers, as in the aerial imagery and energy of *Antony and Cleopatra*, with Cleopatra at death as 'fire and air' (V ii 291); or on its delicate and tender sweetness, as in the 'piece of tender air', Imogen (*Cymbeline* V v 436–53); wherever such elusive and intangible excellences are our matter, there Ariel is forecast. He is the spirit of love's aspiration 'all compact of fire' in *Venus and Adonis* 1 49. He is made of Biron's speech of elaborate love-psychology with its contrast of 'slow arts' and the quicksilver swiftnesses of love's heightened consciousness, its new delicacy of perception and increased power, all entwined with fire, thoughts of mythology, poetry and music, and the ability (shown by Ariel's music in *The Tempest* at III ii 123–50 and IV i 175–8) to

> ravish savage ears
> And plant in tyrants mild humility;

while at the limit touching, as does Ariel (at V i 19), 'charity' (*Love's Labour's Lost* IV iii 320–65). Closely similar is Falstaff's speech on sherris-sack, which makes the brain 'apprehensive, quick, forgetive, full of nimble, fiery and delectable shapes which, deliverer'd o'er to the voice, the tongue, which is the birth, becomes excellent wit' (*2 Henry Iv* IV iii 107). Ariel is also forecast by other passages on wit (in the modern sense), so often, as is Mercutio's, levelled *against* love; as when the shafts of feminine mockery are compared to the swiftness of 'arrows, bullets, wind, thought' at *Love's Labour's Lost* V ii 262. Ariel exists in a dimension overlooking normal categories of both reason and emotion: he is the 'mutual flame' in which the winged partners of *The Phoenix and the Turtle* transcend their own duality.

Since, moreover, he personifies these subtle and overruling powers of the imagination, he becomes automatically a personification of poetry itself. His sudden appearance depends, precisely, on

Prospero's 'thought' (IV i 164–5; cp. 'the quick forge and working-house of thought', *Henry V* V chor. 23). He is the poetic medium, whatever the subject handled, his powers ranging over the earthy and the ethereal, tragic and lyric, with equal ease. As a dramatic person, he certainly descends from Puck and also, in view of his songs and trickery – he is a 'tricksy spirit' (V i 226; a word associated with Launcelot Gobbo in *The Merchant of Venice* III v 75) – from the jesters Feste, Touchstone, even Lear's Fool; all of whom enjoy a share of the poet's own, critical, awareness, as in certain of Puck's generalized speeches and his final epilogue, the philosophic detachment of Feste's and Touchstone's wit, and the Fool's perceptual clarity. Ariel likewise is apart: he is emotionally detached, though actively engaged, everyone and everything, except Prospero and Miranda, being the rough material of creation on which the Ariel-spirit of poetry works; an opposition seen most starkly in his piping to Caliban.

Ariel is accordingly shown as the agent of Prospero's purpose. He is Prospero's instrument in controlling and developing the action. Through him Prospero raises the tempest, Ariel (like mad Tom in *Lear*) being part of it, acting it (I ii 195–215). He puts people to sleep, so tempting the murderers, but wakes them just in time (II i), thunderously interrupts the feast, pronouncing judgement and drawing the moral (III iii). He plays tricks on the drunkards (III ii), hears their plot and leads them to disaster (III ii; IV i 171–84). His music leads Ferdinand to Miranda (I ii). He puts the ship safely in harbour (I ii 226) and later releases and conducts the mariners (V i). He is Prospero's stage-manager; more, he is the enactor of Prospero's conception: Prospero is the artist, Ariel the art. He is a spirit of 'air' (V i 21) corresponding to the definition of poetry as 'airy nothing' in *A Midsummer Night's Dream* (V i 16). His powers range freely over and between the thunderous and the musical, tragic and lyric, extremes of Shakespearian drama.

Caliban condenses Shakespeare's concern, comical or satiric, with the animal aspect of man; as seen in Christopher Sly and the aptly-named Bottom (whose union with Titania drives fantasy to an extreme), Dogberry, writ down 'an ass' (*Much Ado about Nothing* IV ii 75–93), Sir Toby Belch; and Falstaff, especially in *The Merry Wives of Windsor*, where his animality is punished by fairies (that Falstaff should show contacts with both Ariel and Caliban exactly defines the universal nature of his complexity). Caliban also symbolizes all brainless revolution, such as Jack Cade's in *2 Henry VI*, and the absurdities of mob mentality in *Julius Caesar* and *Coriolanus*. So much is fairly obvious; but there is more.

Caliban derives from other ill-graced cursers, a 'misshapen knave' and 'bastard' (V i 268–73) like the deformed Thersites ('bastard begot, bastard instructed, bastard in mind, bastard in valour, in everything illegitimate', *Troilus and Cressida* V vii 17) and bitter as Apemantus; from the 'indigest deformed lump', 'abortive rooting hog', 'poisonous bunch-back'd toad' and 'cacodemon', Richard III (*3 Henry VI* V vi 51; *Richard III* I iii 228, 246, 144; cp. Caliban as 'demi-devil' at V i 272); and from all Shakespeare's imagery of nausea and evil expressed through reptiles or, since we must not forget Sycorax (who may be allowed to sum all Shakespeare's evil women), creatures of black magic, as in *Macbeth*. He derives from all bad passion, as when Lear and Coriolanus are called dragons (*King Lear* I i 124; *Coriolanus* V iv 14). He combines the infra-natural evil of *Macbeth* with the bestial evil of *King Lear*, where man's suicidal voracity is compared to 'monsters of the deep' (*King Lear* IV ii 50). He is himself a water-beast, growing from the ooze and slime of those stagnant pools elsewhere associated with vice, being exactly defined by Thersites' description of Ajax as 'a very land-fish, languageless, a monster' (*Troilus and Cressida* III iii 266). But he has a beast's innocence and pathos too, and is moved by music as are the 'race of youthful and unhandled colts' of *The Merchant of Venice* (V i 71–9; cp. the comparison of the music-charmed Caliban to 'unback'd colts' at IV i 176–8). He sums up the ravenous animals that accompany tempest-passages, the boar, bull, bear; especially the much-loathed boar of *Venus and Adonis*. In him is the ugliness of sexual appetite from *Lucrece* onwards, and also the ugliness vice raises in those who too much detest it, the ugliness of hatred itself and loathing, the ugliness of Leontes. Man, savage, ape, water-beast, dragon, semi-devil – Caliban is all of them; and because he so condenses masses of great poetry, is himself beautiful. He is the physical as opposed to the spiritual; earth and water as opposed to air and fire. That he may, like Ariel, be considered in closest relation to Prospero himself is witnessed by Prospero's admission: 'This thing of darkness I acknowledge mine' (V i 275).

These three main persons present aspects of Timon. Besides Prospero's resemblance already observed, Ariel's thunderous denunciation (at III iii 53) recalls Timon's prophetic fury, both addressed to a society that has rejected true nobility for a sham, while Caliban reproduces his naked savagery and the more ugly, Apemantus-like, affinities of his general hatred. This especial inclusiveness marks Timon's archetypal importance.

To turn to the subsidiary persons. Alonso and his party present a varied assortment of more or less guilty people. We have, first, a striking recapitulation of *Macbeth*, Antonio persuading Sebastian to murder the sleeping king in phrases redolent of Duncan's murder:

> What might,
> Worthy Sebastian? O! what might? – No more:
> And yet methinks I see it in *thy face*
> What thou should'st be. *The occasion speaks thee*; and
> My strong imagination sees a *crown*
> Dropping upon thy head. (II i 199)

We remember 'Your face, great thane, is as a book . . .'; 'Nor time, nor place, did then adhere and yet you would make both; they have made themselves . . .'; and 'all that impedes thee from the golden round . . .' (*Macbeth* I v 63; I vii 51; I v 29). Antonio's

> O!
> If you but knew how you the purpose cherish
> Whiles thus you mock it . . . (II i 218)

is a crisp capitulation of Lady Macbeth's soliloquy on her husband's divided will (I v 17–30). *Macbeth* is resurrected in both phrase and verse-texture:

> And by that destiny to perform an *act*
> Whereof what's past is *prologue*, what to come
> Is yours and my discharge. (II i 247)

Compare Macbeth's 'happy *prologues* to the swelling *act* of the imperial theme' and Lady Macbeth's 'Leave all the rest to me' (*Macbeth* I iii 128; I v 74). Death and sleep are all but identified in both (II i 255–7; *Macbeth* II ii 54). Antonio's attitude to conscience ('Ay, sir, where lies that?' at II i 271) parallels Lady Macbeth's, while her 'Who dares receive it other?' (*Macbeth* I vii 77) is expanded into Antonio's scornful certainty that 'all the rest' will

> take suggestion as a cat laps milk;
> They'll tell the clock to any business that
> We say befits the hour . . . (II i 283)

– where even the cat, a comparatively rare Shakespearian animal, harks back to 'the poor cat i' the adage' (*Macbeth* I vii 45). In both plays the victim's weariness is brutally advanced as an assurance of sleep: compare Duncan's 'day's hard labour', which shall 'invite' him to sound sleep (*Macbeth* I vii 62) with 'now they are oppressed with travel' (III iii 15). That *Macbeth* should be singled out for so elaborate a re-enactment is not strange, since, standing alone in point of absolute and abysmal evil, it shares only slightly (via Sycorax) in the general recapitulation covered by Caliban, whom Prospero specifically acknowledges. Thus poetic honesty leaves Antonio's final reformation doubtful.

Alonso is less guilty, nor is there here any so vivid correspondence to be observed. Sebastian blames him for insisting on marrying his daughter Claribel against her and his subjects' will to an African (II i 119–31); and, since Gonzalo partly sanctions the criticism, we must, it would seem, perhaps with some faint reference to Desdemona's ill-starred marriage, regard Alonso's action as a fault. He was also a silent accomplice to Antonio's original treachery, and Ariel later asserts that he is being punished for it by his son's loss (III iii 75). As one of Shakespeare's many autocratic fathers and also as a king rather pathetically searching for his child, he is a distant relative of Lear. Both are purgatorial figures: he realizes his 'trespass' (III iii 99).

The faithful and garrulous old lord Gonzalo is a blend of Polonius, Adam and Kent. The courtiers Adrian and Francisco are not particularized. The wit of Antonio and Sebastian on their first entry needs, however, a remark.

It is cynical and cruel. The points made are of slight importance except for the extraordinary reiteration of 'widow Dido' (II i 73–97). There is presumably a sneer at an unmarried woman who has been deserted by her lover being given the status of 'widow'; and this we may tentatively relate to *Antony and Cleopatra*, wherein 'Dido and her Aeneas' are once compared to the protagonists (IV xii 53) and which in Cleopatra's phrase 'Husband, I come!' (V ii 289) reaches a compact self-interpretation in direct answer to such cynicism as Antonio's. The whole dialogue, starting with criticism of Gonzalo's and Adrian's insistence on the isle's fertility (the island varies mysteriously according to the nature of the spectator) and leading through ridicule of Gonzalo's phrase 'widow Dido' and his identification of Tunis and Carthage, to a final flowering in his Utopian dream, serves very precisely to define an opposition of cynic and romantic.[2] The points at issue are less important than the points of view:

> *Antonio.* He misses not much.
> *Sebastian.* No. He doth but mistake the truth totally. (II i 54)

That is cynical keenness in good form; and our dialogue takes us accordingly to the threshold at least of *Antony and Cleopatra*, the supreme answer of romanticism, wherein human love, though criticized as filth, wins through to glory. There is further corroboration: not only do the phrases 'such a paragon to their queen', 'miraculous harp' and 'impossible matter' (II i 71, 83, 85) raise, ironically or otherwise, suggestion of the marvellous harking back to *Antony and Cleopatra*, but we have one direct reminder:

> *Sebastian.* I think he will carry this island home in his *pocket*, and give it his son for an apple.
> *Antonio.* And, sowing the kernels of it in the sea, bring forth more *islands*. (II i 86)

Compare Cleopatra's dream, with its 'realms and *islands* were as plates dropt from his *pocket*' (*Antony and Cleopatra* V ii 91). We find the romantic extreme, whether in jocular cynicism or in visionary earnest, reaching definition in similar terms. Certainly one expects some trace of the earlier play, some honest facing in this austere work of its golden sexuality; and perhaps the easiest way to honour it was through the self-negating cynicism of an Antonio.[3]

To return to the marriage of Claribel to the King of Tunis. Any further correspondences (outside *Othello*) may again be sought in *Antony and Cleopatra*, where a west–east conflict in relation to marriage is strongly developed; and again in the Prince of Morocco, in *The Merchant of Venice* (see also *The Winter's Tale* V i 156–67). Criticism of the marriage originates from Sebastian, the cynic being naturally hostile, as in *Othello*, to the eastern glamour; while Gonzalo changes his view later, regarding it as part of the general happiness (V i 209). To Shakespeare Africa and the Orient are at once glamorous and dangerous (Sycorax came from Angier), with something of the disturbing magic wielded by the Indian fairies in *A Midsummer Night's Dream*: perhaps that is why Antonio seems to regard Tunis as an *infinite* distance from Milan.

The central experience of this group is the offering and sudden withdrawal of the mysterious banquet, with Ariel's appearance as a harpy and speech of denunciation.

Feasts are regularly important throughout Shakespeare, but are so obvious that one accepts them without thought. It is the mark of greatest literature to play on such fundamentals of human existence and we must remember their importance in Homer and the New Testament; in the one direct, in the other, in event, miracle and parable, carrying symbolic overtones. Shakespeare ends his two morality farces, *The Taming of the Shrew* and *The Merry Wives of Windsor*, with feasts, acted or announced, to convey a sense of general good-will succeeding horse-play. In *Romeo and Juliet* a feast and dance relate neatly to the family feud, raising questions of daring, adventure and hospitality. There is a rough feasting in Arden and Belarius' cave, both characterized by hospitality. Eating and drinking are continually given dramatic emphasis, with various ethical implications: they are important throughout *Antony and Cleopatra*, with one gorgeous feast-scene celebrating union after hostility, though nearly ruined by treachery. An elaborate banquet occurs in *Pericles*, with Thaisa as 'queen of the feast' (II iii 17) pointing on, as we have seen, to Perdita as 'mistress of the feast' (IV iii 68) in *The Winter's Tale*. Important examples occur in *Timon of Athens* and *Macbeth*. In *Timon* there are two: the first (I ii) conceived as a sacrament of love and friendship (with New Testament reminiscence at line 51), crowned by Timon's speech and negatively underlined by Apemantus' cynicism; the second (III vi), planned as a deadly serious practical joke, in which Timon, after raising his false friends' hopes, speaks an ironic grace, overturns (probably) their tables, and douses them with luke-warm water. In *Macbeth*, we have first the irony of the feasting of Duncan (I vii), and later on (IV i) the *inverted* good of the 'hell-broth' brewed by the Weird Women; and, in between (III iv), the feast to which Banquo has been carefully invited and which he attends as a ghost, smashing up the conviviality and social health so vividly emphasized in the text, and thus denying to Macbeth's tyrannous and blood-stained rule all such sacraments of brotherhood. These two *broken* feasts in *Timon of Athens* and *Macbeth*, related to the two main Shakespearian evils of unfaithfulness and crime, are key-scenes; and their shattering stage-power derives precisely from the simplicity of the effects used, planted squarely as they are on fundamentals.

The meaning of the feast offered but denied to Alonso, Sebastian and Antonio will now be clear; and also its relevance to the Shakespearian world.

The 'solemn and strange music' (III iii 18) of the feast is followed by Ariel's appearance as a Harpy to 'thunder and lightning' (III iii 53). The sequence recalls the Vision in *Cymbeline*, and Ariel's harpy-appearance drives home the similarity. Like Jupiter, he enters as a figure of overruling judgment, speaking scornfully of the lesser beings who think to dispute the ordinances of 'fate' (III iii; cp. 'How dare you ghosts . . .' *Cymbeline* V iv 94). Both epitomize the Shakespearian emphasis on thunder as the voice of the gods, or God. So Ariel acts the more awe-inspiring attributes of Shakespeare's tempest-poetry before our eyes, and in a long speech drives home its purgatorial purpose.

Besides Alonso and his party, we have the comic group of Stephano and Trinculo, in association with Caliban. The comedy is delightful, but scarcely subtle. Stephano the butler is an unqualified, almost professional, drunkard, with nothing of the philosophic quality of Falstaff or the open if unprincipled *bonhomie* of Sir Toby. Both those are, in their way, gentlemen, and yet their new representative (as drunkard) is of a low type socially; as are Dogberry, Bottom and the Gravediggers, though Stephano is a poor equivalent, lacking natural dignity. Trinculo is an equally poor successor to Touchstone, Feste, Yorick and Lear's Fool. Note that their representative quality is nevertheless emphasized by their joint embodiment of the two main sorts of clown: the natural and the artificial.

The Tempest is an austere work. The poet, while giving his clowns full rein in comic appeal, allows them no dignity. In writing of Autolycus we have observed Shakespeare's tendency there, as with Falstaff, earlier, to show his humorist as disintegrating; both as losing dignity and revealing ugly tendencies. So, too, with Sir Toby: in spite of his admirable 'cakes and ale' (*Twelfth Night* II iii 125) he is carefully made to lose dignity towards the play's conclusion, the balance of conviviality and reproof being carefully held.

Both Falstaff and Autolycus, as their glow of humour pales, show themselves as rather cheaply ambitious: whilst bearers of the comic spirit, they are, for a while, the superiors of kings; but when they, in their turn, ape the courtier, join in the vulgar scramble for show, they fall lower than their meanest dupes. Falstaff in *2 Henry IV* is enjoying his advance, ordering new clothes, being the grand man. Here the distinction is subtle; but the way is open for his final disintegration in *The Merry Wives of Windsor.* So, too, with Autolycus: he dresses as a courtier, apes a courtier's grandiosity and trades sadistically on the Shepherd's and Clown's anguish. He is finally shown as cringing to his former dupe. Now, remembering, too, Hamlet's disgust at the heavy drinking of Cladius' court, observe what happens to our comic trio, especially Stephano.

First, he drinks and sings maudlin songs. Next, he becomes a petty tyrant and engages in a bloody plot, aiming to make himself lord of the island. He is a burlesque of the power-quest, with all the absurdity of a barbaric despotism, having his foot licked by Caliban and posing as king, resembling Marlowe's Tamburlaine and the Macbeth of

> Now does he feel his title
> Hang loose upon him, like a giant's robe
> Upon a dwarfish thief. (*Macbeth* v ii 20)

Stephano parodies the essential absurdity of tyrannic ambition. Now he and his companions are lured by Ariel to a filthy pool:

> at last I left them
> I' the filthy-mantled pool beyond your cell,
> There dancing up to the chins, that the foul lake
> O'erstunk their feet. (iv i 181)

Stagnant water occurs regularly to suggest filth and indignity. Poor Tom in *King Lear* has been led by the foul fiend 'through fire and through flame, through ford and whirlpool, o'er bog and quagmire'; and an utmost degradation is suggested by his eating 'the swimming frog, the toad, the tadpole, the wall-newt and the water' and drinking 'the green mantle of the standing pool' (*King Lear* III iv 50; 132, 137). The lascivious Falstaff is ducked in *The Merry Wives of Windsor*; in flowing water, certainly, but the dirty-linen basket supplies the rest. There is also the final entry of the absurd braggart, Parolles, in *All's Well that Ends Well*, bedraggled, with filthy clothes, and admitting that he is 'muddied in Fortune's mood' and smelling 'somewhat strong of her strong displeasure'; with a developed dialogue on bad smells, an 'unclean fish-pond', 'carp', etc. (v ii 1–27). Notice that (i) lust – there is direct association of pools to sexual vice at *The Winter's Tale* I ii 195 and *Cymbeline* I iv 103 – and (ii) braggadocio are involved. Stephano, the would-be tyrant, meant to possess Miranda after murdering Prospero; Caliban has already tried to rape her; and all three are accordingly left in the 'filthy-mantled pool'.

Our buffoons are next tempted, like Autolycus, by an array of 'trumpery' (IV i 186), of 'glistering apparel' (IV i 193). Rich clothes were a more pressing masculine temptation in Shakespeare's day than in ours. One of Faustus' ambitions was to clothe Wittenberg's students in silk, and *Macbeth*'s power-quest is characterized in terms of 'a giant's robe' (*Macbeth* V ii 21; cp. *The Tempest* II i 267). Shakespeare reiterates his scorn for the latest (usually foreign) fashions, for all tinsel of clothes, speech, or manners, in play after play; as with Claudio, Sir Andrew and his 'flame-colour'd stock' (*Twelfth Night* I iii 146), Kent's 'a tailor made thee' (*King Lear* II ii 59), Osric, and many others. The prim Malvolio is fooled in his yellow stockings; Christopher Sly dressed absurdly in a nobleman's robes; Katharina the Shrew tormented with finery. This vein of satire beats in our present symbolic incident: the two fools are ensnared by a tinsel glitter, though Caliban, being closer to nature, has more sense (the temptation is perhaps slightly out of character for the others too, whose job here is, however, to parody their social superiors). All three are next chased off by Prospero's hounds. The pool and the show of garments will be now understood, but what of the hounds? Hounds are impregnated with a sense of healthy, non-brutal, and (like Shakespeare's horses) man-serving virility, occurring favourably at *Venus and Adonis* 913–24; *Henry V* III i 31; and *Timon of Athens* I ii 198. Hunting is a noble sport, though sympathy can be accorded the hunted hare (at *Venus and Adonis* 679–708, and *3 Henry VI* II v 130). Courteous gentlemen, such as Theseus and Timon, necessarily hunt, especially important being the long description of Theseus' *musical* hounds, with reference also to those of Hercules, baying the bear in Crete (*A Midsummer Night's Dream* IV i 112–32). Hounds are adversaries to the bear and (in *Venus and Adonis*) the boar, both 'tempest-beasts', and, though the fawning of dogs is used satirically, hounds, as such, may be musically, almost spiritually, conceived: hence their picturesque names in *The Tempest*: 'Mountain', 'Silver', 'Fury' and 'Tyrant'.[4] They are spirit-essences directed against the bestial Caliban and his companions.

So, too, the fleshly and 'corrupt' Falstaff was punished by fairies or supposed fairies in *The Merry Wives of Windsor* by pinching, conceived as a punishment of 'sinful fantasy', 'lust' and 'unchaste desire' by spirits (V v 96–108). Here Caliban regularly (I ii 327–32, 371–3; II ii 4), and now Stephano and Trinculo, too, are thoroughly *pinched* and given cramps and aches (IV i 258–61).[5]

Such is Shakespeare's judgement on drunkenness, sexual lust and braggart ambition. Such evils have, variously, held dignity, as in Falstaff's speech on sherris-sack (*2 Henry IV* IV iii 92), the riotous love of Antony and Cleopatra and, for the power-quest, *Macbeth*; but it is a tight-rope course; one slip and the several vices appear in their nakedness. That naked essence, in all its lewd and ludicrous vulgarity, is here emphasized.

There remain Ferdinand and Miranda. These are representative of beautiful and virtuous youth as drawn in former plays (Marina, Florizel and Perdita, Guiderius and Arviragus), though lacking something of their human impact. Our new pair illustrate humility (as in Ferdinand's log-piling), innocence, faith and purity; their words being characterized by utter simplicity and sincerity. They are whittled down to these virtues with slight further realization, and in comparison with earlier equivalents must be accounted pale. As elsewhere, essences are abstracted and reclothed. Except for Prospero, Ariel and Caliban, the people scarcely exist in their own right. The real drama consists of the actions and interplay of our three major persons with the natural, human and spiritual powers in which their destiny is entangled.

Prospero, who controls this comprehensive Shakespearian world, automatically reflects Shakespeare himself. Like Hamlet, he arranges dramatic shows to rouse his sinning victims' conscience: the mock-feast (whose vanishing, as we have seen, recalls Macbeth's ghost-shattered banquet), brought in by a 'living drollery' of 'shapes' (III iii 21); and the masque of goddesses and dancers (IV i), which, like the Final Plays themselves (of whose divinities these goddesses are pale reflections), is addressed to the purer consciousness (Ferdinand's). This tendency, as in *Hamlet*, reflects some degree of identification of the protagonist with the playwright, whose every work is a parable. Prospero himself delivers what is practically a long prologue in Act I, and in his own person speaks the epilogue. He is, even more than the Duke in *Measure for Measure*, a designer of the drama in which he functions as protagonist. We have seen how many of Shakespeare's tragic themes are covered by him; and that his farewell might have been spoken by Shakespeare is a correspondence demanded by the whole conception.

He addresses (V i 33–57) the various powers (drawn from folk-lore and called, with a grand humility, 'weak') by whose aid he has 'bedimm'd the noontide sun' (as 'the travelling lamp' is strangled in *Macbeth* II iv 7) and loosed the 'mutinous winds' to 'set roaring war' between sea and sky, thereby recalling such tempests throughout the great tragedies, in *Julius Caesar, Othello, Macbeth, King Lear,* with their many symbolic undertones of passionate conflict here crisply recapitulated in thought of war betwixt 'sea' and 'sky'. He has used 'Jove's own bolt' to blast (as at *Measure for Measure* II ii 116 and *Coriolanus* V iii 152) Jove's tree, the oak, recalling Jupiter the Thunderer in *Cymbeline*. From such images the speech moves inevitably to:

> Graves at my command
> Have wak'd their sleepers, op'd, and let them forth
> By my so potent art. (V i 48)

The statement, with its parallel in the resurrections of *Pericles* and *The Winter's Tale* and the less vivid restoration of Imogen in *Cymbeline*, may seem to apply more directly to Shakespeare than to Prospero; though the miraculous preservation of the ship and its crew must be regarded as an extension of earlier miracles. Prospero's speech, ending in 'heavenly' or 'solemn' (V i 52, 57) music, forms a recapitulation of Shakespeare's artistic progress from tempest-torn tragedy to resurrection and music (cp. the 'music of the spheres' at *Pericles* V i 231, and the resurrection music of *Pericles* III ii 88, 91; and *The Winter's Tale* V iii 98) corresponding to its forecast in *Richard II*.

Prospero uses his tempest-magic to draw his enemies to the island, and there renders them harmless. He wrecks and saves, teaches through disaster, entices and leads by music, getting them utterly under his power, redeeming and finally forgiving. What are the Shakespearian analogies? The poet himself labours to master and assimilate that unassuaged bitterness and sense of rejection so normal a lot to humanity (hence the popularity of *Hamlet*) by drawing the hostile elements within his own world of artistic creation: and this he does mainly through tragedy and its thunderous music; and by seeing that, in spite of logic, his creation is good. By destroying his protagonists, he renders them deathless; by expressing evil, in others and in himself, he renders it innocent. And throughout this tumult of creative activity, turning every grief to a star, making of his very loathing something 'rich and strange', there is a danger: a certain centre of faith or love must be preserved, this centre at least kept free from the taint of that rich, wild, earthy, lustful, violent, cursing, slimy yet glittering thing that is creation itself, or Caliban; that uses cynicism (born of the knowledge of lust) to ruin Desdemona, though not Othello's love for her; that tries in vain, but only just in vain, to make of Timon an Apemantus. Therefore Prospero keeps Miranda intact, though threatened by Caliban, just as Marina was threatened in the brothel of Mitylene. Alone with her he had voyaged far to his magic land, cast off in a wretched boat,

> To cry to the sea that roar'd to us; to sigh
> To the winds whose pity, sighing back again,
> Did us but loving wrong. (I ii 149)

What an image of lonely, spiritual voyage, like that of Wordsworth's Newton 'voyaging through strange seas of thought, alone'; while echoing back, through the long story of Shakespearian 'sea-sorrow' (I ii 170), to the Nordic origins of our literature in *The Wanderer* and *The Seafarer*. Prospero, unlike Lear, Pericles and Leontes, guards his Miranda, and with her survives on his island of poetry, with Ariel and Caliban. Who are these? The one, clearly, his art, his poetry in action; the other, the world of creation, smelling of earth and water, with the salt tang of the physical, of sexual energy, and with, too, all those revulsions and curses to which it gives birth. Prospero finds both Ariel and Caliban on the island, releasing the one (as genius is regularly characterized less by inventiveness than by the ability to release some dormant power) and aiming to train the other; and both must be strictly controlled. Prospero, Ariel, Caliban, Miranda: all are aspects of Shakespeare himself. Prospero, corresponding to the poet's controlling judgement, returns to Milan, uniting his daughter, his human faith, to his enemy's son; and Shakespeare's life-work, in *Henry VIII*, draws to its conclusion.

It is, indeed, remarkable how well the meanings correspond. Prospero has been on the island for twelve years (I ii 53); and it is roughly twelve years since the sequence of greater plays started with *Hamlet*. Before that, Ariel had been prisoned in a tree for another twelve years (I ii 279); again, roughly, the time spent by Shakespeare in his earlier work, before the powers of bitterness and abysmal sight projected him into the twilit, lightning-riven and finally transcendent regions; rather as Herman Melville passed from *Typee* and *White Jacket* to *Moby Dick, Pierre* and his later poetry. And now, as the end draws near, Ariel cries (as does Caliban too) for freedom from ceaseless 'toil':

> *Prospero*. How now! moody?
> What is't thou canst demand?
> *Ariel*. My liberty.
> *Prospero*. Before the time be out? No more! (I ii 244)

Prospero dominates Ariel and Caliban with an equal severity: as Shakespeare may be supposed to have willed, sternly, the safe conclusion of his labour in *Henry VIII*.

That labour is not all easy. Prospero, though still, is not static. Like Hamlet's, his very centrality is dynamic, drawing others to him, like Timon in his retirement, radiating power: or rather those earlier spiritual radiations are here given appropriate, symbolic, action, just as, according to Shelley's definition, poetry itself holds, in its very reserve, its stillness, a myriad radiations.

NOTES

1. See G. Wilson Knight, *The Crown of Life* (1947), p. 187.
2. According to Vergil Dido was widowed before Aeneas' arrival at Carthage and Gonzalo here, as in his identification of Tunis and Carthage, is correct. The cynic's sneer is based on lack of information.
3. My suggestion must remain tentative; but it has at least some confirmation from my brother's reading of Vergil's poetic methods. (See W. F. Jackson Knight, *Roman Vergil* (1944).)
4. The use of such names as 'Tyrant' and 'Fury' does not lower the animals' status, since the implied humanizing serves as an idealization; as with battleships, where the names H.M.S. *Furious* or H.M.S. *Venomous*, by attributing living status to a machine, witness a respect not usually offered to ill-temper and snakes.
5. Compare the fairies' song 'Pinch him black and blue' in Lyly's *Endimion*.

Reuben A. Brower The Mirror of Analogy

The Mind, that Ocean where each kind
Does streight its own resemblance find;
Yet it creates, transcending these,
Far other Worlds, and other Seas . . .

ANDREW MARVELL

Of *The Tempest*, we may say what Ferdinand said of the masque,

This is a most majestic vision, and
Harmonious charmingly.

The harmony of the play lies in its metaphorical design, in the closeness and completeness with which its rich and varied elements are linked through almost inexhaustible analogies. It is hard to pick a speech at random without coming on an expression that brings us by analogy into direct contact with elements that seem remote because of their place in the action or because of the type of experience they symbolize. Opening the play at the second act we read,

Four legs and two voices; a most delicate monster!

The last phrase is comic enough as used of Caliban and as issuing from the lips of Stephano, a 'most foul' speaker. But 'delicate' evokes a more subtle incongruity by recalling characters and a world we might suppose were forgotten. Stephano is parodying Prospero when he rebukes Ariel as 'a spirit too delicate / To act her [Sycorax's] earthy and abhorr'd commands' and when he says,

delicate Ariel,
I'll set thee free for this!

We have in Stephano's words not only the familiar Shakespearean balancing of comic and serious, but a counterpointing of analogies that run throughout the play. 'Delicate' as the antithesis of 'earth' points to the opposition of Ariel and Caliban and to the often recurring earth–air symbolism of *The Tempest*. 'Delicate' used of this remarkable island creature echoes also the 'delicate temperance' of which the courtiers spoke and 'the air' that 'breathes . . . here most sweetly'. 'Monster' – almost another name for Caliban – balances these airy suggestions with an allusion to 'the people of the island . . . of monstrous shape' and thereby to the strain of fantastic sea lore in *The Tempest*, which is being parodied in this scene.

So viewed, Shakespeare's analogies may perhaps seem too much like exploding nebulae in an expanding though hardly ordered universe. But Shakespeare does not 'multiply variety in a wilderness of mirrors'; he makes use of a few fairly constant analogies that can be traced through expressions sometimes the same and sometimes extraordinarily varied. And the recurrent analogies (or continuities) are linked through a key metaphor into a single metaphorical design. Shakespeare is continually prodding us – often in ways of which we are barely conscious – to relate the passing dialogue with other dialogues into and through a super-design of metaphor.

In concentrating on how the design is built up, I am not forgetting that it is a metaphorical design in a *drama*, that we are interested in how Shakespeare has linked stages in a presentation of changing human relationships. Toward the end of the chapter I hope to show how wonderfully the metaphorical design is related to the main dramatic sequence of *The Tempest*, especially in the climactic speeches of Acts IV and V.

The play moves forward, we should remember, from a scene of tempest to a final promise of 'calm seas, auspicious gales', and through a series of punishments or trials to a series of reconciliations and restorations. Although, as Dr. Johnson might say, there is a 'concatenation of events' running through Prospero's 'project' and though the play has a curiously exact time schedule, there is often little chronological or logical connection between successive dialogues or bits of action. To be sure, Shakespeare has the Elizabethan conventions on his side, but the freedom of his dramatic composition in *The Tempest* never seems merely conventional or capricious because the linkage of analogy is so varied and so pervasive.

The surest proof of the pervasiveness of Shakespeare's design lies in the mere number of continuities that can be discovered in the play. But some are more important than others because they can be traced through more expressions or in more scenes and because they express analogies more closely related to the key metaphor. The six main continuities, roughly labeled to indicate their character, are: 'strange-wondrous', 'sleep-and-dream', 'sea-tempest', 'music-and-noise', 'earth-air', 'slavery-freedom', and 'sovereignty-conspiracy'.

All of these continuities appear during the second scene of Act I, which is an exposition of Shakespeare's metaphorical and dramatic designs for the entire play. Near the close of the scene, Ariel's two songs offer wonderfully concentrated expressions of both designs. 'Come unto these yellow sands' calms the 'fury' of the waves and Ferdinand's 'passion', thus charting in brief the course of the action. 'Full fathom five' is anticipatory in a very different fashion. It presents in miniature the main lines of the metaphorical design and sounds the key note of 'sea change', Shakespeare's most direct expression of the key metaphor of *The Tempest*. (See I ii 1–186.)

As we trace the first two continuities ('strange-wondrous', 'sleep-and-dream'), the reader can appreciate how unobtrusively they emerge from the developing dramatic pattern. Prospero's narrative, with which the scene opens, tells us of the past and describes the present situation while symbolizing the quality of *The Tempest* world. Prospero explains that his enemies have come to this shore 'by accident most strange', and Miranda, who falls to sleep at the end of his tale, accounts for her lapse by saying,

> The strangeness of your story put
> Heaviness in me.

Prospero's tale was strange indeed: it included a ruler 'rapt in secret studies', a 'false uncle' who 'new created / The creatures' of the state, the miraculous voyage of Prospero and Miranda (who was 'a cherubin') and their safe arrival 'by Providence divine'. This 'strangeness' is best defined by Alonso's remarks near the end of the play:

> These are not natural events; they strengthen
> From strange to stranger . . .
>
> This is as strange a maze as e'er men trod;
> And there is in this business more than nature
> Was ever conduct of . . .

They are 'unnatural' in a broad seventeenth-century sense of the term; that is, outside the order which includes all created things. The theme is almost constantly being played on: 'strange', 'strangely', or 'strangeness' occur altogether some seventeen times, and similar meanings are echoed in 'wondrous', 'monstrous', 'divine'.

Of all the analogies of the play this is probably the vaguest, the nearest in effect to the atmospheric unity of nineteenth-century Romantic poetry. But a more precise metaphor of strangeness appears, the 'strangeness' of 'new created creatures'. From the 'accident most strange' of the shipwreck we come to Alonso's ponderous woe:

> O thou, mine heir
> Of Naples and of Milan! what strange fish
> Hath made his meal on thee?

and then to Trinculo's discovery of Caliban – 'A strange fish!' With a similar comic antiphony, Miranda finds Ferdinand 'a thing divine', and Ferdinand replies, 'O you wonder'; while a little later Caliban hails Trinculo as his god and cries, 'Thou wondrous man'. The full significance of these strange births will appear later.

The vague 'strangeness' of the island world is closely allied to a state of sleep, both continuities appearing in Miranda's remark about the 'heaviness' that came over her while listening to Prospero's story. The feeling that we are entering on an experience of sleep-and-dream arises beautifully out of the dramatic and rhythmic texture of the opening dialogue between father and daughter. The movement of these speeches with their oddly rocking repetitions is in key with the sleepy incredibility of the events about to be described: 'Canst thou remember . . . thou canst . . . I can . . . thy remembrance . . . my remembrance . . . thou remember'st . . . Twelve year since, Miranda, twelve year since . . .' Throughout the story Prospero is continually reminding Miranda to 'attend' to the telling, and it seems perfectly natural that at the end she should be 'inclin'd to sleep'. (Note in passing how neatly Shakespeare has broken a long narrative into dialogue and also given a distinct impression of Prospero's firmness and of Miranda's innocent dependence.) Miranda's images of the past come back to her 'rather like a dream', and Prospero seems to be drawing their story from a world of sleep, 'the dark backward and abysm of time'.

With the next scene (the mourning King and his courtiers) we meet one of Shakespeare's typical analogical progressions. The sleep which affects the courtiers is, like Miranda's, a strange 'heaviness'. Their dialogue runs down, psychologically and rhythmically, through three echoes of Miranda's words:

> *Gonzalo*. Will you laugh me asleep, for I am very heavy? . . .
> *Sebastian*. Do not omit the heavy offer of it . . .
> *Alonso*. Thank you. Wondrous heavy.
> *Sebastian*. What a strange drowsiness possesses them!

The conversation that follows between the conspirators shows how Shakespeare uses an analogy to move to a new level of action and experience and to make them harmonious with what precedes and follows. Sebastian and Antonio begin by talking about actual sleep and waking: why are they not drowsy like the others? Then Antonio shifts to talking of sleepiness and alertness of mind, and from that to imagining that he sees 'a crown dropping' upon Sebastian's head. The wit becomes more complex as Sebastian describes Antonio's talk as 'sleepy language' – without meaning – though indicating that it does have meaning. 'There's meaning in thy snores.' This dialogue, which readers are liable to dismiss as so much Elizabethan wit, has its place within the play's metaphorical pattern. The plotting takes on a preposterous dreamy-sleepy character like that of Prospero's narrative and Miranda's recollections. Through such verbal trifling Shakespeare maintains the continuous quality of his imagined world.

References to similar wakings and sleepings, to dreams and dreamlike states, abound from here to the end of the play, where the sailors are 'brought moping . . . even in a dream', and the grand awakening of all the characters is completed. But up to that point confusion between waking and sleep is the rule, being awake is never far from sleep or dream. In *The Tempest* sleep is always imminent, and more than once action ends in sleep or trance.

The witty talk of the conspirators glides from conceits of 'sleep' to conceits of 'the sea', to talk of 'standing water' and 'flowing' and 'ebbing'. The 'good Gonzalo', in consoling the King, speaks in similar figures:

> It is foul weather in us all, good sir,
> When you are cloudy.

Recurrent expressions of 'sea and tempest', like those of 'sleep and dream', are numerous and have a similar atmospheric value of not letting us forget the special quality of life on Prospero's island. But they also have far more important effects, for many of them become metaphors which are more precisely and more variously symbolic and which link more kinds of experience together.

By tracing two groups of 'tempest' expressions, metaphors of 'sea-swallowing' and images of 'clouds', we may understand how these more complex analogies are built up. We may also see how Shakespeare moves from narrative fact to metaphor, from image or metaphor referring only to narrative fact to metaphor rich in moral and psychological implications. As in creating the analogies of 'strangeness' and 'sleep', Shakespeare starts from a dramatic necessity: the audience must be told what the situation was in the storm scene with which the play opens, and they must learn through an actor (Miranda) how they are to take it. (See I ii 1–186.) Although there is a hint of magic in Miranda's vision of the tempest, she pictures it as a violent actuality:

> Had I been any god of power, I would
> Have sunk the sea within the earth, or e'er
> It should the good ship so have swallow'd and
> The fraughting souls within her.

As if there were an inner rhythm in these responses, this metaphor, like others we have been tracing, recurs in the plotting episode. Antonio is speaking of Ferdinand's sister Claribel, left behind in Tunis:

> she that from whom
> We all were sea-swallow'd, though some cast again,
> And by that destiny to perform an act
> Whereof what's past is prologue, what to come
> In yours and my discharge.

In this new context 'sea-swallow'd' does several things at once. It brings back Miranda's horrified impression; but the magical nature of the storm now being known, the phrase reminds us that there was no 'sea-swallowing', no actual sinking of 'fraughting souls'. Next, with a curiously Shakespearean 'glide and a jump' via the pun on 'cast', 'sea-swallow'd' merges into another metaphor (they are now 'cast' as actors in destiny's drama). 'Sea-swallowing' has become a metaphor that expresses destiny's extraordinary way of bringing Sebastian to the throne.

The irony of Antonio's words, which is clear to the audience is made explicit later in the solemn speech in which Ariel explains the purpose of the tempest:

> You are three men of sin, whom Destiny –
> That hath no instrument this lower world
> And what is in 't – the never-surfeited sea
> Hath caused to belch up you . . .

Few passages could show better how Shakespeare carries his analogies along and at the same time completely renews them. The 'belching up' recalls the wreck and the casting ashore and the earlier connection with destiny. But the sea's action is now described in much grosser terms and with grim sarcasm, while the oddly compact grammar makes 'the never-surfeited sea' very nearly a synonym for 'Destiny'. The violence though increased is now religious and moral; the imagery has become expressive of the strenuous punishment and purification of 'three men of sin'. So by the continuity of his varying metaphor Shakespeare has expressed an unbroken transition from actual storm to the storm of the soul. This sequence, which expresses both physical and metaphysical transformations, points very clearly to the key metaphor of *The Tempest*.

The recurrent cloud images present a similar sequence as they take on various symbolic meanings in the course of the play. 'Cloud' does not actually occur in the opening storm scene, but when Trinculo sees 'another storm brewing' and speaks of a 'black cloud', we are reminded of the original tempest. The cloud undergoes an appropriate change in Trinculo's speech; it 'looks like a foul bombard that would shed his liquor'. This comic cloud is very different from 'the curl'd clouds' on which Ariel rides, though they too are associated with storms. The clouds of Caliban's exquisite speech are those of Ariel and the deities of the masque:

> and then, in dreaming,
> The clouds methought would open and show riches
> Ready to drop upon me . . .

Clouds – here linked with magical riches – become in Prospero's 'cloud-capp'd towers' speech a symbol for the unsubstantial splendor of the world. One of the subordinate metaphors there, the 'melting into air' and the 'dissolving' of the clouds, is picked up in Prospero's later words about the courtiers:

> The charm dissolves apace;
> And as the morning steals upon the night,
> Melting the darkness, so their rising senses
> Begin to chase the ignorant fumes that mantle
> Their clearer reason.

This dissolution of night clouds (suggested also by 'fumes') is a figure for the change from madness to sanity, from evil ignorance to the clear perceptions of reason. Although the cloud images of the play are so varied, they have a common symbolic value, for whether they are clouds of tempest or of visionary riches or of the soul, they are always magically unsubstantial. The reader is led to feel some touch of likeness among experiences as different as a storm at sea, a bit of drunken whimsy, a vision of heavenly and earthly beauty, and a spiritual regeneration. The cloud sequence, as an arc of metaphor, is in perfect relation to the gradual dramatic movement from tempest and punishment to fair weather and reconciliation, the images having meanings more and more remote from any actual storm.

The 'cloudlike' change in the distracted souls of the guilty nobles was induced (as if in reminiscence of Plato) by *Solemn music* –

> A solemn air and the best comforter
> To an unsettled fancy.

Many of the expressions referring to music, like the stage direction above, are not explicitly metaphorical, but along with the continuities of 'sleep' and 'strangeness' they help maintain the magical character of the action. The music is always the music of spirits and always a sign of more than natural events.

The one fairly constant musical metaphor[1] in *The Tempest* is the symbolic opposition of confused noises, especially storm sounds, and harmonious music. The key word and the central impression of the opening scene is certainly 'noise'[2] in the modern sense. The impression is carried over in the first words of the next scene:

> If by your art, my dearest father, you have
> Put the wild waters in this roar, allay them.

Miranda's request is soon answered by Ariel's first song, 'the wild waves' are 'whist'. The '*solemn and strange music*' heard when the '*strange Shapes*' bring a banquet to the courtiers makes Alonso say, 'What harmony is this? my good friends, hark!' Gonzalo replies:

'Marvelous sweet music!' By contrast, when Ariel enters shortly after, in order to inform the 'three men of sin' of their punishment by the storm, there is an offstage sound of *Thunder and lightning*. The masque vision which Ferdinand finds 'harmonious charmingly' is rudely interrupted by *a strange, hollow, and confused noise* which symbolizes the stormy anger expressed by Prospero in the speeches that follow. When in the next scene he prepares to forgive his enemies, he abjures the 'rough magic' by which he

> call'd forth the mutinous winds,
> And 'twixt the green sea and the azur'd vault
> Set roaring war . . .

As the *solemn music* is played the clouds of ignorance 'dissolve', and so the musical metaphor, like the sea metaphor, has moved from outer to inner weather.

The music analogy has some close links with the earth-air continuity which we glanced at in the introductory chapter of the book. Ferdinand, following Ariel's 'yellow sands' song, asks, 'Where should this music be? i' th' air, or th' earth?' And a little later:

> This is no mortal business, nor no sound
> That the earth owes: I hear it now above me.

The connection of air and music can never be long forgotten: Ariel and his spirits of 'thin air' are the musicians of the island.

The earth-air, Caliban-Ariel antithesis coincides at points with what we might call a slavery-freedom continuity, for Caliban is in Prospero's words both 'slave' and 'earth'. Ariel too is called a 'slave' by Prospero, and for the time of the play he is as much a slave as Caliban. (Both are called 'slaves' in I ii, the scene of metaphorical exposition.) He is always asking for his freedom, which is at last granted, his release being symbolically expressed in the airy rovings of his final song. He flies into perpetual summer and, like air, becomes merged with the elements. By contrast, the 'high-day, freedom!' of which Caliban sings is ironically enough simply a change of masters.

The 'slaves' and 'servants' of the play suffer various kinds of imprisonment, from Ariel in his 'cloven pine' to Ferdinand's mild confinement, and before the end of Act IV everyone except Prospero and Miranda has been imprisoned in one way or another. During the course of Act V all the prisoners except Ferdinand (who has already been released) are set free, each of them by Prospero's special command.

A sovereignty-conspiracy analogy parallels very closely the slavery-freedom analogy, some of the same persons, e.g. Ferdinand and Caliban, appearing as both slaves and conspirators. 'That foul conspiracy / Of the beast Caliban, and his confederates' is of course a parody version of the 'Open-ey'd Conspiracy' of Sebastian and Antonio. Ferdinand, too, is charged fantastically by Prospero with plotting against his island rule. Talk of kings and royalty turns up in many scenes, being connected usually with the denial of kingship, as in 'good Gonzalo's' speech on his golden-age commonwealth where 'he would be king' and yet have 'no sovereignty'. Though no single explicit metaphor for conspiracy or usurpation is often repeated, Shakespeare rings many changes on the theme as he moves from plot to plot. Prospero's brother, we recall, is said to have 'new created the creatures' of state. Antonio's seizure of power is called a 'substitution': 'crediting his own lies', he began to believe 'he was indeed the duke', and from merely playing a part he went on to become 'absolute Milan'. The figure is picked up in the somnolent dialogue of Sebastian and Antonio:

> I remember
> You did supplant your brother Prospero.

In the second of the scenes in which Caliban and his fellows plot to overthrow the island 'tyrant', Sebastian's 'supplant' is recalled with a difference:

> *Caliban.* I would my valiant master would destroy thee; I do not lie.
> *Stephano.* Trinculo, if you trouble him any more in his tale, by this hand, I will supplant some of your teeth.

The figure recurs a little later in a more serious context:

> . . . you three
> From Milan did supplant good Prospero.

In Act V after various supplantings, serious and comic, accomplished or merely projected, all true kings are restored and all false ones dethroned.

The two continuities, sovereignty-conspiracy and slavery-freedom, are also alike in the fact that their metaphorical force is expressed through scenes that are just one step removed from allegory. The more serious of the restorations and releases convey similar kinds of moral meaning. Ferdinand's release from 'wooden slavery' signifies that he is a true lover and a true prince. In being freed from madness Alonso has escaped from 'heart-sorrow' and regained his rightful rank and a 'clear life ensuing'. Both continuities convey an impression of topsyturvydom in the order of things, an unnatural interchange of status among creatures of every kind. Both express a return to stability after a disturbance of degree.

What then is the key metaphor through which the various continuities are linked, and how are they connected through it? Shakespeare's most direct expression of his key metaphor is 'sea change', the key phrase of Ariel's song. But what does Shakespeare mean by 'sea change'? Ariel sings of 'bones' being made into 'coral' and of 'eyes' becoming 'pearls'. 'A change into something rich and strange', we now understand, is a change 'out of nature'. 'Sea change' is a metaphor for 'magical transformation', for metamorphosis. The key metaphor of the play is 'change' in this special sense, and 'change' is the analogy common to all of the continuities we have been tracing. (I am not forgetting that they are also expressive of many other relationships, or that Shakespeare is often playing with two or three metaphors at once, as in the various figures of 'sea-swallowing'. But all are at least expressive of change, or changeableness.)

Through the first rather vague analogies we traced, of 'strangeness' and 'sleep-and-dream', numerous events and persons in the play are qualified as belonging to a realm where anything may happen. Expressions of 'strangeness' and 'sleep', like many of the references to sea and music, suggest 'far other Worlds and other Seas', where magical change is to be expected. A more particular metaphor of change is expressed through the stress on the 'strangeness' of 'new creations' and on the confusion between sleep and dream and waking. The island is a world of fluid, merging states of being and forms of life. This lack of dependable boundaries between states is also expressed by the many instances of confusion between natural and divine. Miranda says that she might call Ferdinand

> A thing divine; for nothing natural
> I ever saw so noble

Ferdinand cannot be sure whether she is a goddess or a maid, and Caliban takes Trinculo for a 'brave god'. There is a further comic variation on this theme in Trinculo's difficulty in deciding whether to classify Caliban as fish or man, monster or devil.

But 'change' is most clearly and richly expressed through the sequence of tempest images (especially 'cloud' and 'sea-swallowed') and through the noise-music antithesis. All kinds of sounds, harmonious and ugly, like the manifestations of sea and storm, are expressive of magical transformation. 'The fire and cracks / Of sulfurous roaring' (imagery in which both storm and sound analogies are blended) 'infects' the courtiers' 'reason', and *solemn music* induces the 'clearing' of their understanding. The 'music' and the 'tempest' continuities, taken together as metaphors of 'sea change', are perhaps the most extensive of all the analogies in their organizing power. They recur often, they connect a wide diversity of experiences, and they express in symbolic form some of the main steps in the drama, in particular, the climactic moments of inner change: Ariel's revelation to the courtiers of their guilt, Alonso's first show of remorse, and the final purification.

The earth-air or Caliban-Ariel antithesis may seem to have very little to do with metamorphosis. But the relation of this theme to the key metaphor is clear and important. Air, Ariel, and his music are a blended symbol of change as against the unchanging Caliban, 'the thing of darkness'. He can be punished, but hardly humanized; he is, says Prospero,

> A devil, a born devil, on whose nature
> Nurture can never stick; on whom my pains,
> Humanely taken, are all lost, quite lost.

The other continuities parallel to earth-air, of slavery-freedom and conspiracy-sovereignty, are frequently expressive of major and minor changes of status among the inhabitants and temporary visitors on Prospero's island.

But the interconnection of Shakespeare's analogies through the key metaphor cannot be adequately described, since we are able to speak of only one point of relationship at a time. We can get a better sense of the felt union of various lines of analogy in *The Tempest* by looking at the two passages where Shakespeare expresses his key metaphor most completely, the 'Full fathom five' song and Prospero's 'cloud-capp'd towers' speech.

Rereading Ariel's song at this point, we can see how many of the main continuities are alluded to and related in the description of 'sea change' and how the song anticipates the metaphorical design that emerges through the dialogue of the whole play. The total metaphorical pattern is to an amazing degree an efflorescence from this single crystal:

> Full fathom five thy father lies;
> Of his bones are coral made:
> Those are pearls that were his eyes:
> Nothing of him that doth fade,
> But doth suffer a sea change
> Into something rich and strange.
> Sea nymphs hourly ring his knell:
> *Burthen:* 'Ding-dong!'
> Hark! now I hear them – Ding-dong, bell.

In addition to the more obvious references to the deep sea and its powers and to the 'strangeness' of this drowning, there are indirect anticipations of other analogies. 'Fade' prefigures the 'dissolving cloud' metaphor and the theme of tempest changes, outer and inner. 'Rich', along with 'coral' and 'pearls', anticipates the opulent imagery of the dream-world passages and scenes, the 'riches ready to drop' on Caliban and the expressions of wealth and plenty in the masque. ('Rich' and 'riches' occur no less than five times in the masque.) The song closes with the nymphs tolling the bell, the transformation and the 'sea sorrow' are expressed through sea music. Ferdinand's comment reminds us that the song has connections with two other lines of analogy:

> The ditty does remember my drown'd father.
> This is no mortal business, nor no sound
> That the earth owes: – I hear it now above me.

The song convinces Ferdinand that he is now King of Naples (the first of the interchanges of sovereignty), and it is a 'ditty' belonging not to the 'earth', but to the 'air'.

The sense of relationship between the many continuities is still more vividly felt in the lines of Prospero's most memorable speech:

> You do look, my son, in a mov'd sort,
> As if you were dismay'd: be cheerful, sir:
> Our revels now are ended. These our actors,

As I foretold you, were all spirits and
Are melted into air, into thin air:
And, like the baseless fabric of this vision,
The cloud-capp'd towers, the gorgeous palaces,
The solemn temples, the great globe itself,
Yea, all which it inherit, shall dissolve
And, like this insubstantial pageant faded,
Leave not a rack behind. We are such stuff
As dreams are made on, and our little life
Is rounded with a sleep.

In Prospero's words Shakespeare has gathered all the lights of analogy into a single metaphor which sums up the metaphorical design and the essential meaning of *The Tempest.* The language evokes nearly every continuity that we have traced. 'Melted into air', 'dissolve', 'cloud', and 'rack' bring us immediately to Ariel and tempest changes, while 'vision', 'dream', and 'sleep' recall other familiar continuities. 'Revels', 'gorgeous palaces', and 'pageant' (for Elizabethans closely associated with royalty) are echoes of the kingly theme; and 'solemn' is associated particularly with the soft music of change. The 'stuff' of dreams is at once cloud-stuff (air) and cloth, both images being finely compressed in 'baseless fabric'. Taken with 'faded' these images refer obliquely to the garments so miraculously 'new-dyed ... with salt water', one of the first signs of 'sea change' noted by Gonzalo. Within the metaphor of tempest-clearing and of cloudlike transformation, Shakespeare has included allusions to every important analogy of change in the play.

But it is through the twofold progress of the whole figure that the change metaphor is experienced and its most general meaning fully understood. We read first: that like the actors and scenery of the vision, earth's glories and man shall vanish into nothingness. Through a happy mistake we also read otherwise. By the time we have passed through 'dissolve', 'insubstantial', and 'faded', and reached 'leave not a rack behind', we are reading 'cloudcapped towers' in reverse as a metaphor of tower-like clouds. 'Towers', 'palaces', 'temples', 'the great globe', 'all which it inherit' are now taken for cloud forms. Through a sort of Proustian merging of icon and subject, we experience the blending of states of being, of substantial and unsubstantial, or real and unreal, which is the essence of *The Tempest* metamorphosis.

Similar meanings are expressed through the closing dream figure, which grows equally out of the metaphorical context of the speech and the play. 'Rounded', we should take with Kittredge as 'surrounded', but without losing the force of round, as in Donne's 'surrounded with tears'. 'Our little life' is more than sentimental, it is our little life (microcosm) in contrast with 'the great globe' (macrocosm). There may also be an over-image in 'surrounded' of the world in classical myth and geography with its encircling ocean, sleep being the stream that 'rounds' the lesser world. In relation to the metaphorical design of the play, 'rounded with a sleep' and the notion of life ending in dreams express again the sense of confusion between sleep and dream and waking. This metaphor which completes the figure of cloud-change is Shakespeare's most perfect symbol for the closeness of states that to our daylight sense are easily separable. Although the vision here expressed goes far beyond the play, it is still a natural extension of the dramatic moment and a fulfilment of the metaphor that has been implicit since the noisy opening lines of *The Tempest*.

But if Shakespeare's total metaphor is in a sense present everywhere, it is also a design that develops in close relation to the main dramatic movement of the play. As we have noted more than once, a particular metaphor will be varied to fit a new dramatic situation and so serve to express the situation more fully and to anticipate the next step in the development of the drama. The best example of this adaptation of metaphor comes in a speech in which Shakespeare seems to be playing capriciously with his noise-music theme. At first sight the passage seems inconsistent with the symbolic contrast between storm noise and music:

> *Alonso.* O, it is monstrous! monstrous!
> Methought the billows spoke and told me of it;
> The winds did sing it to me; and the thunder,
> That deep and dreadful organ pipe, pronounc'd
> The name of Prosper: it did bass my trespass.

It is admittedly odd that the confused noise of the tempest should, in Alonso's soul, compose a harmony – however gloomy – but the paradox fits in perfectly with the developing structure of the play. Alonso has just been told by Ariel that the storm had a purpose as an instrument of Destiny. Since at this moment remorse first appears in the play and the inner clearing begins, it is exactly right that the storm sounds should seem harmonious and so point forward to the events of the fourth and fifth acts. No use of metaphor in *The*

Tempest reveals more clearly Shakespeare's exact sense of the movement of his drama, of the changing human relations and feelings he is presenting.

In building up his metaphorical design, Shakespeare prepares us for the moment in *The Tempest* when the major shift in dramatic relationships takes place. The moment comes in the speech in which Prospero describes the behaviour of the King and the courtiers as they slowly return from madness to sanity. The first important step toward this climax, Alonso's acknowledgment of his guilt, was expressed through a metaphor combining both sea and musical changes. The next step, Ferdinand's release from his tempest-trials and from dreamlike enchantment, is expressed through the masque, which is an elaborate dramatization of metamorphosis, Ariel's 'meaner fellows', 'the rabble', being now transformed into majestic Olympian goddesses. Once again, familiar continuities appear, and again they are transformed to fit a new occasion. 'Earth', for example, is no longer 'barren place and fertile', but the earth enriched by human cultivation and symbolized now by Ceres – not by Caliban, who is 'nature resisting nurture'. Iris summons this new Earth in the gorgeous speech beginning 'Ceres, most bounteous lady, thy rich leas . . .', lines in which we hear a quite new majesty of tone and movement. The couplet form sets the dialogue apart from human speech, while the longer periods, the added stresses, the phrasal balancings are especially appropriate to 'that large utterance of the early gods'. (Here is one of many instances of how Shakespeare adapts his sound patterns to his metaphorical and dramatic designs.) Prospero's visionary speech that ends 'the revels' is not simply a concentration of metaphor without reference to the dramatic development. It announces the changes to come, it gives a rich expression of their meaning, and it anticipates the dreamlike flux of the psychological events of the last act.

If we now read Prospero's words in Act V, in which he describes the great changes as they take place, we see many references back to Shakespeare's metaphorical preparation for this moment. We also realize that various lines of action and various lines of analogy are converging almost simultaneously. The speech opens with Prospero's farewell to his art, after which he turns his thoughts to 'restoring the senses' of the courtiers, whom Ariel has just gone to release:

A solemn air and the best comforter
To an unsettled fancy, cure thy brains,
Now useless, boil'd within thy skull! There stand,
For you are spell-stopp'd.
Holy Gonzalo, honorable man,
Mine eyes, even sociable to the show of thine,
Fall fellowly drops. The charm dissolves apace;
And as the morning steals upon the night,
Melting the darkness, so their rising senses
Begin to chase the ignorant fumes that mantle
Their clearer reason. O good Gonzalo!
My true preserver, and a loyal sir
To him thou follow'st, I will pay thy graces
Home, both in word and deed. Most cruelly
Didst thou, Alonso, use me and my daughter:
Thy brother was a furtherer in the act;
Thou'rt pinch'd for 't now, Sebastian. Flesh and blood,
You, brother mine, that entertain'd ambition,
Expell'd remorse and nature; who, with Sebastian –
Whose inward pinches therefore are most strong –
Would here have kill'd your king; I do forgive thee,
Unnatural though thou art! Their understanding
Begins to swell, and the approaching tide
Will shortly fill the reasonable shores
That now lie foul and muddy. Not one of them
That yet looks on me, or would know me. Ariel,
Fetch me the hat and rapier in my cell: [*Exit* ARIEL
I will discase me, and myself present,
As I was sometime Milan. Quickly, spirit;
Thou shalt ere long be free.

If this is a climactic moment, what changes in dramatic relationships are taking place, what is happening dramatically? The 'men of sin', like Ferdinand, have come to the end of the trials which began with the storm and continued through various 'distractions'. Now, as Prospero explains, they are undergoing a moral as well as a mental regeneration, they are 'pinch'd' with remorse and are being forgiven. The twofold regeneration is further dramatized in the speeches that follow: 'th' affliction of Alonso's mind amends', he resigns Prospero's dukedom and 'entreats' him to pardon his 'wrongs'.

But these are the prose facts, the bare bones of the changes in dramatic relationships. We cannot feel the peculiar quality of what is taking place or grasp its meaning apart from the metaphorical language through which it is being expressed. nd the expressions acquire their force and precision from the whole metaphorical preparation we have been tracing. The courtiers' senses are restored by 'an airy charm', by magic similar to that which was worked by Ariel and his spirits. The allusions to 'heavenly music' and 'a solemn air', in contrast to the 'rough magic' that Prospero has abjured, remind us that these changes will be musically harmonious, like the songs of Ariel, and not noisy and confused like the storm sent to punish these men and reveal their 'monstrous' guilt. Towards the end of the speech, the imagery recalls the tempest metaphor, but it is altered so as to express the mental and moral change that is taking place. The return of understanding is like an approaching tide that covers the evidence of a storm (both 'foul' and 'muddy' have storm associations from earlier occurrences).

But the metaphor that best expresses this clearing is the one for which the preparation has been most complete:

> The charm dissolves apace;
> And as the morning steals upon the night,
> Melting the darkness, so their rising senses
> Begin to chase the ignorant fumes that mantle
> Their clearer reason.

'Dissolving' and 'melting' and 'fumes' take us back at once to the grand transformations of the masque speech, to the earlier cloud transformations both serious and comic; and they take us back further to the association of clouds with magical tempests, inner storms, and clearing weather. We read of the moral and psychological transformations with a present sense of these analogies. They are qualified for us as a dreamlike dissolution of tempest clouds, as events in the 'insubstantial' region where reality and unreality merge.

It is through such links that Shakespeare concentrates at this climactic moment the fullest meaning of his key metaphor. There is of course no separation in the reader's experience between the dramatic fact and the metaphorical qualification. The images that recur in Prospero's speech take us back to felt qualities, but to felt qualities embedded in particular dramatic contexts. 'Melting', for example, carries us to the spiritlike dissolution of 'spirits . . . melted into air, into thin air'; but it also reminds us of the masque pageantry and of Prospero's calming of Ferdinand's fears. We hear

Prospero's soothing and mysterious tone in both the earlier and later uses of the word. The dramatic links and the analogical links are experienced at once, which is to say that metaphorical design and dramatic design are perfectly integrated.

We can now realize that metamorphosis is truly the key metaphor to the *drama*, and not the key metaphor to a detachable design of decorative analogies. Through the echoes in Prospero's speech of various lines of analogy, Shakespeare makes us feel each shift in dramatic relationships as a magical transformation, whether it is the courtiers' return to sanity, or Prospero's restoration to his dukedom, or Ariel's flight into perpetual summer. While all of the 'slaves' and 'prisoners' are being freed, and while all of the 'sovereigns' are being restored, the sense of magical change is never wholly lost. The union of drama and metaphor in *The Tempest* is nowhere more complete than in the last act of the play.

The larger meaning of Shakespeare's total design, which was anticipated in the cloud and dream metaphor of Prospero's visionary speech, is most clearly and fully expressed in these final transformations. In a world where everywhere may become something else, doubts naturally arise, and in the swift flow of change the confusion about what is and what is not becomes fairly acute. When Prospero 'diseases' himself and appears as Duke of Milan, Gonzalo says with understandable caution:

> Whether this be
> Or be not, I'll not swear

And Prospero answers:

> You do yet taste
> Some subtilties o' the isle, that will not let you
> Believe things certain.

Whereas in the earlier acts the characters had often accepted the unreal as real (spirits, shipwrecks, drownings, visions), they now find it difficult to accept the real as truly real. The play concludes with their acceptance of the unexpected change to reality. But for the spectator there remains the heightened sense of the 'thin partitions' that 'do divide' these states. The world that common sense regards as real, of order in nature and society and of sanity in the individual, is a shimmering transformation of disorder. 'We shall

all be changed, in a moment, in the twinkling of an eye.' (This or something like it is as near as we can come to describing the total attitude conveyed by *The Tempest*.)

Thus *The Tempest* is, like Marvell's 'Garden', a Metaphysical poem of metamorphosis, though the meaning of change is quite different for the two writers. It is worth noting too that Shakespeare 'had Ovid in his eye', a fact that is obvious from the echoes of Golding's famous translation. There could be no better proof of Shakespeare's maturity than the contrast between the 'sweet witty' Ovidianism of 'Venus and Adonis' and the metaphorical design of *The Tempest*, which gives philosophic meaning to a drama of Ovidian metamorphosis. We remember 'a lily prison'd in a jail of snow' as an isolated 'beauty', but hardly as an apt symbol of the amorous relations of Venus and Adonis, or as symbolic of some larger meaning in their story. (Indeed a 'jail of snow' is rather inept for the fervid goddess of the poem.) 'Those were pearls that were his eyes' revives Ariel's sea music, Ferdinand's melancholy, and a world of fantasy and transshifting states of being. The increased concentration in meaning of the image from *The Tempest* is a sign of a growth in the command of language which is command of life for a poet. As Arnold said of Wordsworth, Shakespeare now 'deals with more of *life*' and 'he deals with *life*, as a whole, more powerfully'. His maturity and power appear in the variety of experience so perfectly harmonized through the imaginative design of *The Tempest*.

NOTES

1. The music and tempest metaphors have been traced in a very different fashion and with quite different aims by G. Wilson Knight in *The Shakespearian Tempest* (1932). My analysis (which I had worked out before reading Professor Knight's essay) has a more limited purpose: to show a continuity of analogy and a development of metaphor parallel to that of the other continuities I have traced.

2. The scene is full of expressions such as: *A tempestuous noise of thunder and lightning heard*, 'roarers', 'command these elements to silence', *A cry within*, 'A plague upon this howling! they are louder than the weather, or our office', 'insolent noisemaker', *A confused noise within*, etc.

Frank Kermode Introduction to *The Tempest* (1954)

NATURE

I. *Natural Men.* The only undisputed source for any part of *The Tempest* is Montaigne's essay 'Of Cannibals'; there are unmistakeable traces of Florio's translation in the text. It has been argued, most recently by A. Lovejoy,[1] that Shakespeare intends a satirical comment upon Montaigne's apparent acceptance of the primitivistic view that a natural society, without the civilized accretions of law, custom, and other artificial restraints, would be a happy one.

Montaigne's essay as a whole is relevant to the play, and it would appear that critical comment has been hampered by a failure to understand this. The essay, like the play, is concerned with the general contrast between natural and artificial societies and men, though Montaigne assumes, in his 'naturalist' way, that the New World offers an example of naturally virtuous life uncorrupted by civilization, whereas Shakespeare obviously does not. Montaigne's general position is stated thus:

> They [the Indians] are even savage, as we call those fruits wilde, which nature of her selfe . . . hath produced: whereas indeed . . . those which our selves have altered by our artificiall devices, and diverted from their common order, we should rather terme savage. In those are the true and most profitable vertues, and naturall properties most lively and vigorous, which in these we have bastardized, applying them to the pleasure of our corrupted taste. And if notwithstanding, in divers fruits of those countries that were never tilled, we shall finde, that in respect of ours they are most excellent, and as delicate unto our taste; there is no reason, art should gaine the point of honour of our great and puissant mother Nature . . .[2]

This is a simple 'primitivism', and it uses the traditional horticultural analogy, equally available to those who held that the gardener's art corrupted and those who believed it improved the stock.[3] The dispute is central to *The Winter's Tale*, and is debated by Polixenes, who takes the view that Art acts to the improvement of Nature;*

* IV iv. Nature transcends Art when the statue of Hermione moves.

Perdita, who disagrees, is herself the product of careful breeding, of virtuous stock, which can no more be concealed by her rustic milieu than can the nobility of the salvage man and Pastorella in *The Faerie Queene*, book VI, or of the King's sons in *Cymbeline*.

These apparently antithetical views on the natural life to some extent controlled the reports of the voyagers upon whom Montaigne and Shakespeare both depend. They tended to describe the natives as purely virtuous or purely vicious. From Eden to Harcourt they repeat the theme of Montaigne's commonwealth; and yet they also speak of the brutality of the natives, of their treachery, ugliness, and infidelity. The *True Declaration* called them 'human beasts' and the experienced Captain John Smith 'perfidious, inhuman, all Savage'.[4] Literary men saw in the favourable reports a rich affirmation of a traditional theme of poetry; hence the enthusiasm of Drayton, the talk of 'sun-burnt Indians, That know no other wealth but Peace and Pleasure';[5] but a more central humanism expressed the other view, as did Sandys in his comparison of the Indians with the Cyclops, with its emphasis on the social achievement of Art:

> ... The *Cyclops* were a salvage people ... unsociable amongst themselves, & inhumane to strangers: And no marvaile, when lawlesse, and subject to no government, the bond of society; which gives to every man his owne, suppressing vice, and advancing vertue, the two maine columnes of a Commonwealth ... Man is a politicall and sociable creature: they therefore are to be numbered among beasts who renounce society, whereby they are destitute of lawes, the ordination of civility. Hence it ensues, that man, in creation the best, when averse to justice, is the worst of all creatures. Such *Polyphemus*; ... more salvage ... are the *West Indians* at this day.[6]

Both these attitudes to primitive man are deeply rooted in the past; and both found some support in the behaviour of the natives, which was, as a rule, very amiable at first – as Caliban's was with Prospero and Stephano – but under provocation, and sometimes spontaneously, treacherous later. Behind all these observations are the two opposing versions of the natural; on the one hand, that which man corrupts, and on the other that which is defective, and must be mended by cultivation – the less than human, which calls forth man's authoritative power to correct and rule. This latter is the view which suits best the conscience of the colonist. In practice everybody except a few missionaries treated the savages literally as lesser breeds without the law; sun- and devil-worshippers, often cannibals, they were also in occupation of fertile territory, and it was at once virtuous and expedient to convert and exploit them. In 1493, for example, the Spanish Ambassador at the Papal Court announced the discoveries of Columbus on behalf of his sovereigns; 'Christ', he said, 'has placed under their rule the Fortunate Isles.'[7] Prospero's assumption of his right to rule the island, 'to be the lord on't', is the natural assumption of a European prince, as Purchas on 'The Lawfulness of Discoveries' demonstrates.[8] The natives were worth some trouble; although they had no rational language, they did not lack certain mechanic arts, like the building of dams for fish, upon which the European settler long remained dependent. Many stratagems were devised to expedite the subjection of the natives. Stephano's claim to be descended from the moon was commonly made by unscrupulous voyagers who seized the chance of turning to account the polytheism of the Indians.[9] There is ample testimony to the corrupting effect upon natives of contact with dissolute Europeans – Christian savages sent to convert heathen savages, as Fuller put it.[10] Ronsard seems to have been the first to voice this complaint,[11] and of course it is another element in the situation which interested both Montaigne and Shakespeare. Reports of such barbarism would tend to reinforce the nostalgic primitivism of the literary men, and lead them once more to reflect upon an ancient theme:

> not all
> That beare the name of men . . .
> . . . Are for to be accounted men: but such as under awe
> Of reasons rule continually doo live in vertues law;
> And that the rest doo differ nought from beasts, but
> rather bee
> Much woorse than beasts, bicause they do abace theyr
> owne degree.[13]

Gonzalo's half-serious talk about his commonwealth serves to introduce into the play the theme of the natural life in a guise more appropriate to pastoral poetry which takes a 'soft' view of Nature. It is over-simple to assume that this perennial theme is destroyed by the cheap jeers of Antonio and Sebastian. There are points in the play at which Shakespeare uses Caliban to indicate how much baser the corruption of the civilized can be than the bestiality of the natural, and in these places he is using his natural man as a criterion of civilized corruption, as Montaigne had done. At the end of the play we learn Gonzalo's stature; he is not only the good-natured calm old man of the wreck, the cheerful courtier of the second act, and the pure soul of the third; he pronounces the benediction, and we see that he was all the time as right as it was human to be, even when to the common sense of the corrupt he was transparently wrong – wrong about the location of Tunis, wrong about the commonwealth, wrong about the survival of Ferdinand. And we see that Nature is not, in *The Tempest*, defined with the single-minded clarity of a philosophic proposition.[13] Shakespeare's treatment of the theme has what all his mature poetry has, a richly analytical approach to ideas, which never reaches after a naked opinion of true or false.

The poetic definition of Nature in the play is achieved largely by a series of antitheses with Caliban constantly recurring as one term. He represents the natural man. This figure is not, as in pastoral generally, a virtuous shepherd, but a salvage and deformed slave.

II. *A Salvage and Deformed Slave.* Caliban's name is usually regarded as a development of some form of the word 'Carib', meaning a savage inhabitant of the New World; 'cannibal' derives from this, and 'Caliban' is possibly a simple anagram of that word.[14] But though he is thus connected with the Indian savage, he is also associated, as were the uncivilized inhabitants of the Indies, with the wild or salvage man of Europe, formerly the most familiar image of mankind without the ordination of civility.

The origins of this type are obscure,[15] but the wild man was a familiar figure in painting, heraldry, pageant, and drama.[16] Several varieties are distinguished; the kind which survived in the drama was a satyr-type, like Bremo in the old play *Mucedorus*, which was revived by Shakespeare's company in 1610. Bremo abducts a virgin; unchastity was a conventional attribute of salvage men, which Shakespeare skilfully exploits. These creatures were believed to occupy an 'intermediate position in the moral scale, below man, just as the angels were above him . . . they are the link between . . . the settled and the wild, the moral and the unmoral'.[17] The term 'salvage', used of Caliban in the Folio 'Names of the Actors', has thus a restricted meaning, as it has in Spenser. Caliban is a salvage man, and the West Indians were salvage men of a topical kind; hence the Indian element in this natural man.

The next thing the 'Names of the Actors' says about Caliban is that he is deformed. He is what Thersites called Ajax, 'a very land-fish, languageless, a monster'.[18] There were reports from the Indies of curious specimens, and these reports may have influenced some of the things that are said about Caliban in the play;[19] but his deformity is visualized in terms of Old World monsters. Caliban's birth, as Prospero insists, was inhuman; he was 'a born devil', 'got by the devil himself upon thy wicked dam'. He was the product of sexual union between a witch and an incubus, and this would account for his deformity, whether the devil-lover was Setebos (all pagan gods were classified as devils) or, as W. C. Curry infers, some aquatic demon.[20]

Caliban's mother, though associated with reports of devil-worship and witchcraft in the New World, belongs to the Old. She is a powerful witch, deliberately endowed with many of the qualities of classical witches,[21] but also possessing a clearly defined place in the contemporary demonological scheme. She is a practitioner of 'natural' magic, a goetist who exploited the universal sympathies, but whose power is limited by the fact that she could command, as a rule, only devils and the lowest orders of spirits. Prospero, on the other hand, is a theurgist, whose Art is to achieve supremacy over the natural world by holy magic. The Neo-Platonic mage studies the harmonic relationship of the elementary, celestial, and intellectual worlds,[22] and conceives it

> no way irrational that it should be possible for us to ascend by the same degrees through each World to the same very original world itself, the Maker of all things, and First Cause, from whence all things are, and proceed . . .[23]

His object is to 'walk to the skie', as Vaughan put it, before death, by ascending through the created worlds to the condition of the angels. His Art is supernatural; the spirits he commands are the daemons of Neo-Platonism, the criterion of whose goodness is not the Christian one of adherence to, or defection from, God, but of immateriality or submersion in matter. He deals with spirits high in the scale of goodness, and if lesser spirits ('weak masters') are required, the superior daemon controls them on his behalf. He is '*divinorum cultor & interpres*, a studious observer and expounder of divine things', and his Art is 'the absolute perfection of Natural Philosophy'.[24] Natural Philosophy includes the arts of astrology, alchemy, and ceremonial magic, to all of which Prospero alludes.[25]

We shall return to the special powers and the learning of the mage Prospero; the point here is that his Art,* being the Art of supernatural virtue which belongs to the redeemed world of civility and learning, is the antithesis of the black magic of Sycorax.[26] Caliban's deformity is the result of evil natural magic, and it stands as a natural criterion by which we measure the world of Art, represented by Prospero's divine magic and the supernaturally sanctioned beauty of Miranda and Ferdinand.

The last thing the 'Names of the Actors' says about Caliban is that he is a slave. We have seen the readiness with which the white man took charge of the New World; Prospero arrived on his island 'to be the lord on 't'. If Aristotle was right in arguing that 'men . . . who are as much inferior to others as the body is to the soul . . . are slaves by nature, and it is advantageous for them always to be under government', and that 'to find our governor we should . . . examine into a man who is most perfectly formed in soul and body . . . for in the depraved and vicious the body seems to rule rather than the soul, on account of their being corrupt and contrary to nature',[27] then the black and mutilated cannibal must be the natural slave of the European gentleman, and, *a fortiori*, the salvage and deformed Caliban of the learned Prospero.

Caliban is, therefore, accurately described in the Folio 'Names of the Actors'. His origins and character are natural in the sense that they do not partake of grace, civility, and art; he is ugly in body, associated with an evil natural magic, and unqualified for rule or nurture. He exists at the simplest level of sensual pain and pleasure, fit for lechery because love is beyond his nature, and a natural slave of demons. He hears music with pleasure, as music can appeal to the beast who lacks reason;[28] and indeed he resembles Aristotle's bestial man. He is a measure of the incredible superiority of the world of Art, but also a measure of its corruption. For the courtiers and their servants include the incontinent Stephano and the malicious Antonio. Caliban scorns the infirmity of purpose exhibited by the first, and knows better than Antonio that it is imprudent to resist grace, for which, he says, he will henceforth seek. Unlike the incontinent man, whose appetites subdue his will, and the malicious man, whose will is perverted to evils ends, 'the bestial man has no sense of right and wrong, and therefore sees no difference between good and evil. His state is less guilty but more hopeless than those of

* Always spelled with the capital in the Folio text. This is a recognized method of indicating that it is a technical usage.

incontinence and malice, since he cannot be improved'.[29] Men can abase their degree below the bestial; and there is possibly a hint, for which there is no support in Aristotle, that the bestial Caliban gains a new spiritual dimension from his glimpse of the 'brave spirits'. Whether or no this is true, he is an extraordinarily powerful and comprehensive type of Nature; an inverted pastoral hero, against whom civility and the Art which improves Nature may be measured.

ART

I. *Buds of Nobler Race.* The civilized castaways of *The Tempest* are brought into close contact with a representative of Nature uncontrolled by Art. How do they differ from Caliban, and how is this difference expressed?

It is useful to compare Spenser's treatment of two salvage men in *The Faerie Queene*.[30] The one who carries off Amoret in Book IV is an unamiable personification of greedy lust – 'For he liv'd all on ravin and on rape' (IV vii 5). The full description leaves no doubt that this is the wild man of the entertainments, and that his are the 'natural' activities of lust and cannibalism. The salvage man who treats Serena so gently in the sixth book is quite different; though he cannot speak he shows a tenderness which is, apparently, against his nature. The reason is, that 'he was borne of noble blood' (VI v 2); we do not hear how he came to be languageless and salvage, but we know he owes his gentleness to his gentle birth.

> O what an easie thing is to descry
> The gentle bloud, how ever it be wrapt
> In sad misfortunes foule deformity
> And wretched sorrowes, which have often hapt!
> For howsoever it may grow mis-shapt,
> Like this wyld man being undisciplynd,
> That to all virtue it may seeme unapt,
>   Yet will it shew some sparkes of gentle mynd,
> And at the last breake forth in his owne proper kynd.
> (VI v 1)

That gentle birth predisposed a man to virtue, even if it was not absolutely necessary to virtue, was part of the lore of courtesy. *Fortes creantur fortibus* ... – argument as to the mode of inheriting, and of cultivating, *nobilitas*, runs through the history of moral philosophy from Aristotle through Dante to the Renaissance. It is true that, with evidence to the contrary continually before their eyes, philosophers could not uniformly maintain that where there was high birth there was virtue, taking nobility to mean the *non vile*, 'the perfection of its own nature in each thing';[31] and in Italy there was a growing tendency to judge of nobility by actual manners and merit, rather than by family. As early as the *Convito* the conditions of its development are described as much more complex than the racial theory of its provenance allows,[32] but more commonplace thought constantly recurs to the biological analogy; *est in juvencis, est in equis, patrum Virtus* – as Polixenes conceived that there were 'buds of nobler race'.

The question is debated in the first book of Castiglione's *Courtier* by Canossa and Pallavicino.[33] The arguments are conventional, but they serve to illustrate the theory of natural nobility which animates Spenser's portrait of the salvage man. Nature makes the work of greatness easier, and the penalties of failure heavier, for the high-born; 'because nature in every thing hath deepely sowed that privie seed, which giveth a certaine force and propertie of her beginning, unto whatsoever springeth of it, and maketh it like unto herselfe. As we see by example . . . in trees, whose slippes and grafts alwaies for the most part are like unto the stock of the tree they cam from: and if at any time they grow out of kinde, the fault is in the husbandman';[34] which is to say, in the individual nobleman – a fault of nurture, not of nature. Thus Canossa, though not to the satisfaction of Pallavicino, accounts also for the Antonios of the world. He allows an important place to education, believing, with Prospero and against Socrates, the pedagogues could be found capable of nursing the seed:[35]

> Therefore even as in the other artes, so also in the vertues, it is behofefull to have a teacher, that with lessons and good exhortations may stirre up and quicken in us those moral vertues, whereof wee have the seede inclosed and buried in the soule.[36]

If the seed is not there (and here Prospero's experience confirms him) the husbandman loses his labour, and brings forth only 'the briers and darnell of appetites' which he had desired to restrain. Canossa omits all the other factors which might be brought into consideration – 'the complex nature of the seed', 'the disposition of the dominant Heaven' – which Dante two centuries before had attempted to calculate, and takes account only of nature and of nurture. This leaves an opening for Pallavicino's reply, and Castiglione had, of course, to arrange matters to suit his dialectic scheme.

But for Spenser moral virtues inhabit the simpler, the ideal, world of romance, and his salvage man differs from his kind in that he has the seed implanted by nature, though not husbanded by nurture.

There is a striking version of the theory by Edward Phillips, the nephew of Milton. Phillips, in a passage so much above his usual manner that critics have seen in it the hand of his uncle, identifies two forces which distinguish the better part of mankind from the more brutish:

> ... the first is that *Melior natura* which the Poet speaks of, with which whoever is amply indued, take that Man from his Infancy, throw him into the Desarts of *Arabia*, there let him converse some years with Tygers and Leopards, and at last bring him where civil society & conversation abides, and ye shall see how on a sudden, the scales and dross of his barbarity purging off by degrees, he will start up a Prince or Legislator, or some such illustrious Person: the other is that noble thing call'd *Education*, this is, that Harp of *Orpheus*, that lute of *Amphion*, so elegantly figur'd by the Poets to have wrought such Miracles among irrational and insensible Creatures, which raiseth beauty even out of deformity, order and regularity out of Chaos and confusion, and which, if throughly and rightly prosecuted, would be able to civilize the most savage natures, & root out barbarism and ignorance from off the face of the Earth: those who have either of these qualifications singly may justly be term'd *Men*; those who have both united in a happy conjunction, *more* than *Men*; those who have neither of them in any competent measure ... *less* than *Men* ...[37]

Phillips here takes the view expressed by Dante, Pallavicino, and many others, that the want of nature can be partially supplied by Education, and in this respect differs from those who, like Canossa and, as we shall see, the romance-writers, held more rigidly to the notion of the seed without which all husbandry is not only wasted but even harmful, since it promotes the growth of undesirable weed-like qualities. The unknown poet's *melior natura* provides an excellent label for all the ideas associated with 'buds of nobler race', and his 'Education' enables us to see Prospero's 'nurture' in its proper context. Miranda, as Prospero early informs us, is endowed not only with the *melior natura*, but with education:

> here
> Have I, thy schoolmaster, made thee more profit
> Than other princess' can, that have more time
> For vainer hours, and tutors not so careful. (I ii 171–4)

She has both these qualities of nobility 'united in a happy conjunction'. Caliban has neither, and there is in the structure of the play a carefully prepared parallel between the two characters to illustrate this point; Caliban's education was not only useless – on *his* nature, which is nature *tout court*, nurture would never stick – but harmful. He can only abuse the gift of speech; and by cultivating him Prospero brings forth in him 'the briers and darnell of appetites' – lust for Miranda, discontent at his inferior position, ambition, intemperance of all kinds, including a disposition to enslave himself to the bottle of Stephano. And there is in his 'vile race' that 'which *good* natures Could not abide to be with' (I ii 361–2, my italics); in other words there is a repugnance between the raw, unreclaimed nature which he represents, and the courtier-stock with which he has to deal, endowed as it is with grace, and nurtured in refinement through the centuries, in the world of Art.[38]

II. *Prospero's Art*. At the risk of introducing 'distincts' where there is no 'division' it may be said that Prospero's Art has two functions in *The Tempest*. The first is simple; as a mage he exercises the supernatural powers of the holy adept. His Art is here the disciplined exercise of virtuous knowledge, a 'translation of merit into power',[39] the achievement of 'an intellect pure and conjoined with the powers of the gods, without which we shall never happily ascend to the scrutiny of secret things, and to the power of wonderfull workings'.[40] This Art is contrasted with the natural power of Sycorax to exploit for evil purposes the universal sympathies. It is a technique for liberating the soul from the passions, from nature; the practical application of a discipline of which the primary requirements are learning and temperance, and of which the mode is contemplation. When Prospero achieves this necessary control over himself and nature he achieves his ends (reflected in the restoration of harmony at the human and political levels) and has no more need of the instrument, 'rough magic'.[41]

The second function is symbolic. Prospero's Art controls Nature; it requires of the artist virtue and temperance if his experiment is to succeed; and it thus stands for the world of the better natures and its qualities. This is the world which is closed to Caliban (and Comus); the world of mind and the possibilities of liberating the soul, not the world of sense, whether that be represented as coarsely natural or charmingly voluptuous.[42] Art is not only a beneficent magic in contrast to an evil one; it is the ordination of civility, the control of appetite, the transformation of nature by breeding and learning; it is even, in a sense, the means of Grace.

Prospero is, therefore, the representative of Art, as Caliban is of Nature. As a mage he controls nature; as a prince he conquers the passions which had excluded him from his kingdom and overthrown law; as a scholar he repairs his loss of Eden; as a man he learns to temper his passions, an achievement essential to success in any of the other activities.

Prospero describes his efforts to control his own passion in V i 25–7 –

> Though with their high wrongs I am struck to th' quick,
> Yet with my nobler reason 'gainst my fury
> Do I take part.

In an age when 'natural' conduct was fashionably associated with sexual promiscuity, chastity alone could stand as the chief function of temperance, and there is considerable emphasis on this particular restraint in *The Tempest*. The practice of good magic required it;[43] but in this it is again merely the practical application of civility. Prospero twice, and Juno again, warn Ferdinand of the absolute necessity for it, and Ferdinand's ability to make pure beauty 'abate the ardour of his liver'[44] is in the strongest possible contrast to Caliban's straightforward natural lust for it. The unchaste designs of Stephano arouse Prospero's anger also; it is as if he were conducting, with magically purified book and rod,[45] the kind of experiment which depended for its success on the absolute purity of all concerned; and indeed, in so far as his aims were a dynastic marriage and the regeneration of the noble, this was so.

This is characteristic of the way in which the magic of Prospero translates into more general terms. The self-discipline of the magician is the self-discipline of the prince. It was the object of the good ruler to make his people good by his own efforts; and that he might do so it was considered necessary for him to acquire learning, and to rid himself 'of those troublous affections that untemperate mindes feele'.[46] The personal requirements of mage and prince are the same, and Prospero labours to regain a worldly as well as a heavenly power. Like James I in the flattering description, he 'standeth invested with that triplicitie which in great veneration was ascribed to the ancient *Hermes*, the power and fortune of a *King*, the knowledge and illumination of a Priest, and the Learning and universalitie of a Philosopher'.[47]

Learning is a major theme in the play; we learn that Miranda is capable of it and Caliban not, and why this should be so; but we are also given a plan of the place of learning in the dispositions of providence. Prospero, like Adam, fell from his kingdom by an inordinate thirst for knowledge; but learning is a great aid to virtue, the road by which we may love and imitate God, and 'repair the ruins of our first parents',[48] and by its means he is enabled to return. The solicitude which accompanied Adam and Eve when 'the world was all before them' went also with Prospero and Miranda when they set out in their 'rotten carcass of a butt'.

> By foul play, as thou say'st, were we heav'd thence,
> But blessedly holp hither. (I ii 62–3)

They came ashore 'by Providence divine'; and Gonzalo leaves us in no doubt that Prospero's fault, like Adam's, was a happy one:

> Was Milan thrust from Milan, that his issue
> Should become kings of Naples? O rejoice
> Beyond a common joy! . . . (V i 205–7)

He had achieved the great object of Learning, and regained a richer heritage.[49] But he is not learned in only this rather abstract sense; he is the learned prince. Like Boethius, he had been a natural philosopher, and had learnt from Philosophy that 'to hate the wicked were against reason'. He clearly shared the view that 'no wise man had rather live in banishment, poverty, and ignominy, than prosper in his own country . . . For in this manner is the office of wisdom performed with more credit and renown, where the governors' happiness is participated by the people about them.' And Philosophy, though ambiguously, taught both Boethius and Prospero 'the way by which thou mayest return to thy country'.[50]

There is nothing remarkable about Prospero's ambition to regain his own kingdom and strengthen his house by a royal marriage. To be studious and contemplative, but also to be able to translate knowledge into power in the active life, was the object of his discipline; the Renaissance venerated Scipio for his demonstration of this truth, and Marvell's Horatian Ode speaks of Cromwell in the same terms.

> The chiefe Use then in man of that he knowes,
> Is his paines taking for the good of all . . .
> Yet *Some seeke knowledge, merely but to know,*
> And idle Curiositie that is . . .[51]

Prospero is not at all paradoxical in presenting himself at the climax as he was 'sometime Milan'. Yet he does not intend merely to look after his worldly affairs; every third thought is to be his grave. 'The end of the active or doing life ought to be the beholding; as of war, peace, and as of paines, rest.'[52] The active and contemplative lives are complementary.

In all respects, then, Prospero expresses the qualities of the world of Art, of the *non vile.* These qualities become evident in the organized contrasts between his world and the world of the vile; between the worlds of Art and Nature.

NOTES

1. *Essays in the History of Ideas* (1948) p. 238. Lovejoy calls Shakespeare's source 'the locus classicus of primitivism in modern literature'. See also M. T. Hodgen, 'Montaigne and Shakespeare again', in *Huntington Library Quarterly*, XVI (1952–3) 23–42.
2. *Montaigne's Essays*, transl. John Florio (1892 ed.) I 219.
3. For the early history of the idea, see A. Lovejoy and G. Boas, *Primitivism in Antiquity* (1935); Democritus alludes to it (ibid. pp. 207–8) and it is commonplace in Renaissance literary criticism (e.g., *The Arte of English Poesie*, ed. Willcock and Walker (1936) p. 304 – the gardener does what 'nature of her selfe would never have done: as to make the single gillifloure double'). One view, that Art is an agent of Nature, and necessary to the development of created nature – the view of Polixenes – is set over against the other, that Art (meaning anything that interferes with Nature) can only corrupt, which is the view of Perdita, of the Mower in Marvell's 'Mower against Gardens' and of Montaigne in this essay.
4. R. R. Cawley, *The Voyagers and Elizabethan Drama* (1938) pp. 346 ff.
5. Beaumont and Fletcher, *Four Plays in One* (Cambridge, 1905–12) X 360.
6. George Sandys, *Ovids Metamorphoses Englished* (1632) p. 477.
7. G. Chinard, *L'Exotisme américain dans la littérature française au XVIe siècle* (1911) p. 4.
8. Samuel Purchas, *Purchas his Pilgrimes* (1625) I (1906 ed.).
9. Cawley, *PMLA* XLI 714 ff.
10. Cawley, *Voyagers*, p. 193. See also Jonson's *Staple of News*, in *Works*, ed. Herford and Simpson, V 245.
11. Chinard, op. cit. p. 118.

12. Arthur Golding, *The XV Bookes of P. Ovidius Naso, entytuled Metamorphosis* (1567), *Epistle*, lines 55–62.

13. E. C. Knowlton in his 'Nature and Shakespeare' (*PMLA* LI (1936) 719 ff.), argues that Shakespeare attributes to Perdita in *The Winter's Tale* 'a kind of rightness', but that his own view was probably that of Polixenes.

14. E. K. Chambers favours the derivation from *cauliban*, a Romany word meaning 'blackness' (*William Shakespeare* (1930) I 494). There are also the Chalybeates, savage cannibals of the ancient world, whom Virgil mentions twice, and whom Pliny situates near the Coraxi.

15. It is discussed by R. Withington, *English Pageantry* (1918) I 72 ff., and by E. Welsford, *The Court Masque* (1927) p. 6. Possibly the practice of abandoning children in forests had something to do with it; some of the survivors, perhaps subnormal to begin with, might have led a bestial life in the woods. Linnaeus classified such survivors as a distinct species, *homo ferus*. Conceivably the Γορίλλα observed by Hanno the Carthaginian has some part in the tradition.

16. Pictorially the wodehouse, or wodewose, flourished in the thirteenth and fourteenth centuries (R. van Marle, *Iconographie de l'Art Profane* (1931) I 183–91). The earliest recorded dramatic specimen is in a Paduan entertainment of 1208 – *magnus Ludus de quodam homine salvatico* (P. Neri, in *Giornale Storico della Letteratura Italiana*, I ix 49; cited by L. Edwards, 'The Historical and Legendary Background of the Wodehouse and Peacock Feast Motif in the Walsokne and Braunche Brasses', in *Monumental Brass Society Transactions*, VIII part vii 300–11). Then they occur with great frequency. In England, there is a wild man in the Christmas entertainment of Edward III in 1347, and they are common in Tudor entertainments, such as the progresses and receptions of Elizabeth. (See J. Nichol, *Royal Progresses* (1823) *passim*.)

17. L. Edwards, loc. cit. This idea persisted into the eighteenth century; Lovejoy quotes a poem which includes the lines, 'De l'homme aux animaux rapprochant la distance, Voyez l'Hommes des Bois lier leur existence' (*The Great Chain of Being* (1936) p. 236).

18. *Troilus and Cressida* III iii 265.

19. The closest resemblance is in a beast reported by dos Sanctos in 1597, which had the 'eares of a Dog, armes like a Man without haire, and at the elbows great Finnes like a fish', which the native assistants had believed to be 'the sonne of the Devill'. (Quoted by J. E. Hankins, 'Caliban the Bestial Man', in *PMLA* LXII (1947) 794.)

20. W. C. Curry, *Shakespeare's Philosophical Patterns* (1936) pp. 148–55.

21. Some of the classical *loci* are: Virgil, *Eclogue* VIII, Horace, *Epode* V, Lucan, *Pharsalia*, I; Ovid, *Met.* VII 199–207; Seneca, *Medea*, 755–66. These witches had a share in the development of the witches of Renaissance literature. Lyly's *Endimion* has a witch, Dipsa, who says she can 'darken the Sunne by my skil, and remoove the Moone out of her course'. This traditional power is mentioned in the Faust books, and by Reginald Scot.

22. For detailed discussion of these topics, see R. H. West's invaluable *The Invisible World* (1939), the fullest treatment of the supernatural in Elizabethan drama; and Hardin Craig, *The Enchanted Glass* (1936) chap. 1.

23. Cornelius Agrippa, *Occult Philosophy*, transl. J. F. (1651) I i.
24. Agrippa, op. cit. III xi.
25. e.g. I ii 181–4; V i 1, and the many allusions to ceremonial magic – book, rod, cloak of invisibility, which are the instruments of the 'rougher magic' which the mage at a later stage renounces, as Prospero does before confronting Alonso.
26. This highly important distinction is lost if Prospero is called a black magician, as he often is. The arguments against this view are conclusive but there is no space for them here; they can be deduced from the works of West and Curry. It has been objected that Shakespeare could not have presented at the Court of James I a play openly alluding to a system of magic to which the King was notoriously opposed. But James was well accustomed to such treatment; he himself was often presented as a beneficent magician, and he took pleasure in Jonson's *Masque of Queens*, a brilliant iceberg whose hidden part is a craggy mass of occult learning. He no more took exception to this than he did to the presentation of pagan gods, whom he theoretically regarded as devils, because he understood the equation between a fiction of beneficent magic and the sacred power he himself professed as an actual king.
27. *Politics*, 1254 a–b.
28. Cf. Horace, *De Arte Poetica*, lines 391–2: Silvestres homines sacer interpresque deorum / caedibus et victu foedo deterruit Orpheus.
29. See the valuable essay of J. E. Hankins in *PMLA* LXII.
30. The Nature–Art Debate is a leading motive in Spenser; its most complete study is that of R. H. Pierce in *Journal of English and Germanic Philology*, XLIV. A. Thaler (*Shakespeare Association Bulletin*, X) compares with Caliban the son of Hag (*The Faerie Queene* III vii) who lusts after Florimell. J. A. S. McPeek (*Philological Quarterly*, XXV) adds that the beast sent after Florimell is freckled and doglike.
31. *Il Convito. The Banquet* of Dante Alighieri, trans. E. P. Sayer (1887) p. 226. See the curtain-lecture in Chaucer's *Wife of Bath's Tale*.
32. Ibid., see e.g. p. 241. Dante devotes the fourth and last extant section of the work to this subject. In the earlier *De Monarchia* he allowed more force to heredity. For a short survey of the changing theory see Burckhardt, *The Civilization of the Renaissance in Italy* (1944 English ed.) pp. 217 ff.
33. The same theme, with many variations, is regularly treated in later works on courtesy and the education of princes and nobles. See e.g. *ΗΡΩ-ΠΑΙΔΕΙΑ*, or *The Institution of a Young Noble Man*, by James Cleland (1607), esp IV 7. Peacham (*Compleat Gentleman*, 1622+) defines nobility as 'the Honour of blood', 'it selfe essential and absolute'. He treats also of the loss of it through vice, and of the irrepressible appearance of nobility in children (ed. Gordon (1906) pp. 2, 3, 9, 14).
34. *The Courtier* (1528), trans. Hoby (1561), 1928 ed. (Everyman) p. 31.
35. This expression occurs so frequently in discussions of this sort that it will perhaps be useful to remind the reader that it had far more force than the modern idea of analogy would allow it, and also that the word 'seed' was also used as symbolizing the element of divine law implanted at birth in the human breast. This connotation is present in *Convito*, IV.

36. Castiglione, *The Courtier.*

37. Preface to *Theatrum Poetarum* (1675) in *Critical Essays of the Seventeenth Century*, ed. J. E. Spingarn (1908) III 257. See also Peacham, op. cit., where learning is treated as an essential adjunct to birth – the gentleman is to be not merely ἐυγενής but also πολυμαθής. De la Primaudaye, *Academie Francoise* (1585+), a widely read book, has a chapter on the subject (XVI) called *De la nature et de la Nourriture.* Bacon uses the phrase *melior natura* in 'Of Atheism'.

38. 'Nature' and its compounds are used in a wide range of meanings in *The Tempest*, as they always are in literature. I have shown how it is used in connexion with Caliban (his 'vile race' opposed to the race *non vile* – the stock etymology of *nobile*) and there is also some play on the idea that this nature is 'monstrous' – i.e. un-natural – a paradox which involves the concept of another and higher nature. 'Lord, that a monster should be such a natural' (III ii 30–1) where the pun depends upon the colloquial 'natural' (= 'idiot'). Miranda puts the paradox the other way round when she sees Ferdinand, and thinks he is a spirit, 'For nothing natural I ever saw so *noble*' (I ii 421–2), where the *Melior natura* is contrasted with the *vile* she recognized in Caliban. There is here of course a strong admixture of 'natural' meaning 'not supernatural'. This meaning recurs in the last Act, when Alonso, hearing that the ship is safe, says, 'These are not natural events' (V i 227) where we think at once that they are due to Prospero's Art. In V i 157 'natural breath' is of course simply 'human' breath, though the reading 'These words/Are natural breath' (*The Tempest*, ed. Sir Arthur Quiller-Couch and J. D. Wilson (New Shakespeare Series: 1921)) modifies it slightly. There are three other meanings (though it should be pointed out that this schematization inevitably entails over-simplification): Antonio, who is of noble race, and should have the better nature, exhibits 'an evil nature' (I ii 93) in his ambition. This is a disposition to do evil which can inhere in good stock for reasons given below. He is called 'unnatural' (V i 79) by Prospero as he forgives him; the primary meaning here is 'unfraternal, neglecting the ties of blood', but there is also the sense of 'degenerate, a betrayer of his race and of the better nature'. See also V i 78–9. Finally, *natura naturans* occurs in a form we have learned to recognize, in Gonzalo's 'all things in common nature should produce' and 'nature should bring forth of it own kind . . .' (i.e. without culture) II i 155, 158–9.

39. West, *The Invisible World*, pp. 41–5.

40. Agrippa, op. cit. III, iii.

41. *The Tempest*, severe and refined as it is, is still a development of folk-tales in which magicians and their agents have not a precise status in academic demonology. Hence Prospero shows certain unschematic resemblances to the simple magicians of Italian popular comedy and Ayrer's *Die Schöne Sidea*, and Ariel is not the unalloyed Platonic daemon of *Comus*. Nice distinctions are, however, impossible here.

42. Despite the attention given to verbal echoes of *The Tempest* in *Comus*, the deep indebtedness of Milton to the play has not been understood. Shakespeare is of course less formally allegorical, but the play is almost as important to Milton as *The Faerie Queene*.

43. Cf. Jonson's comic use of this law in *The Alchemist*.

44. IV i 56. C. Leech, in his *Shakespeare's Tragedies* (1950), finds the repetition of Prospero's warning 'impertinent' and thinks it 'cannot be understood other than pathologically'; this is the starting-point, as I understand it, of his demonstration that '*The Tempest* gave the fullest and most ordered expression of the Puritan impulse in Shakespeare'.

45. The book, so highly valued by Prospero and Caliban, as well as the rod, occur in all demonology, popular and learned; they were required to be of virginal purity.

46. Castiglione, *The Courtier*, p. 277.

47. Cleland, *The Institution of a Young Man* (1612) II i.

48. Milton, *Of Education*, in *Prose Works*, ed. Hughes, p. 31.

49. For a somewhat similar reading, though different in detail, see N. Coghill, 'The Basis of Shakespearian Comedy', *Essays and Studies* (1950) pp. 1–28.

50. The *Consolation of Philosophy*, IV Prose 5, V Prose 1 (Loeb ed. p. 335, 365).

51. Fulke Greville, *A Treatie of Humane Learning* (1603–5) st. 144–5; ed. G. Bullough (1938) I 190.

52. Castiglione, op. cit. p. 280. See also Bacon, *Advancement of Learning* (World's Classics ed.) pp. 11–12, 15–16, 42. The theme is a humanist commonplace.

Leslie A. Fiedler Caliban as the American Indian (1973)

To be sure, the world 'slave' is ambiguous in Shakespeare, meaning sometimes (as in the case of Iago) one so vile that only total subjugation to another seems an appropriate fate, and sometimes one actually thus subjugated (like Othello), whether he deserves it or not. Read either way, however, Caliban's label raises themes of colonialism and race; and taken all together, such themes evoke the place in which, for two hundred years, white Europeans had been confronting them in fact as well as theory, the land already called by Shakespeare's time 'America,' though he uses the word only once in a joke and never in *The Tempest*.

There seems little doubt, however, that America was on Shakespeare's mind, particularly at the point in Act II when he puts into the mouth of that kindly but ineffectual old wind-bag, Gonzalo, the speech beginning, 'Had I the plantation of this isle, my lord –' and ending, 'I would with such perfection govern, sir, / To excel the Golden Age.' There is something especially pathetic about the constantly interrupted speech of one who, having been unable to save Prospero and Miranda (he contented himself with smuggling the Duke's favorite books aboard their rotting ship), can now scarcely hold his listeners' attention long enough to make his points. But they are important points, all the same.

> I' the commonwealth I would by contraries
> Execute all things, for no kind of traffic
> Would I admit, no name of magistrate.
> Letters should not be known; riches, poverty,
> And use of service none; . . .
>
>   all men idle, all;
> And women too, but innocent and pure; . . .
> All things in common nature should produce
> Without sweat or endeavor.

And when Shakespeare allows this vision to be mocked through the foul mouths of the bad brothers, Sebastian and Antonio, it is Montaigne's dream of a communist utopia in the New World he is allowing them to vilify. For the very words he attributes to Gonzalo he has lifted from Florio's translation of the French skeptic, whose skepticism seems to have failed him for once in his essay 'Of the Cannibals.'

Montaigne had begun by reading the accounts of returned travelers from Brazil about the life lived by man-eating savages on the banks of the Amazon and, comparing their way of life with that lived by his European neighbors, had moved toward a kind of cultural relativism. 'Chacun appelle barbarie,' he commented, 'ce qui n'est pas de son usage' ('Each calls "savagery" customs different from his own'). It is the observation of a protoanthropologist, a contributor to the *Encyclopédie* born before his time. And beginning thus, he inevitably ends up with a sentimental paradox worthy of Rousseau: that the New World barbarians are, in some sense, less barbarous than the European ones, providing at least, for all their cannibalism, models for a perfect commonwealth, the Golden Age restored. If there is the merest hint of irony in all this, it is quite gone from Gonzalo's version, which leaves all the ironical qualification to his interlocutors, who observe aside, 'The latter end of his commonwealth forgets the beginning.' And this can be read as meaning not only that the old councillor, carried away by his own rhetoric, forgets how he has begun his speech before concluding it but also that he has forgotten the Fall in the garden with which the whole history of human society began.

Certainly Shakespeare is on their side in the debate, utter, even hopeless villains though they may be, for the events of the play prove them, not Gonzalo, right. Indeed, that old man himself, who has begun by observing of the New World, 'Here everything is advantageous to life,' ends by confessing, 'All torment, trouble, wonder, and amazement / Inhabits here. Some heavenly power guide us / Out of this fearful country!' The pun on 'maze' is clearly intended, the image it suggests being picked up later by Alonso who says, 'This is as strange a maze as e'er men trod.' Indeed, the maze seems as central to the mythology of the West in *The Tempest* as the riddle is to the mythology of the East. And with its emergence, the two archetypal equations which underlie the play's action are made completely manifest: the East = the past = incest = the riddle; the West = the future = rape and miscegenation = the maze. 'And there is in this business more than nature / Was ever conduct of,' Alonso continues. 'Some oracle / Must rectify our knowledge.' But Prospero proves 'oracle' enough, unriddling the enigma, unwinding the maze in his actions as well as his words.

To seek the past, the fable of his life signifies, is to leave action for books and to end up enisled with a nubile daughter in an ultimate travesty of the endogamous family, an incestuous *ménage à deux*. But in place of the East he dreams, the common source of Rome and Carthage and the 'mouldy tale' of *Apollonius of Tyre*, he wakes to find the West, a beach more strange and fearful than the 'still-vexed Bermoothes.' Here rape and miscegenation threaten the daughter too dearly loved in an ultimate travesty of the exogamous family. And instead of himself – that is, the past – repeated in the child that daughter bears, he can look forward only to total strangers, monsters as grandchildren – that is, a future utterly alien to anything he knows.

The identification of incest with the riddle is traditional enough to seem convincing, even without the testimony of Claude Lévi-Strauss; but that of miscegenation-rape with the maze may seem at first arbitrary and implausible. Yet a moment's reflection on the myth of Crete reminds us that the latter identification, too, is rooted in ancient mythology; for at the center of the first of all mazes, the labyrinth, there lay in wait the Minotaur, bestial product of woman's lust to be possessed, without due rite or ceremony, by the horned beast, monstrously hung but bereft of human speech. And Caliban is, in effect, a New World Minotaur, inheritor by *Mutterrecht* of a little world which proves, therefore, a maze to all European castaways, even those who dream it Paradise regained. But Caliban exists in history as well as myth, or more properly, perhaps, represents myth in the process of becoming history: the Minotaur rediscovered in the Indian.

His very name is meant to indicate as much, since it is 'cannibal' anagrammatized and 'cannibal' is derived from 'Carib,' first tribal Indian name made known to Europe. Caliban seems to have been created, on his historical side, by a fusion in Shakespeare's imagination of Columbus's first New World savages with Montaigne's Brazilians, Somers's native Bermudans, and those Patagonian 'giants' encountered by Pigafetta during his trip around the world with Magellan, strange creatures whose chief god was called, like Caliban's mother's, 'Setebos.' But to say that Caliban was for Shakespeare an Indian means that he was a problem, since the age had not been able to decide what in fact Indians were. And, in a certain sense, *The Tempest* must be understood as an attempt to answer that troubling question on the basis of both ancient preconceptions and new information about the inhabitants of the Americas.

That Caliban seems to be part fish has always troubled some readers of Shakespeare, though the characterization is apt enough for a native of the hemisphere which medieval scholars had believed to be all water. He is portrayed finally as a creature of the mud flats who has managed to climb onto land at long last, but has not yet acclimatized himself to the higher elements of air and fire. Humanoid without being quite human, though a step above what he himself describes as 'apes / With foreheads villainous low,' he is as the play draws to its close called more and more exclusively 'monster': 'servant-monster,' 'brave monster,' 'man-monster,' or simply 'monster' unqualified. And the point is to identify him with a kind of subhuman freak imagined in Europe even before the discovery of red men in America: the *homme sauvage* or 'savage man,' who, in the nightmares of Mediterranean humanists, had been endowed with sexual powers vastly in excess of their own. Such monstrous virility

ıting him not with canni-
as Prospero reminds us
ɔloitation and appropria-

, and lodged thee
k to violate

nswers:

> Oh ho, oh ho! Would 't had been done!
> Thou didst prevent me. I had peopled else
> The isle with Calibans.

He becomes thus the first nonwhite rapist in white man's literature, ancestor of innumerable Indian warriors and skulking niggers who have threatened ever since in print, as well as on stage and screen, the fragile honor of their oppressors' daughters. And it is his unredeemable carnality which, as both Prospero and Miranda insist, condemns him to eternal slavery, since, incapable of being educated to virtue, he must be controlled by force. 'A devil, a born devil, on whose nature / Nurture never can stick,' the master of arts describes him. And his daughter, more explicitly racist, concurs: 'But thy vile race, / Though thou didst learn, had that in't which good natures / Could not abide to be with.'

This charge Caliban never directly answers, though with his usual generosity, Shakespeare permits him an eloquent plea on his own behalf, less relevant, perhaps, but quite as moving as Shylock's.

> This island's mine, by Sycorax my mother,
> Which thou takest from me. When thou camest first,
> Thou strokedst me, and madest much of me, wouldst give me
> Water with berries in 't. And teach me how
> To name the bigger light, and how the less,
> That burn by day and night. And then I loved thee,
> And showed thee all the qualities o' th' isle. . . .
> Cursèd be I that did so! . . .
> For I am all the subjects that you have,
> Which first was mine own king. And here you sty me
> In this hard rock whiles you do keep from me
> The rest o' th' island.

There is, moreover, a kind of music in Caliban's speech, one is tempted to say a 'natural rhythm,' quite remote from Shylock's tone; for the Jew is postulated as an enemy of all sweet sound, whereas the New World savage is a singer of songs and a maker of poems, especially when he remembers the virginal world he inhabited before the coming of patriarchal power.

Prospero thinks of his island kingdom as a place to be subdued, hewed, trimmed, and ordered, so that, indeed, the chief use of his slave is to chop down trees and pile logs for the fire. But Caliban remembers a world of unprofaned magic, a living nature, in which reality had not yet quite been separated from dream, nor waking from sleeping:

> Be not afeared. The isle is full of noises,
> Sounds and sweet airs that give delight and hurt not.
> Sometimes a thousand twangling instruments
> Will hum about my ears, and sometimes voices,
> That, if I then had waked after long sleep,
> Will make me sleep again. And then, in dreaming,
> The clouds methought would open and show riches
> Ready to drop upon me, that when I waked,
> I cried to dream again

Once awakened from the long dream of primitive life, fallen out of the mother into the world of the father, there is no falling back into that intra-uterine sleep, only the hope for another kind of happiness, a new freedom on the farther side of slavery. Even drunk, Caliban remains a poet and visionary, singing that new freedom in a new kind of song.

> No more dams I'll make for fish.
> Nor fetch in firing
> At requiring,
> Nor scrape trencher, nor wash dish.
> 'Ban, 'Ban, Cacaliban
> Has a new master – Get a new man.
> Freedom, heyday! Heyday, freedom! Freedom,
> heyday, freedom.

Particularly in its Whitmanian long last lines – howled, we are told by the two mocking European clowns who listen – he has created something new under the sun: the first American poem.

And what has this in common with the Old World pastoral

elegance of the marriage masque, in which Prospero compels certain more 'temperate' spirits to speak for the top of his mind, even as the rebellious Caliban does for the depths of his soul.

> You nymphs, called Naiads, of the wandring brooks,
> With your sedged crowns and ever-harmless looks,
> Leave your crisp channels, and on this green land
> Answer your summons. Juno does command.
> Come, temperate nymphs. . . .

They simply cannot see eye to eye, the bookman and the logman, for while one is planning marriage, the other is plotting rape, since the savage (as even Gonzalo seems to know, providing that 'Letters should not be known. . . .' in his commonwealth) prefers freedom to culture and would rather breed new Americans in passion than himself become a new European in cold blood. But against Prospero's 'art' he is powerless and must abide, therefore, enslaved and desexed until some outside deliverer comes to his rescue.

That outside deliverer turns out to be, alas, the team of Stephano and Trinculo, the scum of the Old World promising themselves unaccustomed glory in the New and attempting to use against their old masters the New World savage, converted by whisky to their cause. But a drunken revolution is a comic one, and joining the clowns who would be kings, Caliban turns drunken, too, which is to say, becomes a clown himself. Indeed, the subject of drunkenness haunts *The Tempest* early and late quite as compulsively as it does *Macbeth* or *Othello*. But it has lost its tragic implications, providing only occasions for jokes, from the first scene, with its sodden sailors, to the last, from which Stephano and Trinculo exit 'reeling ripe' and prophesying that they will remain 'pickled forever.' 'What a thrice-double ass / Was I,' Caliban comments toward the play's close, 'to take this drunkard for a god.' And we remember how only a little while before, he had cried, 'That's a brave god, and bears celestial liquor,' thus preparing to become the first drunken Indian in Western literature.

Together with Stephano and Trinculo, in any case, he had plotted a slave's revolt against what Shakespeare believed to be proper authority. Caliban, in fact, was the tactician of this fool's rebellion, suggesting, out of his fantasies of revenge, means to destroy their common enemy: 'with a log / Batter his skull, or paunch him with a stake, / Or cut his weasand with thy knife.' But especially he insists that they must first take from the master of arts the instruments which give him a fatal advantage over them all: his books, which is to say, those symbols of a literate technology with which the ruling classes of Europe controlled the subliterates of two worlds. The theme recurs almost obsessively in his speeches: 'Having first seized his books.... Remember / First to possess his books, for without them / He's but a sot.... Burn but his books.' Yet the revolt is foredoomed because Stephano and Trinculo prove interested only in the trashy insignia of power, while Caliban is dreaming not just the substitution of one master for another but the annihilation of all authority and all culture, a world eternally without slaves and clowns.

Moreover, Prospero has been aware of what they plotted from the very start, only awaiting the proper moment to quash it. By the time he has hunted them down, however, with dogs called 'Fury' and 'Tyrant,' the whole history of imperialist America has been prophetically revealed to us in brief parable:* from the initial act of expropriation through the Indian wars to the setting up of reservations, and from the beginnings of black slavery to the first revolts and evasions. With even more astonishing prescience, *The Tempest* foreshadows as well the emergence of that democracy of fugitive white slaves, deprived and cultureless refugees from a Europe they never owned, which D. H. Lawrence was so bitterly to describe. And it prophesies, finally, like some inspired piece of science fiction before its time, the revolt against the printed page, the anti-Gutenberg rebellion for which Marshall McLuhan is currently a chief spokesman.

Thus fallen into history, however, has Shakespeare not also fallen out of his own myth, for what, after all, has America to do with *Apollonius of Tyre*, the guilt of expropriating ex-Europeans with that of incestuous fathers? It is easy enough to perceive on the literal level of his fable common images which betrayed Shakespeare from legend to chronicle: the sea voyage itself, for instance, along with the attendant circumstances of storm and shipwreck and miraculous salvation. In the most general sense, moreover, both the Old World

* Appropriately enough, one of the hounds pursuing two runaway slave girls in Harriet Beecher Stowe's *Uncle Tom's Cabin* is also called 'Fury,' whether in tribute to the prescience of Shakespeare (whom Mrs Stowe knew well) or by apt coincidence it is hard to be sure.

of Apollonius and the New World of Caliban are worlds inhabited by terrifying and hostile strangers, or conversely, ones in which the castaway European feels himself a stranger in a strange land. Indeed, the word 'strange' appears everywhere in *The Tempest*, not only in the speeches of the shipwrecked Neapolitans but in the stage directions as well: 'strange drowsiness,' 'strange beast,' '*strange music*,' '*strange Shapes*,' 'strange stare,' 'strange story' – all climaxing in Alonso's description of Caliban: 'This is a strange thing as e'er I looked on.'

These last words are only spoken, however, after Prospero's unknotting of the web he has woven; before, it is themselves and their plight which the displaced Europeans find superlatively 'strange.' And the sense of total alienation stirs in them not only 'wonder, and amazement' but 'trouble' and 'torment,' too, which is to say, the pangs of guilt. It is not merely that all of them are in fact guilty of treachery and usurpation in respect to each other but that having entered so alien a realm, however inadvertently, they become also guilty, on the metaphorical level, of rape and miscegenation. They are all, in short, Calibans, for America was at once virgin and someone else's before they came – and this they dimly surmise.

The figure of Caliban, at any rate, casts its shadow upon two utopian visions at once: that of Montaigne-Gonzalo, on the one hand, and that of Shakespeare-Prospero, on the other, the dream of a political utopia and the vision of sexuality redeemed. Inside the skin of every free man, Mark Twain was to observe three centuries later, there is a slave; and Shakespeare has concurred in advance, adding, and a monster as well! But all this Prospero has somehow temporarily forgotten, as the play which Shakespeare let him write moves – inexorably, it seems – toward its intended happy endings.

Frances A. Yates Prospero and Some Contemporaries (1975)

We have now to think about magic in *The Tempest*. What kind of magic is it? This is a problem which has been considerably discussed in recent years and I am not bringing forward any very new or startling discovery in observing that Prospero, as a magus, appears to work on the lines indicated in that well-known textbook of Renaissance magic, the *De occulta philosophia* of Henry Cornelius Agrippa. Frank Kermode was a pioneer in pointing to Agrippa as a power behind Prospero's art in his introduction to *The Tempest* in the Arden edition, first published in 1954. Prospero as a magus, says Kermode, exercises a discipline of virtuous knowledge; his art is the achievement of 'an intellect pure and conjoined with the powers of the gods without which [and this is direct quotation by Kermode from Agrippa] we shall never happily ascend to the scrutiny of secret things, and to the power of wonderful workings'. In short, Prospero has learned that 'occult philosophy' which Agrippa taught and knows how to put it into practice. Moreover, like Agrippa, Shakespeare makes very clear in *The Tempest* how utterly different is the high intellectual and virtuous magic of the true magus from low and filthy witchcraft and sorcery. Prospero is poles apart from the witch Sycorax and her evil son. Indeed, Prospero as the good magus has a reforming mission; he clears the world of his island from the evil magic of the witch; he rewards the good characters and punishes the wicked. He is a just judge, or a virtuous and reforming monarch, who uses his magico-scientific powers for good. The triumph of a liberal and Protestant Reformation in *Henry VIII* has its counterpart in *The Tempest* in the triumph of a reforming magus in the dream world of the magical island.

Prospero's magic is then a good magic, a reforming magic. But what exactly is the intellectual structure or system within which his magic works? Here we have to turn to Agrippa's definitions which can be simplified, rather drastically, as follows.

The universe is divided into three worlds: the elemental world of terrestrial nature; the celestial world of the stars; the supercelestial world of the spirits or intelligences or angels. Natural magic operates in the elemental world; celestial magic operates in the world of the stars; and there is a highest, religious, magic which operates in the supercelestial world. The lofty religious magus can conjure spirits or intelligences to his aid. The enemies of this kind of magic called it diabolical conjuring, and indeed the pious believers in it were always aware of the danger of conjuring up evil spirits, or demons, instead of angels. Prospero has the conjuring power, and he performs his operations through the spirit, Ariel, whom he conjures. Of the two branches, Magia and Cabala, set out in Agrippa's handbook of Renaissance magic, Prospero would seem to use mainly the Cabalistic conjuring magic, rather than the healing magic of Cerimon, or the profound natural magic which pervades *The Winter's Tale*.

It is inevitable and unavoidable in thinking of Prospero to bring in the name of John Dee, the great mathematical magus of whom Shakespeare must have known, the teacher of Philip Sidney, and deeply in the confidence of Queen Elizabeth I. In his famous preface to Euclid of 1570, which became the Bible of the rising generations of Elizabethan scientists and mathematicians, Dee sets out, following Agrippa, the theory of the three worlds, emphasizing, as does Agrippa, that through all the three worlds there runs, as the connecting link, number. If I may paraphrase what I have myself said elsewhere, Dee was in his own right a brilliant mathematician, and he related his study of number to the three worlds of the Cabalists. In the lower elemental world, he studied number as technology and applied science. In the celestial world his study of number was related to astrology and alchemy. And in the supercelestial world, Dee believed that he had found the secret of conjuring spirits by numerical computations in the tradition of Trithemius and Agrippa. Dee's type of science can be classified as 'Rosicrucian', using this word, as I have suggested that it can be used, to designate a stage in the history of the magico-scientific tradition which is intermediate between the Renaissance and the seventeenth century.

The commanding figure of Prospero represents precisely that Rosicrucian stage. We see him as a conjuror in the play, but the knowledge of such a Dee-like figure would have included mathematics developing into science, and particularly the science of navigation in which Dee was proficient and in which he instructed the great mariners of the Elizabethan age.

Now, if the first version of *The Tempest* appeared around 1611, the date at which Shakespeare chose to glorify a Dee-like magus is significant. For Dee had fallen into deep disfavour after his return from his mysterious continental mission in 1589, and he was completely cast off by James I after his accession. When the old Elizabethan magus appealed to James in 1604 for help in clearing his reputation from charges of conjuring devils, James would have nothing to do with him, in spite of his earnest protests that his art and science were good and virtuous and that he had no commerce with evil spirits. The old man to whose scientific learning the Elizabethan age had been so deeply indebted was disgraced in the reign of James and died in great poverty in 1608.

Seen in the context of these events, Shakespeare's presentation of a scientific magus in an extremely favourable light takes on a new significance. Prospero is far from diabolic; on the contrary, he is the virtuous opponent of evil sorcery, the noble and benevolent ruler who uses his magico-scientific knowledge for good ends. Prospero might be a vindication of Dee, a reply to the censure of James. And the contemporary scientists and mathematicians who were working in the Dee tradition were to be found, not in the circle of the King, but in that of his son, Prince Henry. The Prince was eager to build up a navy, as Dee used to advise Elizabeth to do, and he patronised and encouraged scientific experts like William Petty who built for him his great ship, the *Royal Prince*. Mathematicians and navigators of the Elizabethan age, Walter Raleigh and his friend Thomas Hariot, were imprisoned by James in the Tower, but were encouraged by Prince Henry. Thus here the line of inquiry which seeks to establish that Shakespeare's Last Plays belong in the atmosphere and aspirations surrounding the younger royal generation makes contact with this other line of inquiry into the magico-philosophical influences in the plays. Prospero, the magus as scientist, would belong with Prince Henry and his interests, and not with those of his unscientific father with his superstitious dread of magic.

Thus I am suggesting new contexts in which to see *The Tempest*. This play is not an isolated phenomenon but one of the Last Plays, and other Last Plays breathe the atmosphere of learned magic, the medical magic of Cerimon in *Pericles*, the deep Hermetic magic of *The Winter's Tale*, the incantatory singing of *Henry VIII*. All such magics connect with one another and belong to the late period of Renaissance magic. *The Tempest* would be one of the supreme expressions of that vitally important phase in the history of the European mind, the phase which borders on, and presages, the so-called scientific revolution of the seventeenth century. Prospero is so clearly the magus as scientist, able to operate scientifically within his world view, which includes areas of operation not recognized by science proper.

There is also, and this is very important, the element of moral reform in Prospero's outlook and aims, the element of Utopia, an essential feature of the scientific outlook of the Rosicrucian period, in which it was seen to be necessary to situate the developing magico-scientific knowledge within a reformed society, a society broadened by new moral insights to accept the broadening stream of knowledge. Prospero as scientist is also Prospero the moral reformer, bent on freeing the world of his island from evil influences.

Finally, we should see *The Tempest* in the context of *Henry VIII*, in which the reforming conciliatory themes of the Last Plays are presented through real historical personages. Henry VIII is seen as the monarch of the Tudor imperial reform, casting out vices in the person of Wolsey, and presenting a Reformation, originally Protestant, but in which the old hardness and intolerance has been done away in an atmosphere of love and reconciliation.

From these various lines of approach, *The Tempest* would now appear as the corner-stone of the total edifice of the Last Plays, the play presenting a philosophy which connects with all their themes and reflects a movement, or a phase, which can now be more or less identified among the currents of European intellectual and religious history. It is the Rosicrucian movement, which was to be given open expression in the manifestos published in Germany in 1614 and 1615.

In my book, *The Rosicrucian Enlightenment*, I have argued that this movement was connected with the currents stirring around the Elector Palatine and his wife. These were ostensibly Protestant, as befitted the head of the Union of German Protestant Princes, but drew on Paracelsist alchemy and other Hermetic influences for spiritual nourishment. The manifestos envisage a general moral and religious reform of the whole world. These strange hopes were to be extinguished in utter disaster, with the brief reign in Prague in 1619–20 of the 'Winter King and Queen' and the subsequent total defeat and exile of the unfortunate pair. Thus ended in ignominy and confusion the movement which had been building up around them in London, a movement very much weakened by the death of Prince Henry. Not only their own party in England but many in Europe had fixed their hopes on these two. And it would be wrong to say that all came to an end with the disaster, for the movement lived on, taking other forms, and leading eventually to important developments.

Shakespeare has often been derided for his absurd geographical error in giving a 'sea coast' to Bohemia in *The Winter's Tale*, but may his object have been to provide a setting for the frightful storm in which the infant Princess arrives in Bohemia? Shakespeare took the name 'Bohemia' from Greene's novel, *Pandosto*, the plot of which he was adapting. Yet there is something strangely prophetic in his choice of a story about Bohemia, foreshadowing the terrible tempest of the Thirty Years' War which would break out in Bohemia following the shipwreck of the Winter King and Queen. Is it possible that Shakespeare may have known more of what was going on in Bohemia than do critics of his geographical ignorance? Might he, for example, have had some contact with Michael Maier, Paracelsist doctor and Rosicrucian, who was moving between Prague and London in the early years of the century, linking movements in England with movements in Germany and Bohemia?

A main feature of the 'new approach' to Shakespeare's Last Plays presented here has been the argument that the hopes of a younger generation which the plays seem to express may allude to hopes in relation to a real historical generation, Prince Henry, and, after his death, Princess Elizabeth and her husband. Taken at its face value, this argument would amount to yet another 'topical allusion' detected in the plays, a type of investigation which has been very much used and abused. Even if the topical allusion to the younger royal generation is fairly substantially based, what does it amount to in relation to Shakespeare's genius, to the understanding of his mind and art? Topical-allusion hunting for its own sake is but an empty sport unless it can open doors to new approaches to matters more profound.

And it is precisely this, or so I believe, that this topical allusion can do. The other new approach attempted has been to the thought of the Last Plays, to the philosophy of nature with religious and reforming undercurrents, with association with scientific movements of the kind propagated by John Dee, with spiritual and mental enlightenment. And it is just such a movement as this which seems to have been associated in German circles with the Elector Palatine and with his disastrous Bohemian enterprise.

The German Rosicrucian movement was certainly not newly invented in connection with the Elector Palatine and his wife. It was something already in existence with which they, or the movement associated with them, became somehow involved. There are various influences from England on the movement which I have tried to bring out in my book, influences from Philip Sidney's mission to Germany and to the imperial court, influences from visits of the

Knights of the Garter, influences from John Dee's sojourn in Bohemia. The second Rosicrucian manifesto of 1615 has included in it a discourse on secret philosophy which is based on Dee's *Monas hieroglyphica*. The works of the Englishman, Robert Fludd, a leading exponent of Rosicrucian philosophy, were published at Oppenheim, a town in the territory of the Elector Palatine. And, most curious of all from the theatrical point of view, there appears to have been an influence of English actors, or of plays acted by travelling English actors in Germany, on the ideas and modes of expression of the Rosicrucian publications.

The man known to be behind the movement, Johann Valentin Andreae, states in his autobiography that in his youth, around 1604, he wrote plays in imitation of English comedians, and at about the same time he wrote the first version of his strange work, *The Chemical Wedding of Christian Rosencreutz*, first published, in German, in 1616. This is a mystical romance reflecting ceremonial orders of chivalry in a setting which I believe I have identified as the castle and gardens of the Elector Palatine at Heidelberg, reflecting his court there and the presence in it of his English wife, the Princess Elizabeth. Andreae's style in all his writings is dramatic, infused with theatrical influences. The story of Christian Rosencruetz and his Order, told in the manifestos (which were not actually written by Andreae though inspired by him), is said to be a fiction or a play. And the mysterious doings in the castle grounds in *The Chemical Wedding* include a play, the plot of which is given as follows (I quote from the résumé of it in my book):

> On the sea-shore, an old king found an infant in a chest washed up by the waves: an accompanying letter explained that the King of the Moors had seized the child's country. In the following acts, The Moor appeared and captured the infant, now grown into a young woman. She was rescued by the old king's son and betrothed to him, but fell again into the Moor's power. She was finally rescued again but a very wicked priest had to be got out of the way. . . . When his power was broken the wedding could take place. Bride and bridegroom appeared in great splendour and all joined in a Song of Love:
>
> This time full of love
> Does our joy much approve. . . .

The plot reminds one of the plots of Last Plays, with shipwrecked infants who grow up to have adventures in which evil influences are surmounted, stories reflecting a passage of time from an older generation to a younger, and ending in general love and reconciliation. And, if I am right in my suggestions, this play described in *The Chemical Wedding* is supposed to be enacted in a setting reflecting the court of the Elector Palatine and the Princess Elizabeth at Heidelberg. It is as though Shakespearean dramatic influences in London at the time of their wedding were being reflected back to them through a mystical haze. The extremely simple plot of the comedy described in *The Chemical Wedding* is punctuated by Biblical allusions, as though the fiction had some reference to the religious problems of the day.

This is only one example of the curious reflections of plays, perhaps of plays staged by English players in Germany, in the German Rosicrucian literature. Was there some connection between players and Rosicrucian ideas? Ought we to look for light on Shakespeare in these directions? Did the Last Plays deliver a message the meaning of which we have lost? Are the connections between the Last Plays and the new generation of Prince Henry and his sister much more than topical allusions in the ordinary sense? Might they introduce us to ways of unravelling Shakespeare's position in the religious, intellectual, magical, political, theatrical movements of his time? Or, more than that, might they help us to penetrate to Shakespeare's inner religious experiences?

A French writer who has made a study of the Rosicrucian literature in relation to Shakespeare thinks that *The Chemical Wedding* reflects rituals of initiation through enaction of the mystery of death. He believes that some of Shakespeare's plays – he mentions particularly Imogen's death-like sleep and resurrection in *Cymbeline* – reflect such experiences, conveyed through esoteric allusion in the imagery. He sees influences of 'spiritual alchemy' in the imagery of *Cymbeline*. The Rosicrucian method of using the play or the fiction as the vehicle through which to indicate an esoteric meaning would also be Shakespeare's method. I mention Arnold's book here not because I think it reliable as a whole, or in detail (it is not), but because the general drift of his comparative study of Rosicrucian literature and of Shakespeare may not be altogether wide of the mark.

Shakespeare died in 1616 and so did not live to hear the news of the events of 1620, the defeat at the Battle of the White Mountain, the flight of the Winter King and Queen of Bohemia, the outbreak of the Thirty Years' War. Perhaps that was the terrible storm which he prophetically dreaded.

It is strange that Shakespearean scholarship seems to have paid so much more attention to the biographical, the literary, or the critical aspects of its vast subject than to investigating Shakespeare's work in relation to the thought movements of his age. It is perhaps time that it should break out of the limits it has imposed on itself and begin to ask new questions. Even very familiar topics might appear in a new light if approached from new angles. I will give one example.

In 1623, Shakespeare's fellow-actors published that famous volume, the First Folio edition of his plays. *The Tempest* is the first play in the volume, which is dedicated to William Herbert, Earl of Pembroke, and his brother. We all know how this dedication has been worn threadbare by eager detectives pursuing clues to Shakespeare's personal history, but other questions might be asked about the First Folio. What was the attitude of its dedicatees to events and movements of the times? Pembroke and his brother had taken a conspicuous part in urging most strongly the support of the King and Queen of Bohemia in the great crisis of their lives, a support which was not forthcoming from James I. And one might also take into account the fact that, after their defeat and the collapse of their movement, violent propaganda was made against imaginary 'Rosicrucians' as diabolical 'conjurors'. The scare about Rosicrucians was in full swing in Paris in 1623, the year in which Heminges and Condell fearlessly placed *The Tempest* in the forefront of their collection of Shakespeare's plays. I suggest that inquiries along these lines about the First Folio and its dedicatees might be rewarding, because they might be historically related to contemporary events and movements.

Trevor R. Griffiths Caliban on the Stage (1983)

At the end of the nineteenth century, two major actors played the part of Caliban in ways which made explicit many of the various strands of interpretation we have examined thus far. F. R. Benson and Beerbohm Tree each wielded tremendous influence but in very different contexts: Benson, by reason of his tireless touring for fifty years, left his impression on generations of actors and audiences throughout Britain, whereas Tree captured the fashionable and influential London audience. Benson first played Caliban in the 1890s and, although he was not (as he believed) the first actor 'to bring out his responsive devotion to music, songs and sweet airs that give delight and hurt not', he was the first consciously to play the part 'as a sort of missing link'. Constance Benson, who was not altogether impressed by the performance, records that Benson took his missing-link conception seriously enough to spend 'many hours watching monkeys and baboons in the zoo, in order to get the movements in keeping with his "make-up"'. Attired in a 'curious costume', which his wife all too accurately described as 'half monkey, half coco-nut', the future knight would swarm up trees, hang head down from branches and gibber at Trinculo. His devotion to animal realism extended to carrying a real fish in his mouth, an almost Stanislavskian ploy which caused considerable distress to both Benson and his casts when the property master forgot to change it often enough.

Benson was to admit later that he probably carried this athleticism as Caliban to extremes, and it certainly tended to overshadow the other elements in his performance when he first essayed the part at Stratford in 1891. The *Illustrated Sporting and Dramatic News* (2 May) was moved to contrast Shakespeare's Caliban with Benson's:

> Shakespeare's Caliban is a monster, but human. The product of superstition and ignorance, he is surly, brutal, cunning, servile, lustful and vindictively cruel. The best use to which he can put the language he has been taught is the uttering of horrible curses against his teacher, whom he at once fears and hates. His chief pleasure is eating, and he is ready to sell his soul for drink to Stephano and be his slave for ever if he will kill Prospero and give

him Miranda. Mr Benson's Caliban is a comic and amusing one; it provoked peal after peal of merry laughter. He was a kind of man-monkey performing various acrobatic feats, and passing through a series of grotesque antics, grimacing and gesticulating, grinning and chattering and making a series of discordant, inarticulate noises expressive of delight, or, when the master showed his whip, of mingling rage and terror, slavishly licking the dust from the footsteps of the drunken butler as he implores him to be his god.

However much one may take issue with this picture of Shakespeare's Caliban, it is clear that, despite Benson's own later claim to have done justice to the responsive side of Caliban, the initial critical response to his portrayal was shaped by his athletic antics. A 'Lady Visitor', writing in the Stratford *Herald* (1 May) found Benson's Caliban inferior to Cathcart's in Charles Calvert's Manchester revival. She felt that Benson saw him as 'not even on a level with the beasts' and despite 'the evidence of much careful study and thought' she was moved to ask

what purpose is served by such an impersonation? Is it artistic? Is it not straining the text to its utmost limits of coarseness, to say the least of it? And, if we might venture to point out, there *are* better things even in the vile and hateful slave Caliban, as Shakespeare gives him to us, than Mr Benson ever hinted at. It is possible from time to time to feel pity mix with our loathing for the ill-used, down-trodden wretch, who, having had his peaceful island wrested from him, is wantonly tortured and tormented for not obeying the despot, who has despoiled him of all his possessions with alacrity and cheerfulness.... In Mr Cathcart's Caliban we had this subtle discrimination. There was no need of apish jabberings, nor display of athletic powers; certainly no attempt to set before the audience, from a Darwinian point of view, a hideous and degraded, and after all, only hypothetical phase of evolution.

In the same journal a correspondent under the name of 'Druid' also objected to Benson's conception of the character: 'His idea seemed that of a man monkey or monkey man; mine was that of a monster of vice and ignorance of the human kind, distorted and deformed not in body only, but in mind and heart.' In all these judgements, and in the Bensons' own comments, there is no sense of an ideological framework underlying the interpretation. The idea of Caliban as man-monkey or missing link is handled perfectly neutrally, although the 'Lady Visitor' in her charitable feelings for Caliban's sufferings at the hands of the despotic Prospero shows some inkling of an understanding of the ramifications of the play.

When Benson offered his *Tempest* production at the Lyceum in London in 1900, the first professional performance in the capital for twenty-five years, his performance once again elicited baffled admiration for its athleticism. Gordon Crosse, for example, commented in his diary only on the more technical aspects of Benson's performance in 1900:

Caliban is on the whole one of *Mr Benson*'s good parts. It gives him a chance of displaying his athletic propensities in monkey like feats of climbing etc, without marring the effect; and he plays it with sincerity as well as with realism. His get-up was good, but his face should have been coloured to match: a pink and white countenance looking out from all that hairiness was inappropriate. In the comic scenes he played artistically, and was amusing without clowning.

In his published collections, however, Crosse's judgement extended to Benson's conception of the part: 'It added to the realism of his missing-link Caliban that he could clamber nimbly up a tree and hang head downwards from a branch, chattering with rage at Prospero.' This judgement is an amalgamation of his reactions to the 1900 performance and to the one he saw at the King's, Hammersmith, in 1924, when he wrote in his diary: 'His own Caliban was as monkey-like as ever; a missing link between the ape and the lowest savage.'

As far as I have been able to discover, Crosse was typical in not developing his description of Benson's Caliban beyond this categorization. Often critics made references to Benson's Caliban in terms which might have led to further comment on the wider implications of his interpretation, but the point is never fully developed. The *Era* (7 April 1900), for example, used terms like 'simian', 'submission', and 'rebellious' and another journal discussed Benson's make-up as 'a link in the chain between "a wild man of the woods" and an orang-outang', but that is as far as it goes. Similarly the critics were content to describe rather than analyse J. H. Leigh's 1903 Caliban, although the terms they used emphasized familiar aspects of the character. The *Daily Telegraph* (27 October), for example, described it as 'that strange character, Caliban, in which the poet seems to have anticipated Darwin's missing link' and the *Era* (31 October) noted that Leigh emphasized the 'moral, rather than the physical, ugliness of the creature' and presented him as 'more of a man and less of a four-footed animal than usual' (p. 14). Ultimately, as with Darwinism itself, audiences found in Benson's and Leigh's Calibans reflections of their own prejudices. Two points, however, are inescapable: Benson's Caliban was deliberately based on monkeys, making Caliban, the dispossessed native, an ape as well as a sympathetic character; and it was seen by vast numbers over a very lengthy period all over the British Isles, thus fixing an interpretation of Caliban for several generations of actors and audiences.

It is one of the ironies of Benson's work that, however widely influential it may have been elsewhere, it was seldom seen in London and so received much less press coverage than was accorded to a fashionable metropolitan manager like Beerbohm Tree. Tree was an adept publicist and his attention to the press ensured that there would be lengthy and detailed accounts of his productions in the newspapers. These accounts and the souvenir text of Tree's version show that his production represented a very full flowering of many nineteenth-century approaches to Caliban. Indeed, discussion of the role began before the production even opened. In a letter to the *Referee* (4 September 1904), Walter Parke asked the question: 'What was Caliban like?' His answer more than encompassed the whole gallery of nineteenth-century analogues: downtrodden peasants, savages, monkeys, and Saxon serfs:

> Shakespeare describes him merely as 'a savage and deformed slave', which does not imply that he was any more unearthly or uncouth than some of the actual 'natives' whose portraits appear in 'The Living Races of Mankind'. Prospero calls him 'abhorred slave' and, 'a freckled whelp, hag-born', and this seems to indicate that Caliban did not belong to any of the darker races, whose complexions are proof against freckles. A white savage is a prodigy in keeping with the wonders of Prospero's 'Enchanted Isle'.
>
> But Caliban on the stage is frequently an outrageously grotesque being with brick dust complexion, rampant elf-locks, distorted features, teeth like tusks, and a habit of gibbering, howling and grovelling, with ape-like attitudes and gestures. In some illustrations there is a suggestion of scaly limbs and webbed feet, as if he were an amphibious monster of the deep.
>
> Surely this is not a correct portrait, for Caliban, however debased, is still something above the brutes. He has human feelings, and words to express them, and there are moments when he can even win our sympathy. His expressions of sullen malignity and revengeful discontent might have been used by an oppressed Saxon serf in the time of the Normans, or could, perhaps, be heard even in the present day in countries where the peasants are downtrodden, ignorant and superstitious.

Parke's letter exemplifies the ease with which discussions of Caliban could move freely from racial to class ideas, and serves as a further reminder of the character's long association with both racial and class typifications.

Tree's *Tempest* was, in fact, organized round his own performance of Caliban and culminated in a pro-Imperial final tableau. Two weeks before the production even opened, the *Era* (27 August) was informing its readers that Tree 'realises that the "savage and deformed slave" is not a comic character and will enact it accordingly' (p. 14). In practice this meant that Tree's customary massive reorderings and massagings of Shakespeare established Caliban as the star of the show, eating fish, cracking oysters, catching flies, and regarding Ferdinand as a rival in his continued aspirations to Miranda.

The Imperial overtones were most marked in the last act. The *Era* (17 September) described the poetic effect of 'the uncanny figure of Caliban seated on a rock and silhouetted against an azure sky watching the departing vessel sailing away from the enchanted shores sped by auspicious gales' (p. 17); but Tree's own published acting arrangement was much more specific, and clearly indicates that Caliban regrets being deprived of the human companions who have 'gladdened and saddened his island home, and taught him to "seek for grace"'. He turns 'sadly' in the direction of the ship, stretches out his arms to it 'in mute despair' and, as night falls, he is left 'on the lonely rock' as 'a king once more'. The implications of all this are quite clear: Caliban is lost without the civilizing influence exerted upon him by Prospero and his companions; the islander needs the Europeans, the slave needs the master as much as the master needed the slave. Although Benson's 'missing-link' Caliban was political in the sense that analogies had been drawn between 'underdeveloped natives' and the missing link in non-theatrical contexts, Tree expanded the political dimensions of his Caliban, who was clearly the ignorant native to whom the colonist Prospero had brought an enlightenment which he had spurned before learning its true value.

The analogy was not lost on the contemporary audience, but it was somewhat controversial. Indeed, W. T. Stead, visiting his first play at the age of fifty-five, was struck by so many analogies that it is impossible to do them all justice. Nevertheless, several of them are particularly relevant to the current discussions. Under the heading, 'What About Rhodesia?' Stead raised some central questions of Imperialism:

When the man-monster, brutalised by long continued torture, begins, 'This island's mine, by Sycorax my mother, which thou takest from me', we have the whole case of the aboriginal against aggressive civilisation dramatised before us. I confess I felt a sting of conscience – vicariously suffered for my Rhodesian friends, notably Dr Jameson – when Caliban proceeded to unfold a similar case to that of the Matebele. It might have been the double of old King Lobengula rehearsing the blandishments which led to his doom: 'When thou camest first / Thou strok'dst me, and mad'st much of me; would'st give me' – all that was promised by the Chartered Company to secure the charter. Who could help sympathising with his outburst after recollecting how he had helped the newcomer? (pp. 364–5)

Under the heading 'The Instinct of Paternity' Stead remarks that Caliban's desire to people the isle with Calibans implies 'more of a craving for paternity than the satisfaction of a brute instinct' and has some sternly eugenic reflections: 'Poor Caliban! Ferdinand and Miranda nowadays would have one child, or perhaps two, leaving the task of perpetuating the race almost entirely to Caliban. It is he who fills the isle with progeny. The cultured, the wealthy and refined shrink from the duty of replenishing the earth.' On the same tack, Caliban's profiting from language only to curse is 'a result that not unseldom follows our educating of the common people even in the twentieth century' (p. 365). Ignoring the Calibanization of the theatre, latter-day parables of the fall, and Stead's worries about the raising of the age of consent after his successful campaign, we come to 'Contemporary History in Parable', 'Trinculo-Rosebery', 'Stephano-Chamberlain', 'Mafeking Night', and 'The Khaki Election of 1900'. Out of Tree's interpretation, Stead wrests one which seems to run counter to the emotional appeal of the final tableau. To Stead, Caliban is 'the representative of the democracy, robbed of its rightful inheritance, punished without end for an attempted crime, endowed with just enough education to curse its master, and abandoned by him to a condition of brutish ignorance and hopeless slavery' (p. 365). Rosebery (Trinculo) shelters from the storm under Caliban's gaberdine and 'there for a time they lie. Trinculo-Rosebery with Caliban-Democracy, head to feet – even as it was'. Stephano is 'the incarnate representative of Jingo Toryism' carrying 'the bark-made flagon – I looked to see if it was labelled the *Daily Mail* or *Daily Telegraph* – full of the heady wine of Jingoism!' (p. 366).

Allegory is now in full spate and Caliban, Lobengula only a page before, is now the British electorate deluded by the politicians into attacking the Boers. Stead appears to be unaware of the inherent contradictions of the two analyses:

Then we see the pitiful tragedy of the Jingo fever and the South African War. Both political parties combine to pass the bottle to the poor monster, but even while assisting at the process Trinculo, after Lord Rosebery's fashion, cannot resist a sneer at the shallow wits of the half-witted monster who swallows with trusting simplicity the absurd stories and the heady liquor of his 'brave god'. Nevertheless, despite the Roseberian gibes and sneers, the poor, scurvy monster kisses the foot of the Jingo Party, and finally the scene ends with a deliriously drunken dance, in which Caliban-Democracy, supported by Trinculo-Rosebery and Stephano-Chamberlain, howl in maudlin chorus: ' 'Ban, 'Ban, Ca-Caliban / Has a new master – Get a new man.' As the curtain fell amid the roads of laughter, I remembered I had seen it all before on a much larger scale. It was Mafeking night over again.

From this it is but a short step to the Khaki Election of 1900:

After Mafeking we have a still further development of the close parallel. Caliban-Demos being now well drunk with Jingo wine takes the lead. Just as Mr Chamberlain himself shrank with reluctance from the policy of farm burning and concentration camps, which was nevertheless pressed on ruthlessly by a populace maddened by its daily drench of Jingo journalism, so Caliban incites his drunken god Stephano to murderous exploits. 'Monster', says the sailor sententiously, 'I will kill this man; his daughter and I will be king and queen' – and in that saying I seemed to hear the decision proclaimed to annex the Boer Republics!

In the next scene, in which the worthy trio appear, we have the true and faithful presentment of the Khaki Election of 1900, in which the drunken Caliban, despite the scoffing of Trinculo, in humbly abject fashion licks the shoe of Stephano. (p. 366)

Stead's was the most fully allegorical reading of Tree's production and he certainly turned some aspects of it on its head, but he was responding to a quite obvious invitation from the production's treatment of Caliban. All Stead's allegorizing was too much for the *Era* (22 October 1904), which took the resolutely pragmatic line one might expect from the theatrical tradepaper, only to prove equally susceptible to the allegorical tendency which characterizes so much *Tempest* criticism of all kinds:

It would have been just as easy to see an equivalent of Caliban in the Boer nation, and take Prospero as fore-shadowing Lord MILNER, and Ariel as a composite of Lord ROBERTS, Lord KITCHENER, and the British Army.

Caliban was undoubtedly in possession of the island when Prospero, the 'medicine man', arrived as an emigrant; so were the Boers. To put it mildly, he was somewhat rude and primitive in his ideas; so, admittedly were the Boers. Prospero tried giving him personal independence, but he behaved so badly that his republican arrangements had to be extinguished; thus it was with the Boers. And Mr STEAD – who, of course, believes that eventually we shall be outnumbered by his friends in the Transvaal, and ejected from South Africa – may complacently complete the parallel by pointing to Prospero's exist from the isle after burning his books and breaking his rod. How explicit a prophet SHAKESPEARE was may be proved by Caliban's straightforwardly expressed intention to 'people the isle with Calibans' – evidently a *clairvoyant* allusion to the extinction of the British from South Africa by the sheer force of multiplication of the Dutch. (p. 21)

In all of the *Era*'s comments there is, of course, no mention of any other inhabitants of South Africa but, having disposed to its own satisfaction of Stead's case, the *Era* was moved, without preliminaries, to declare that 'analysed, Caliban is much nearer to a modern decadent Frenchman than he is to the chimpanzee or the Wild Man of the Woods'. One allegorical reading disposed of and another enemy of the Empire sniped at, the *Era* is safe to demolish any associations of Caliban with 'the common herd'. Such direct political controversy is unusual, but after Benson's and Tree's peformances Caliban was established as a barometer of attitudes to imperialism and democracy, if not, *pace* Stead, of attitudes to eugenics or the raising of the age of consent.

During and after the First World War, Caliban continued to be treated along the lines established at the turn of the century. Thus we find Ben Greet's Old Vic programme for 19 November 1917 describing Caliban as 'a solitary savage – a member of an almost prehistoric race with witches as ancestors', neatly encapsulating the Darwinian idea that contemporary 'savage' races exemplified the prehistory of modern civilized man. At the same time there was a swing towards a costuming which, unlike Tree's or Benson's, stressed the fishy side of Caliban. For example, Murray Carrington, a former member of Benson's company, played the role at Stratford in 1919 as 'half-seal, half-man' (*Stage*, 14 August) and George Foss, who directed the play at the Old Vic in 1918, believed that Caliban should be 'slow moving and walrus-like'. Although Foss's production was virtually ruined by war-time difficulties, he was able to develop his analysis of Caliban at some length in his book, *What the Author Meant* (London, 1932). Curiously, his 'walrus-like' description of Caliban's appearance was matched with an analysis of his character which was more generally associated with a missing-link or ape-like appearance:

> The part typifies Demos – just one degree above the beasts, of immense strength but with brutalised, degrading passions that had not been eradicated or refined by education, and with no human sympathies. ... On several occasions throughout the ages Caliban has got free for a little time and indulged in a senseless orgy of blood and destruction. He has 'made a hell of earth' until some strong hand has forced him into subjection again. (p. 40)

With these views it is not surprising that Foss suggests that 'Prospero typifies paternal wise government' (p. 41), and once again we can see how closely linked are ideas of democracy, family, and colonial government. As Greta Jones has remarked, the Victorians in describing subordination 'took much of their imagery from an area where subordination was legitimised – that of the family'. They 'talked in terms of dependence, of development, of benevolent and paternal supervision and of the "child" or the childlike qualities of the "primitive" peoples' (p. 144). Similarly, Foss's Prospero was both the head of a family and a governor doing his best to keep an unruly population in check.

Generally we find that the missing-link/native interpretation was the norm against which the Calibans of the twenties were judged. Sometimes the judgement was overt, as in the case of one journal's reaction to Russell Thorndike's 1919 Old Vic Caliban which, 'though hideous enough to have been studied from the new gorilla at the Zoo, managed to combine the grossness with flashes of almost profound intelligence, just in the way that one feels Shakespeare meant his inspired aboriginal to do'. This production clearly encouraged such a reaction with its concluding tableau of the cast departing 'leaving Caliban to resume his erstwhile savage existence, a lonely and solitary figure' (*Era*, 15 October 1919, p. 6). Sometimes the norm was used to castigate an aberrant actor like Louis Calvert, whose 1921 Caliban in Viola Tree's Aldwych production ('a simple figure like a Neapolitan lazzarone in skins') the *Athenaeum* (11 February) compared unfavourably with Beerbohm Tree's 'plaintive, savage child with the ear for music'. Sometimes it was so deeply engrained as to be almost invisible, as when the *Era* (9 February), reviewing the Aldwych production, described Caliban as a 'tragic blend of brutishness and intelligence' which often 'evoked our pity' (p. 8).

The continued association of the ideas of Caliban as a missing link, as a 'native', and as a gorilla is well exemplified by the *Daily Herald*'s reaction to Robert Atkins's 1921 Old Vic Caliban: 'Less of a beast and more of a savage than is customary, labouring for his words, pawing the air in brutish impotence, he is a Caliban to be remembered next century. No one who has seen it will ever forget the unpent, tempestuous lust for liberty' revealed in his farewell to Prospero and singing of his song (21 February). Similarly, Gordon Crosse thought that Atkins was superlative in showing 'the malevolent brute nature with the dim half-formed human intellect just breaking through'. By the 1924 Old Vic production, however, Atkins's conception was more familiar, and the *Observer* (10 February) objected that 'Caliban began to impinge upon my imagination less as a strange sea-fish than as an only too engrossingly natural gorilla. His was a truly marvellous make-up, a poignantly realistic study of the ape turned human, too close a shot at the missing link'.

Although this critical reaction against missing-link make-ups continued, it did not extend to a rejection of the connotations of such make-ups. Thus in 1926, when there were two *Tempest* productions in London and one at Stratford, we find three different approaches to the part of Caliban. Henry Baynton's Caliban for Robert Courtneidge's company was fishy and monstrous, Randle Ayrton's was beastlike and repulsive at Stratford, and Baliol Holloway's was missing link with fishy and democratic overtones at the Old Vic. Baynton followed Murray Carrington's lines, offering a fishy rather than a gorilla-like monster. St John Ervine praised his effort 'to interpret his author's intentions' by giving Caliban 'a fish-like body, with green scales and a most dejected green face', but objected to the lack of 'mind'. The *Era* (13 January) shared this view; even if the fish costume was rather too clean, it was 'nearer the mark than the shaggy bear costume in which the moon-calf sometimes appears', but the real problem was that, although Baynton 'roared with great spirit' and 'tried to get the monstrous character by breaking up all the lines into pieces', 'he was never able to suggest that his Caliban had ever come under the spell of the island, that he had any realisation of anything greater than the drunken Stephano' (p. 1). At Stratford, Randle Ayrton also tried to convey the beastlike nature of the character by mangling his blank verse with 'staccato and broken utterance' and the result was 'amply repulsive and beast-like in this strange half-man, half-animal creation' (Stratford *Herald*, 20 August). In both these interpretations the monster predominated to the detriment of the overall complexity of the character.

At the Old Vic, however, the contrast between Baliol Holloway's make-up and his acting permitted a more subtle reading. He adopted a particularly gruesome make-up, with an ape's face, 'but more hideous, with hidden, deadly eyes, a monstrous flat nose, long, thick protruding lips, and two prongs of teeth projecting', long 'steel' nails on each finger and toe, and a 'sickly yellowish green' skin covered with long hair to provide the terrifying side of Caliban. In contrast to all this, he used restraint in his acting and thereby 'conveyed more of the symbolical meaning of Caliban'. Holloway apparently saw this 'symbolical meaning' in terms of Caliban's status as an oppressed minority, assuring one interviewer that 'Caliban comes in for a good deal of sympathy from the modern audience' and that 'Caliban was justified in his grudge' against Prospero. The problem with playing against costuming in this way is that the contrast may not be perceived as useful and creative. St John Ervine, for example, felt that Holloway's costume, 'a mixture of hog and gorilla', denied the sensitivity of his playing the part as 'a creature aspiring to be a man', 'one who looks up from his slime and sees the stars'. Ervine also favoured the view that Caliban represented 'the embodied crowd', an opinion which is not unsurprising in the year of the General Strike. When Holloway repeated the role, at Stratford in 1934, his monstrous appearance continued to dominate critical responses, although *The Times* (17 April) thought that he 'kept the offending animal in Caliban vigorously alive while interfusing with its grossness the tragic yearning for humanity without which the monster is maligned'.

In general, however, despite the relative frequency of comments about Prospero's mistreatment of Caliban, there was no developed approach to the colonial subtext in performance or in criticism during the inter-war period. The final large-scale pre-war *Tempest* exemplifies this situation very well. Tyrone Guthrie's 1934 Old Vic *Tempest* was given major press coverage because of the presence in the cast of Charles Laughton as Prospero and Elsa Lanchester as Ariel, but Caliban did not bulk large in the critics' responses to the production, and the more extended discussions of Caliban's 'meaning' are to be found in weekly or monthly journals rather than in daily newspapers.

Roger Livesey's scaly and hairy Caliban, perhaps over-liberally covered in black grease-paint, was generally regarded as bringing out both Caliban's pathos and his monstrosity. Peter Fleming extended this to argue that Livesey's 'distinctly aboriginal make-up underlined the parable of Civilization and the Savage which Shakespeare has here prophetically presented' (*Spectator*, 12 January 1934). Similarly Ivor Brown pursued a line that was to become familiar in his reviews of subsequent productions: 'Caliban should be the oppressed aboriginal as well as the lecherous monster, a case for the radical politician's sympathy as well as for Prospero's punishment' (*Observer*, 14 January). Prince Nicolas Galitzine also developed a political insight from the play, objecting to Livesey's Caliban helping with the comedy instead of interpreting 'the message of humanity's suffering, blindness and progress that is so clearly at the disposal of its sub-human prototype' (*Saturday Review*, 20 January). Livesey appears to have been the first Caliban to have actually blacked up, but this excited virtually no critical comment, except for complaints that the black came off on Trinculo and Stephano. George Warrington's remark that one way of staging the *Tempest* was in 'a pantomime-set for "Robinson Crusoe" complete with Caliban's footprints' (*Country Life*, 20 January) may have been inspired by Livesey's costuming and indicates the possibility, at that time, of an equation of Caliban with a black character from another colonial fiction.

Throughout the thirties and forties the broad pattern of incidental references to simian and missing-link Calibans, occasionally expanded to a couple of lines, remained much the same: James Dale 'touchingly suggested the monstrous reaching up to the human' at Stratford in 1938; Jack Hawkins was 'an unregenerate Darwinian orang-outang' at the Old Vic in 1940; and Baliol Holloway, 'getting uglier' was 'still a child-like savage' at Stratford in 1941 and 1942. Among the critics, Ivor Brown was the most consistent propagator of the colonial Caliban, moving on from his analysis of Livesey's performance to see Holloway as a 'dispossessed aboriginal' at Stratford in 1934, Bernard Miles minimizing 'the appeal to sympathy for an oppressed aboriginal' at the Mermaid in 1951, and Michael Hordern as 'a most human and even poignant representative of the Backward and Underprivileged Peoples' at Stratford in 1952.

There were few productions of *The Tempest* in the fifties and sixties. At Stratford, after productions in 1946–47 and 1951–52, there was a gap until 1957 and further longer gaps between the subsequent productions in 1963, 1970, 1974, and 1978. At the Old Vic, the first post-war production was in 1954, the second in 1962, and the third, by the National Theatre, not until 1974. The majority of such productions as there were yielded little in the way of colonial insight until Jonathan Miller's 1970 Mermaid revival, which offered a full-scale colonial analysis. The status quo before Miller's production is well exemplified by the reaction to Oliver Neville's generally undistinguished 1962 Old Vic revival. Only Roger Gellert commented on Caliban in imperial terms: 'Mr Selway looked genuinely and quite solemnly aboriginal, with the wild dignity that this implies. One was all the more inclined to join him in cursing the White Settler' (*New Statesman*, 8 June). This solitary comment is, perhaps, surprising in that the programme made the point that 'the island does not in fact belong to Prospero, but to the man monster Caliban, both by inheritance and by right, for it is Caliban who "knows the best springs", "how to snare the nimble marmoset", and "where to dig for pig-nuts"'. It appears that the production failed to convey the point with enough vigour to elicit a critical-response. In the case of the 1963 production at Stratford the colonial references were again submerged, in this instance beneath the directors' attempts to stress what they saw as the play's deliberate irresolution. This innovatory conception was highly controversial and dominated critical response to the production, so that a programme note which stressed that 'the Elizabethans, like ourselves, had a prickly conscience about the ethics of their colonial enterprise' elicited only the usual incidental use of words like simian or aborigine to describe Roy Dotrice's Caliban, 'black and almost naked, with a forehead as low as that of the Java man' (*The Times*, 3 April 1963).

So, during the great period of British withdrawal from Empire there were few productions of *The Tempest*, and the play's colonial themes were largely uncanvassed. In the early sixties, however, three sociological studies were published in which the Prospero–Caliban relationship was taken as a paradigm of Imperialism. In George Lamming's *The Pleasures of Exile* (1960), Prospero was the colonist and Caliban the West Indian who has an alien language and culture imposed on him. Philip Mason actually took the magician into the title of his analysis, *Prospero's Magic: Some Thoughts on Class and Race* (1962), in which both Ariel and Caliban are seen as black nationalists, with Caliban the more extreme. Mason's book, which is also concerned with the interchangeability of the vocabulary of class and race, was a response to O. Mannoni's *Prospero and Caliban: The Psychology of Colonization* which, however, was not published in English translation until 1964. Mannoni, like Mason and Lamming, used an analogy between Caliban and the natives, and Prospero and the colonists, in his study of the French in Madagascar.

It was partly under the influence of Mannoni's study that Jonathan Miller chose to give serious consideration to the colonial dimension in his 1970 revival of *The Tempest.* Perhaps the new willingness to present the colonial dimension arose from a sense that it was now feasible to approach the colonial elements more dispassionately than had been possible during the retreat from Empire. Miller's production was certainly the most overtly colonial since Tree's, although the analysis of colonialism was far removed from its predecessor's. Apart from Mannoni, Miller's decision to treat the play in terms of colonialism was influenced by his own reading of accounts of the Elizabethan voyages of exploration and a production of Lowell's *The Old Glory*, with its long account of Puritan sailors making Indians drunk. In the programme, which included a lengthy extract from Mannoni, Caliban was without his traditional description as 'a savage and deformed slave' but Ariel was still 'an airy spirit'. In the production, Ariel and Caliban, played for the first time by black actors (Norman Beaton and Rudolph Walker), became examples of two opposing ways in which native black populations responded to the Europeans. Ariel was the accomplished servant who learnt European ways and literally picked up Prospero's broken wand at the end, dressing in European breeches but carrying a Kenyatta flywhisk, whilst Caliban was a detribalized field hand, with faint memories of matrilineal gods, who got drunk with Trinculo and Stephano (whom Miller likened to sergeants getting off the boat at Port Said). The frippery became trade goods and the goddesses were black sopranos.

In general, the critical reaction was extremely favourable to Miller's conception, although the *Financial Times*, 16 June, dismissed the theory on the grounds that 'colonialism, the dominion of one race (as opposed to one nation) over another, is something that Shakespeare had never heard of' and that 'it isn't possible to set any party unequivocally in the position of colonialist or of subject'. Other critics, however, found no difficulty in relating Miller's production specifically to the Bermuda wreck and generally to the subsequent history of colonialism:

Alonso and his courtiers ... are half-bewildered, half-enraptured by an island which seems to them, as the Bermudas seemed to Shakespeare's contemporaries, 'a most prodigious and enchanted place'; and they are almost immediately discontented. They scarcely listen to the old courtier, Gonzalo's, proposals for founding an ideal commonwealth; no sooner have they grasped the possibilities of this magical new world, than they fall – much as the 'Sea Venture's' company did – to plotting murder.

It will be hard after Mr Miller's production, ever again to see *The Tempest* as the fairytale to which we are accustomed – or indeed to see it in any other terms than as Shakespeare's account, prosaic and prophetic, of the impact of the Old World on the New: a confrontation which, beginning in amazed delight, moves so swiftly to drawn swords and 'bloody thoughts' that the opening storm seems only a prelude in a minor key to the 'tempest of dissension' that sweeps Prospero's island. (Hilary Spurling, *Spectator*, 27 June)

As this response (which was much more typical than the *Financial Times*'s) suggests, it is not necessary for an investigation of the colonizing impulse to set up unequivocal colonists and colonized, each acting in accordance with one fixed approach, and, moreover, it is surely desirable that within a complex dramatic structure different characters should manifest different aspects of a central theme. Indeed one of the strengths of Miller's colonial interpretation lay in the way that it embraced all the characters. Thus the often criticized scenes between Caliban, Stephano, and Trinculo were 'transformed from irrelevant low comedy into another expression of the main theme' (*Plays and Players*, 17 August 1970, p. 29). Miranda fitted into the theme by showing 'a mind awakening to many things new and strange' (*Stage*, 18 June) and the *Observer* discovered 'a terrible new irony' in Miranda's 'welcome to the master race'. Perhaps most significantly, the relationship between Caliban and Ariel gained new associations in Miller's interpretation and, as with the other great colonial interpretation, we find that the last vision is of the island's original inhabitants: 'Ariel you'd say is the Uncle Tom, Caliban the black rebel. In fact as the play reminds you, it's Ariel who insists on his liberty, and gains it, Caliban who demands a master to worship and serve. As the Europeans depart, Caliban picks up Prospero's wand and points it icily at his fellow: *uhuru* has begun' (*Observer*, 21 June). In fact it was Ariel who picked up Prospero's wand, but the difference between Tree's tableau and this picture is truly indicative of the aesthetic and political distance between the two productions.

The success of Miller's *Tempest* ensured that the colonial themes would be accorded a greater significance than they had had in the fifties and sixties. Even in productions which operated on different intellectual premises to Miller's, the colonial elements were inescapable. In John Barton's 1970 Stratford production, for example, Ben Kingsley's Ariel was 'a slow moving, secretive native servant, naked except for a G string and a Sioux hairpiece, suggesting the victims depicted in those ancient prints of the Conquest of the America's (*Guardian*, 16 October). Similarly, although the main thrust of Peter Hall's 'emblematic' production for the National Theatre at the Old Vic in 1974 was directed elsewhere, he succeeded in presenting Caliban as a savage, a democrat, and a missing link through an ingenious costume design. Dennis Quilley did full justice to the 'paradoxical dignity' and 'impressive seriousness' of Caliban's 'blunt rhetoric' in a bisected make-up, 'one half the ugly scrofulous monster whom Prospero sees, on the other an image of the noble savage ... striving to break from the first stage into the second. His delivery of the word "freedom" even in the catch ... echoes with more passion and meaning than anything else in the evening'. Quilley's costuming represented a considerable breakthrough in terms of doing full justice to the complexity of Caliban, and would seem to be an entirely appropriate visual representation of the paradoxical elements which make up the character.

Miller's black Ariel and Caliban had been a successful and integral part of the whole conception of his production, but, when Keith Hack used the black actor Jeffrey Kissoon as Caliban at The Other Place in Stratford in 1974, the result was not so happy. Several critics complained that the actor was far too handsome for Caliban, and the *Coventry Evening Telegraph* (23 October) argued that 'in attempting to illustrate the white man's mental and physical cruelty to the black races' Hack had succeeded 'only in being offensive to them'. In this case it would seem that casting a black actor as Caliban misfired, but there is no doubt that the casting was intended to emphasize the play's colonial elements.

Indeed, some emphasis on colonialism is now expected, and Michael Billington castigated the most recent Stratford *Tempest*, directed by Clifford Williams in 1978, for not going far enough 'in mining the play's political-colonial sub-text', despite the blacked-up David Suchet's 'stunning performance with both the anger and the pathos of the unreasonably exploited' as Caliban (*Guardian*, 4 May). Bernard Levin also praised Suchet's performance in terms of its colonial elements: 'no deformed monster but a Man Friday conscious of his usurped rights, and clutching a voodoo figure to help him curse his enemy' (*Sunday Times*, 7 May). Here, with Caliban once more linked with that other great colonial fiction, the story ends for the moment, but there seems to be little likelihood that the 'political-colonial sub-text' of *The Tempest* will not remain an important part of theatrical productions in the future.

In discussing *The Tempest* in terms of theatrical responses to its colonial themes I have, of course, done scant justice to its multi-faceted brilliance, both on the page and in the theatre. I have been more concerned with tracing the often fragmentary process in which approaches to the play have reflected attitudes to colonialism, imperialism, evolution, and democracy. Any analysis of these elements in one play can provide only a partial picture of responses to colonialism or any of the issues of evolution, race, class, and politics which were frequently associated with it. Nevertheless, the various intepretations we have examined, particularly Tree's and Miller's, do show that *The Tempest* has acted as a barometer of the changing fortunes and particular relevances and resonances, critical, social, political, and theatrical, of these themes.

Francis Barker and Peter Hulme
The Tempest and Oppression (1985)

In order to speak of the Shakespearean text as an historical utterance, it is necessary to read it with and within series of *con-texts*. These con-texts are the precondition of the plays' historical and political signification, although literary criticism has operated systematically to close down that signification by a continual process of occlusion. This may seem a strange thing to say about the most notoriously bloated of all critical enterprises, but in fact 'Shakespeare' has been force-fed behind a high wall called Literature, built out of the dismantled pieces of other seventeenth-century discourses. Two particular examples of the occlusive process might be noted here. First, the process of occlusion is accomplished in the production of critical meaning, as is well illustrated by the case of Caliban. The occlusion of his political claims – one of the subjects of the present essay – is achieved by installing him at the very centre of the play, but only as the ground of a nature/art confrontation, itself of undoubted importance for the Renaissance, but here, in Kermode's account, totally without the historical contextualization that would locate it among the early universalizing forms of incipient bourgeois hegemony (Shakespeare 1964, pp. xxxiv–lxiii). Secondly, source criticism, which might *seem* to militate against autotelic unity by relating the text in question to other texts, in fact only obscures such relationships. Kermode's paragraphs on 'The New World' embody the hesitancy with which Shakespearean scholarship has approached the problem. Resemblances between the *language* of the Bermuda pamphlets and that of *The Tempest* are brought forward as evidence that Shakespeare 'has these documents in mind' but, since this must remain 'inference' rather than 'fact', it can only have subsidiary importance, 'of the greatest interest and usefulness', while clearly not 'fundamental to [the play's] structure of ideas'. Such 'sources' are then reprinted in an appendix so 'the reader may judge of the verbal parallels for himself', and the matter closed (Shakespeare 1964, pp. xxvii–xxviii).

And yet such closure proves premature since, strangely, source criticism comes to play an interestingly crucial role in Kermode's production of a site for *The Tempest*'s meaning. In general, the fullness of the play's unity needs protecting from con-textual contamination, so 'sources' are kept at bay except for the odd verbal parallel. But occasionally, and on a strictly *singular* basis, that unity can only be protected by recourse to a notion of source as explanatory of a feature otherwise aberrant to that posited unity. One example of this would be Prospero's well-known irascibility, peculiarly at odds with Kermode's picture of a self-disciplined, reconciliatory white magician, and therefore to be 'in the last analysis, explained by the fact that [he] descend[s] from a bad-tempered giant-magician' (Shakespeare 1964, p. lxiii). Another would be Prospero's strange perturbation which brings the celebratory masque of Act IV to such an abrupt conclusion, in one reading (as we will demonstrate shortly) the most important scene in the play, but here explained as 'a point at which an oddly pedantic concern for classical structure causes it to force its way through the surface of the play (Shakespeare 1964, p. lxxv).' In other words the play's unity is constructed only by shearing off some of its 'surface' complexities and explaining them away as irrelevant survivals or unfortunate academicisms.

Intertextuality, or con-textualization, differs most importantly from source criticism when it establishes the necessity of reading *The Tempest* alongside congruent texts, irrespective of Shakespeare's putative knowledge of them, and when it holds that such congruency will become apparent from the constitution of discursive networks to be traced independently of authorial 'intentionality'.

Essential to the historico-political critique which we are proposing here are the analytic strategies made possible by the concept of *discourse*. Intertextuality has usefully directed attention to the relationship *between* texts: discourse moves us towards a clarification of just what kinds of relationship are involved.

Traditionally *The Tempest* has been related to other texts by reference to a variety of notions: *source*, as we have seen, holds that Shakespeare was influenced by his reading of the Bermuda pamphlets. But the play is also described as belonging to the *genre* of pastoral romance and is seen as occupying a particular place in the *canon* of Shakespeare's works. Intertextuality has sought to displace work done within this earlier paradigm, but has itself been unable to break out of the practice of connecting text with text, of assuming that single texts are the ultimate objects of study and the principal units of meaning. Discourse, on the other hand, refers to the *field* in and through which texts are produced. As a concept wider than 'text' but narrower than language itself (Saussure's *langue*), it operates at the level of the enablement of texts. It is thus not an easy concept to grasp because discourses are never simply observable but only approachable through their effects just as, in a similar way, grammar can be said to be *at work* in particular sentences (even those that are ungrammatical), governing their construction but never fully present 'in' them. The operation of discourse is implicit in the regulation of what statements can and cannot be made and the forms that they can legitimately take. Attention to discourse therefore moves the focus from the interpretative problem of meaning to questions of instrumentality and function. Instead of *having* meaning, statements should be seen as *performative of* meaning; not as possessing some portable and 'universal' content but, rather, as instrumental in the organization and legitimation of power-relations – which of course involves, as one of its components, control over the constitution of meaning. As the author of one of the first modern grammars said, appropriately enough in 1492, 'language is the perfect instrument of empire'.* Yet, unlike grammar, discourse functions effectively precisely because the question of codifying its rules and protocols can never arise: the utterances it silently governs speak what appears to be the 'natural language of the age'. Therefore, from within a given discursive formation no general rules for its operation will be drawn up except against the ideological grain; so the constitution of the discursive fields of the past will, to some degree, need comprehending through the excavatory work of historical study.

To initiate such excavation is of course to confront massive problems. According to what we have said above, each individual text, rather than a meaningful unit in itself, lies at the intersection of different discourses which are related to each other in a complex but ultimately hierarchical way. Strictly speaking, then, it would be meaningless to talk about the unity of any given text – supposedly the intrinsic quality of all 'works of art'. And yet, because literary texts *are* presented to us as characterised precisely by their unity, the text must still be taken as a point of purchase on the discursive field – but in order to demonstrate that, athwart its alleged unity, the text is in fact marked and fissured by the interplay of the discourses that constitute it.

The ensemble of fictional and lived practices, which for convenience we will simply refer to here as 'English colonialism', provides *The Tempest*'s dominant discursive con-texts. We have chosen here to concentrate specifically on the figure of usurpation as the nodal point of the play's imbrication into this discourse of colonialism. We shall look at the variety of forms under which usurpation appears in the text, and indicate briefly how it is active in organizing the text's actual diversity.

* Antonio de Nebrija, quoted in Lewis Hanke, *Aristotle and the American Indians* (Bloomington, Indiana, 1959).

Of course conventional criticism has no difficulty in recognizing the importance of the themes of legitimacy and usurpation for *The Tempest*. Indeed, during the storm-scene with which the play opens, the issue of legitimate authority is brought immediately to the fore. The boatswain's peremptory dismissal of the nobles to their cabins, while not, according to the custom of the sea, strictly a mutinous act, none the less represents a disturbance in the normal hierarchy of power relations. The play then proceeds to recount or display a series of actual or attempted usurpations of authority: from Antonio's successful palace revolution against his brother, Prospero, and Caliban's attempted violation of the honour of Prospero's daughter – accounts of which we hear retrospectively; to the conspiracy of Antonio and Sebastian against the life of Alonso and, finally, Caliban's insurrection, with Stephano and Trinculo, against Prospero's domination of the island. In fact it could be argued that this series *is* the play, in so far as *The Tempest* is a dramatic action at all. However, these rebellions, treacheries, mutinies and conspiracies, referred to here collectively as usurpation, are not *simply* present in the text as extractable 'Themes of the Play'. Rather, they are differentially embedded there, figural traces of the text's anxiety concerning the very matters of domination and resistance.

Take for example the play's famous *protasis*, Prospero's long exposition to Miranda of the significant events that predate the play. For Prospero, the real beginning of the story is his usurpation twelve years previously by Antonio, the opening scene of a drama which Prospero intends to play out during *The Tempest* as a comedy of restoration. Prospero's exposition seems unproblematically to take its place as the indispensible prologue to an understanding of the present moment of Act I, no more than a device for conveying essential information. But to see it simply as a neutral account of the play's prehistory would be to occlude the contestation that follows insistently throughout the rest of the first act, of Prospero's version of true beginnings. In this narration the crucial early days of the relationship between the Europeans and the island's inhabitants are covered by Prospero's laconic 'Here in this island we arriv'd' (I. ii. 171). And this is all we would have were it not for Ariel and Caliban. First Prospero is goaded by Ariel's demands for freedom into recounting at some length how his servitude began, when, at their first contact, Prospero freed him from the cloven pine in which he had earlier been confined by Sycorax. Caliban then offers his compelling and defiant counter to Prospero's single sentence when, in a powerful speech, he recalls the initial mutual trust which was broken by Prospero's assumption of the political control made possible by the power of his magic. Caliban, 'Which first was mine own King', now protests that 'here you sty me / In this hard rock, whiles you do keep from me / The rest o'th'island' (I. ii. 344–6).

It is remarkable that these contestations of 'true beginnings' have been so commonly occluded by an uncritical willingness to identify Prospero's voice as direct and reliable authorial statement, and therefore to ignore the lengths to which the play goes to dramatize its problems with the proper beginning of its own story. Such identification hears, as it were, only Prospero's play, follows only his stage directions, not noticing that Prospero's play and *The Tempest* are not necessarily the same thing.

But although different beginnings are offered by different voices in the play, Prospero has the effective power to impose his construction of events on the others. While Ariel gets a threatening but nevertheless expansive answer, Caliban provokes an entirely different reaction. Prospero's words refuse engagement with Caliban's claim to original sovereignty ('This island's mine, by Sycorax my mother, / Which thou tak'st from me', I. ii. 333–4). Yet Prospero is clearly disconcerted. His sole – somewhat hysterical – response consists of an indirect denial ('Thou most lying slave', I. ii. 346) and a counter accusation of attempted rape ('thou didst seek to violate / The honour of my child', I. ii. 349–50), which together foreclose the exchange and serve in practice as Prospero's only justification for the arbitrary rule he exercises over the island and its inhabitants. At a stroke he erases from what we have called Prospero's play all trace of the moment of his reduction of Caliban to slavery and appropriation of his island. For, indeed, it could be argued that the series of usurpations listed earlier as constituting the dramatic action all belong to that play alone, which is systematically silent about Prospero's own act of usurpation: a silence which is curious, given his otherwise voluble preoccupation with the theme of legitimacy. But, despite his evasiveness, this moment ought to be of decisive *narrative* importance since it marks Prospero's self-installation as ruler, and his acquisition, through Caliban's enslavement, of the means of supplying the food and labour on which he and Miranda are completely dependent: 'We cannot miss him: he does make our fire, / Fetch in our wood, and serves in offices / That profit us' (I. ii.

313–15). Through its very occlusion of Caliban's version of proper beginnings, Prospero's disavowal is itself performative of the discourse of colonialism, since this particular reticulation of denial of dispossession with retrospective justification for it, is the characteristic trope by which European colonial regimes articulated their authority over land to which they could have no conceivable legitimate claim.

The success of this trope is, as so often in these cases, proved by its subsequent invisibility. Caliban's 'I'll show thee every fertile inch o'th'island' (II. ii. 148) is for example glossed by Kermode with 'The colonists were frequently received with this kindness, though treachery might follow', as if this were simply a 'fact' whose relevance to *The Tempest* we might want to consider, without seeing that to speak of 'treachery' is already to interpret, from the position of colonizing power, through a purported 'description'. A discursive analysis would indeed be alive to the use of the word 'treachery' in a colonial context in the early seventeenth century, but would be aware of how it functioned for the English to explain to themselves the *change* in native behaviour (from friendliness to hostility) that was in fact a *reaction* to their increasingly disruptive presence. That this was an explanatory trope rather than a description of behaviour is nicely caught in Gabriel Archer's slightly bemused comment: 'They are naturally given to trechery, howbeit we could not finde it in our travell up the river, but rather a most kind and loving people' (Archer 1979). Kermode's use of the word is of course by no means obviously contentious: its power to shape readings of the play stems from its continuity with the grain of unspoken colonialist assumptions.

So it is not just a matter of the occlusion of the play's initial colonial moment. Colonialist legitimation has always had then to go on to tell its own story, inevitably one of native violence: Prospero's play performs this task within *The Tempest*. The burden of Prospero's play is already deeply concerned with producing legitimacy. The purpose of Prospero's main plot is to secure recognition of his claim to the usurped duchy of Milan, a recognition sealed in the blessing given by Alonso to the prospective marriage of his own son to Prospero's daughter. As part of this, Prospero reduces Caliban to a role in the supporting sub-plot, as instigator of a mutiny that is programmed to fail, thereby forging an equivalence between Antonio's initial *putsch* and Caliban's revolt. This allows Prospero to annul the memory of his failure to prevent his expulsion from the dukedom, by repeating it as a mutiny that he will, this time, forestall. But, in addition, the playing out of the colonist narrative is thereby completed: Caliban's attempt – tarred with the brush of Antonio's supposedly self-evident viciousness – is produced as final and irrevocable confirmation of the natural treachery of savages.

Prospero can plausibly be seen as a playwright only because of the control over the other characters given him by his magic. He can freeze Ferdinand in mid-thrust, immobilize the court party at will, and conjure a pack of hounds to chase the conspirators. Through this physical control he seeks with considerable success to manipulate the mind of Alonso. Curiously though, while the main part of Prospero's play runs according to plan, the sub-plot provides the only real moment of drama when Prospero calls a sudden halt to the celebratory masque, explaining, aside:

> I had forgot that foul conspiracy
> Of the beast Caliban and his confederates
> Against my life: the minute of their plot
> Is almost come. (IV. i. 139–42)

So while, on the face of it, Prospero has no difficulty in dealing with the various threats to his domination, Caliban's revolt proves uniquely disturbing to the smooth unfolding of Prospero's plot. The text is strangely emphatic about this moment of disturbance, insisting not only on Prospero's sudden vexation, but also on the 'strange hollow, and confused noise' with which the Nymphs and Reapers – two lines earlier gracefully dancing – now 'heavily vanish'; and the apprehension voiced by Ferdinand and Miranda:

> FERDINAND This is strange; your father's in some passion
> That works him strongly.
> MIRANDA Never till this day
> Saw I him touch'd with anger, so distemper'd.
> (IV. i. 143–5)

For the first and last time Ferdinand and Miranda speak at a distance from Prospero and from his play. Although this disturbance is immediately glossed over, the hesitation, occasioned by the sudden remembering of Caliban's conspiracy, remains available as a site of potential fracture.

The interrupted masque has certainly troubled scholarship, introducing a jarring note into the harmony of this supposedly most highly structured of Shakespeare's late plays. Kermode speaks of the 'apparently inadequate motivation' for Prospero's perturbation (Shakespeare 1964, p. lxxv), since there is no obvious reason why he should so excite himself over an easily controllable insurrection.

What then is the meaning of this textual excess, this disproportion between apparent cause and effect? There are several possible answers, located at different levels of analysis. The excess obviously marks the recurrent difficulty that Caliban causes Prospero – a difficulty we have been concerned to trace in some detail. So, at the level of character, a psychoanalytic reading would want to suggest that Prospero's excessive reaction represents his disquiet at the irruption into consciousness of an unconscious anxiety concerning the grounding of his legitimacy, both as producer of his play and, *a fortiori*, as governor of the island. The by now urgent need for action forces upon Prospero the hitherto repressed contradiction between his dual roles as usurped and usurper. Of course the emergency is soon contained and the colonialist narrative quickly completed. But, none the less, if only for a moment, the effort invested in holding Prospero's play together as a unity is laid bare.

So, at the formal level, Prospero's difficulties in staging his play are themselves 'staged' by the play that we are watching, this moment presenting for the first time the possibility of distinguishing between Prospero's play and *The Tempest* itself.

Perhaps it could be said that what is staged here in *The Tempest* is Prospero's anxious determination to keep the sub-plot of his play in its place. One way of distinguishing Prospero's play from *The Tempest* might be to claim that Prospero's carefully established relationship between main and sub-plot is reversed in *The Tempest*, whose *main* plot concerns Prospero's anxiety over his *sub*-plot. A formal analysis would seem to bear this out. The climax of Prospero's play is his revelation to Alonso of Miranda and Ferdinand playing chess. This is certainly a true *anagnorisis* for Alonso, but for us a merely theatrical rather than truly dramatic moment. *The Tempest*'s dramatic climax, in a way its only dramatic moment at all, is, after all, this sudden and strange disturbance of Prospero.

But to speak of Prospero's anxiety being staged by *The Tempest* would be, on its own, a recuperative move, preserving the text's unity by the familiar strategy of introducing an ironic distance between author and protagonist. After all, although Prospero's anxiety over his sub-plot may point up the *crucial* nature of that 'sub' plot, a generic analysis would have no difficulty in showing that *The Tempest* is ultimately complicit with Prospero's play in treating Caliban's conspiracy in the full comic mode. Even before it begins, Caliban's attempt to put his political claims into practice is arrested by its implication in the convention of clownish vulgarity represented by the 'low-life' characters of Stephano and Trinculo, his conspiracy framed in a grotesequerie that ends with the dubiously amusing sight of the conspirators being hunted by dogs, a fate, incidentally, not unknown to natives of the New World. The shakiness of Prospero's position is indeed staged, but in the end his version of history remains *authoritative*, the larger play acceding as it were to the containment of the conspirators in the safely comic mode, Caliban allowed only his poignant and ultimately vain protests against the venality of his co-conspirators.

That this comic closure is necessary to enable the European 'reconciliation' which follows hard on its heels – the patching up of a minor dynastic dispute within the Italian nobility – is, however, itself symptomatic of the text's own anxiety about the threat posed to its decorum by its New World materials. The lengths to which the play has to go to achieve a legitimate ending may then be read as the quelling of a fundamental disquiet concerning its own functions within the projects of colonialist discourse.

No adequate reading of the play could afford not to comprehend *both* the anxiety and the drive to closure it necessitates. Yet these aspects of the play's 'rich complexity' have been signally ignored by European and North American critics, who have tended to listen exclusively to Prospero's voice: after all, he speaks their language. It has been left to those who have suffered colonial usurpation to discover and map the traces of that complexity by reading in full measure Caliban's refractory place in both Prospero's play and *The Tempest*.

We have tried to show, within the limits of a brief textual analysis, how an approach via a theory of discourse can recognize *The Tempest* as, in a significant sense, a play imbricated within the discourse of colonialism; and can, at the same time, offer an explanation of features of the play either ignored or occluded by critical practices that have often been complicit, whether consciously or not, with a colonialist ideology.

Three points remain to be clarified. To identify dominant discursive networks and their mode of operation within particular texts should by no means be seen as the end of the story. A more exhaustive analysis would go on to establish the precise articulation of discourses within texts: we have argued for the discourse of colonialism as the articulatory *principle* of *The Tempest*'s diversity but have touched only briefly on what other discourses are articulated and where such linkages can be seen at work in the play.

Then again, each text is more than simply an *instance* of the operation of a discursive network. We have tried to show how much of *The Tempest*'s complexity comes from its *staging* of the distinctive moves and figures of colonialist discourse. Discourse is always performative, active rather than ever merely contemplative; and, of course, the mode of the theatre will also inflect it in particular ways, tending, for example, through the inevitable (because structural) absence of any direct authorial comment, to create an effect of distantiation, which exists in a complex relationship with the countervailing (and equally structural) tendency for audiences to identify with characters presented – through the language and conventions of theatre – as heroes and heroines. Much work remains to be done on the articulation between discursive performance and mode of presentation.

Finally, we have been concerned to show how *The Tempest* has been severed from its discursive con-texts through being produced by criticism as an autotelic unity, and we have tried therefore to exemplify an approach that would engage with the fully dialectical relationship between the detail of the text and the larger discursive formations. But nor can theory and criticism be exempt from such relationships. Our essay too must engage in the discursive struggle that determines the history within which the Shakespearean texts will be located and read: it matters what kind of history that is.

QUESTIONS

1. How important is music in the play?

2. Coleridge described the play as having 'scenic solemnity'. Justify the appropriateness of this description, by considering the spectacular effects in the play.

3. It has been suggested that since Prospero controls the action of the play, it is lacking in dramatic conflict. Do you agree?

4. What symbolic elements do you see in the play?

5. Consider the different aspects of Time as they are used in the play.

6. What part does the theme of service *versus* freedom play in *The Tempest*?

7. Examine Shakespeare's presentation of villainy in the play: is it possible to distinguish between serious and comic wickedness?

8. Trace the interplay of feelings of wonder and disillusion in *The Tempest*.

9. Examine the patterns of parallelism and contrast in the characterisation of the play.

10. How appropriately does Shakespeare distinguish between the major characters of the play in their styles of speech?

11. Do you agree that the play shows Prospero's limitations as well as his virtues?

12. Compare the reactions of Ferdinand and Miranda to each other as lovers.

13. How far does Shakespeare arouse sympathetic feelings towards Caliban?

14. What is Gonzalo's role in the play?

15. What dramatic purposes do Trinculo and Stephano serve, other than the amusement provided by their clowning?

16. How effective is the opening scene as a beginning to the play? What would be lost if it were omitted?

17. Prospero's lengthy exposition in the second scene of the play has been criticised as a crude technique for giving necessary information to the audience. Can you suggest any means of defending its effectiveness?

18. Is the Masque of Ceres an integral part of the play, or an interlude in the main action? Justify its presence in the play.

19. Analyse Prospero's speech after the Masque (beginning 'Our revels now are ended'), showing its theatrical effectiveness and relating it to the main themes of the play.

20. Examine the feelings aroused by the last scene of the play.

21. Do you think *The Tempest* appeals simultaneously to sophisticated and naive tastes?

SELECT BIBLIOGRAPHY

EDITIONS

The standard edition of the play is that by J. F. Kermode in the New Arden Shakespeare (London, 1954). There is also an edition by A. Righter in the New Penguin Shakespeare (Harmondsworth, 1968).

BOOKS AND ARTICLES

Allen, D. C., *Image and Meaning: Metaphoric Traditions in Renaissance Poetry* (Baltimore, Maryland, 1960).

Bentley, G. E., 'Shakespeare and the Blackfriars Theatre', *Shakespeare Survey* I (1948).

Brockbank, J. P., '*The Tempest*: Conventions of Art and Empire', *Later Shakespeare* (eds J. R. Brown and B. Harris, Stratford-upon-Avon Studies 8, London, 1966).

Coghill, N., 'The Basis of Shakespearian Comedy', *Essays and Studies*, N.S. III (1950).

Curry, W. C., *Shakespeare's Philosophical Patterns* (Baton Rouge, Louisiana, 1937).

Felperin, H., *Shakespearean Romance* (Princeton, New Jersey, 1972).

Frye, N., *A Natural Perspective* (New York, 1965).

James, D. G., *The Dream of Prospero* (Oxford, 1967).

Knox, B., '*The Tempest* and Ancient Stage Tradition', *English Stage Comedy* (English Institute Essays 1954, New York, 1955).

Mannoni, O., *Prospero and Caliban: The Psychology of Colonisation* (New York, 1956).

Marx, L., *The Machine in the Garden: Technology and the Pastoral Ideal in America* (New York, 1965).

Nuttall, A. D., *Two Concepts of Allegory: A Study of Shakespeare's 'The Tempest' and the Logic of Allegorical Expression* (London, 1967).

Sisson, C. J., 'The Magic of Prospero', *Shakespeare Survey* XI (1958).

Still, C., *Shakespeare's Mystery Play: A Study of 'The Tempest'* (London, 1921).

Tayler, E. W., *Nature and Art in Renaissance Literature* (New York, 1964).

Traversi, D., *Shakespeare: The Last Phase* (London, 1954).

Welsford, E., *The Court Masque* (London, 1927).

NOTES ON CONTRIBUTORS

W. H. AUDEN was the best known of the 1930s poets.

REUBEN A. BROWER is Professor of English at Harvard University.

HENRY JAMES's Introduction to *The Tempest* is one of his rare excursions into Shakespeare criticism.

FRANK KERMODE is Professor of English at Columbia University, New York.

JOHN MIDDLETON MURRY was a distinguished critic in the early twentieth century, whose works include studies of Swift, Keats and Shakespeare.

E. M. W. TILLYARD was Master of Jesus College, Cambridge, and author of *The Elizabethan World Picture, Shakespeare's History Plays, Shakespeare's Problem Plays* and *Shakespeare's Last Plays*.

G. WILSON KNIGHT was Professor of English at the University of Leeds and one of the most influential Shakespeare critics during the first half of the twentieth century.

LESLIE A. FIEDLER was Professor of English at the State University of New York in Buffalo.

FRANCES A. YATES was Reader in the History of the Renaissance at the University of London.

TREVOR R. GRIFFITHS teaches at the Polytechnic of North London.

FRANCIS BARKER and PETER HULME are lecturers at the University of Essex.

INDEX